D1347889

Frontispiece *J. W. Lindt, Aboriginal man, c.1873*

Colonialism's Culture

Anthropology, Travel and Government

Nicholas Thomas

Polity Press

First published in 1994 by Polity Press
in association with Blackwell Publishers Ltd
Reprinted 1996

Editorial office:
Polity Press
65 Bridge Street
Cambridge CB2 1UR, UK

Marketing and production:
Blackwell Publishers Ltd
108 Cowley Road
Oxford OX4 1JF, UK

ISBN 0 7456 0871 X
ISBN 0 7456 1215 6 (pbk)

British Library Cataloguing-in-Publication Data
A CIP catalogue record for this book is available from the British Library.

Typeset in 11 on 12½pt Baskerville by Best-set Typesetter Ltd, Hong Kong.
Printed and bound in Great Britain by
Hartnolls Limited, Bodmin, Cornwall
This book is printed on acid-free paper.

Contents

List of Illustrations		vii
Preface		ix
Introduction		1
1	From Present to Past: the Politics of Colonial Studies	11
2	Culture and Rule: Theories of Colonial Discourse	33
3	From Past to Present: Colonial Epochs, Agents, and Locations	66
4	Colonial Governmentality and Colonial Conversion	105
5	Imperial Triumph, Settler Failure	143
6	The Primitivist and the Postcolonial	170
Notes		196
Notes to Plates		231
Index		235

for Julian Thomas and Jeannine Jacobson

List of Illustrations

Frontispiece.   J. W. Lindt, Aboriginal man. Albumen print,
   *c.*1873. Courtesy of the Mitchell Library, State Library of
   New South Wales, Sydney   ii
Plate 1   Furniture from Artikeln, published in *The*
   Good Weekend, 1 September 1990, pp. 84–5. Photograph
   by Brendan Read, courtesy of the John Fairfax
   Group   29
Plate 2   Thomas Andrew, 'The Vanquished', *c.*1894.
   Courtesy of the Mitchell Library, State Library of New
   South Wales, Sydney   34
Plate 3   'Mosque at Lucknow'. Aquatint after Henry Salt,
   in *Twenty-four views taken in St Helena, the Cape, India,*
   Ceylon, the Red Sea, Abyssinia and Egypt (London: William
   Miller, 1809). Courtesy of the South Australian Branch
   of the Royal Geographical Society and the State Library
   of South Australia   55
Plate 4   Detail from 'The great bull, a Hindoo Idol, at
   Tanjore', 1798. Aquatint by Thomas and William Daniell
   after Thomas Daniell, in *Oriental Scenery* (London:
   Boydell, 1797–1810), ii, plate 22. Courtesy of the Syndics
   of Cambridge University Library   56
Plate 5   Hudson Lagusu demonstrates use of the sacrificial
   altar. From Geoffrey M. White, *Identity through History:*
   Living Traditions in a Solomon Island Society (Cambridge:
   Cambridge University Press, 1992), plate 2   62
Plate 6   'A Javan of the lower class'. From Thomas
   Stamford Raffles, *The History of Java* (London: Black,

Parbury and Allen, 1817). Courtesy of the Australian
National University Library   87

Plate 7   'A Papuan or native of New Guinea, 10 years
old'. From Thomas Stamford Raffles, *The History of Java*
(London: Black, Parbury and Allen, 1817). Courtesy of
the Australian National University Library   88

Plate 8   'A Study in Black and White'. Crown Studios
postcard, *c.*1908. Courtesy of the Mitchell Library,
State Library of New South Wales, Sydney   130

Plate 9   'Rev. J. F. Goldie with some of the first Converts,
Rubiana, Solomon Islands'. *Australasian Methodist
Missionary Review*, 4 February 1908. Courtesy of the
Mitchell Library, State Library of New South Wales,
Sydney   132

Plate 10   Book spine from Henry M. Stanley, *In Darkest Africa*
(London: Sampson Low, 1890). Courtesy of the
Australian National University Library   135

Plate 11   Tracey Moffatt. *Some Lads II.* 1986. Gelatin silver
photograph, 45.7 × 45.7 cm. Kodak (Australasia) Pty
Ltd Fund 1987. Collection: Australian National Gallery,
Canberra. Reproduced by permission of Tracey Moffatt
and the Australian National Gallery, Canberra   193

Preface

This book is written around a contradiction: colonialism is something that needs to be theorized and discussed, but discussion may be obstructed if we assume that the word relates to any meaningful category or totality. Colonialism needs to be analysed and theorized because its pervasive and enduring ramifications are all too evident, despite decolonization and the increasing frequency with which the term 'postcolonial' is applied to the present. Like modernity or capitalism, colonialism would seem so fundamental to both the larger dynamics of global history and power relations, and to many more immediate aspects of our lives, that the desirability of analysing and reinterpreting 'it' must be obvious. Yet there is an impasse, in much current writing, that arises from too dogged an attachment to 'colonialism' as a unitary totality, and to related totalities such as 'colonial discourse', 'the Other', Orientalism and imperialism.

For reasons I set out in sections of this book, it is becoming increasingly clear that only localized theories and historically specific accounts can provide much insight into the varied articulations of colonizing and counter-colonial representations and practices. Much writing in the field, however, seems less inclined to localize or historicize analysis, than put Fanon and Lacan (or Derrida) into a blender and take the result to be equally appetizing for premodern and modern; for Asian, African and American; for metropolitan, settler, indigenous and diasporic subjects. It is striking also that many writers stress, in principle, the localized character of colonial and postcolonial subjectivities, while resisting much engagement with either localities or subjects. I am not saying that Fanon's interests, or deconstruction, still less 'theory' in general, are unimportant for the kinds of inquiries and critiques that need to be pursued, but that colonialism can only be traced through its plural and particularized expressions. The paramount irony of contemporary colonial studies must be that critics and scholars, who one presumes wish to expose the false universality and hegemony of imperial expansion and modernization, seem unwilling themselves to renounce the aspiration of theorizing globally on the basis of particular strands in European philosophy.

The first half of this book, roughly, outlines the context of this critique and develops it; the second attempts to map out what is general – and peculiar – to some modern colonialisms, thus exemplifying the historicized style of analysis that is advocated, though in a way that must be partial and illustrative rather than exhaustive and extensive, given the aim of this book, which is critically to introduce and review some perspectives on the field.

Although, as I have indicated, sections of this book are written against current trends in colonial discourse theory, its larger approach is constructive rather than negative; my strategy of reading may echo the undisciplined activity of colonial collecting, in its accumulation from diverse sources of insights and strategies that are recontextualized, no doubt often in a fashion that fails to reflect their original authors' or producers' concerns, yet makes them available to new projects and new ends. With respect to the work of Edward Said, Johannes Fabian, Bernard Smith and others, my critiques are not intended to diminish the importance of their texts, but to draw attention to ways in which their approaches might be extended or adapted with respect to different cases or different perspectives. This book is partial not only in the sense that the readings it offers are provisional, but also because it is written from a particular place – from Australia – and out of my own concerns with cultural politics and colonialism in the Pacific region. If these histories must be seen as marginal, in relation to the most important theatres of colonial expansion, rivalry, resistance and decolonization, their peculiarity may draw attention to issues that should have been discussed, but have been marginalized, elsewhere. In the last part of this book I suggest that settler colonialism, in particular, has a burden in the present that needs to be confronted more directly, if the idea of postcoloniality is not to be absolutely meaningless, rather than merely vague and disputed.

This book does not aim to provide the balanced synthesis that a textbook might, but it may provide a useful introduction to the complex range of debates concerning colonial representation that are proceeding at present; in particular, I aim to make it clear why culture is central to these debates in a way that it was not, say, to discussions of colonialism in the 1960s. If it is the particular conjunction of colonial and cultural studies that produces some of the theoretical problems I attempt to diagnose, it is also a cultural orientation that makes current inquiries provocative, unsettling and worth pursuing. Because the book is introductory in this sense I have provided references to further reading (through notes rather than a bibliography, since the former permit contextualization and comment that a straight alphabetical listing does not); these are unavoidably selective, and include very few references to work published after late 1991.

The Australian Research Council gave me the time to write this book, through a Queen Elizabeth II Research Fellowship for 1990–2; I have been based in the Department of Archaeology and Anthropology at the Australian National University, which has provided a congenial environment and generous access to facilities. My understanding of questions around colonialism has benefited from conversations with more people than can possibly be mentioned here, though in many cases my debts are signalled by references to their publications in the endnotes. I must thank Aletta Biersack, Donald Denoon, Harriet Guest, Margaret Jolly, Henrietta Moore and Julian Thomas, for their suggestions or comments on drafts; in Canberra, I have been sustained by the company of Anna, Margaret, Julian and Jeannine.

Introduction

Colonialism: the word's immediate associations are with intrusions, conquest, economic exploitation and the domination of indigenous peoples by European men. Most of the imagery – Lindt's melancholy Aboriginal, the white man's burden, darkest Africa – belongs to the past, and in the late twentieth century formal colonial rule has all but vanished. However, the persistence of neocolonial domination in international and inter-ethnic relations is undeniable. The colonialism that is still with us is expressed in a plethora of crude and more subtle acts, nasty jokes and pervasive inequities, but is perhaps most conspicuous in the frequent military assaults against Third World states or groups within them, acts that aim to preserve spheres of influence, apparent political quiet and conditions that fav-our investment. Thus, the intervention in the Gulf might typify imperialist practice today, as the Vietnam war did in the 1960s and early 1970s.

Such a commonsense understanding of imperialism or neo-colonialism draws attention to its careless violence, to the gross social inequity and immorality in the dominance of a country's affairs by a foreign state or foreign capital. For liberals and radicals in the West, an equation between imperialism and violent exploitation that was supported or condoned by their own governments enabled political protest and prompted critical reflection in academic fields that dealt with colonialism or the Third World. To what extent did disciplines such as anthropology and development economics inform and legitimize the colonial projects of Western governments?

This book is positioned between that kind of public anger and a cooler scholarly project, the continuing reinterpretation of colonial histories and representations. It draws energy from both, but aims also to unsettle both, by raising political questions about modes of academic interpretation, while also using scholarly understandings of colonialism to find left-liberal anticolonialism partial and inadequate. That is not to say that the obvious kinds of imperial violence should not be censured, but that a critique of colonialism – and particularly one of colonial *culture* – must deal with a wider range of events and representations, including some in which the critics themselves are implicated.

This book thus puts forward a series of arguments that are both about ways of analysing colonialism and about the positions and politics of such analyses in the present. Its premiss is a simple assumption that colonialism is not best understood primarily as a political or economic relationship that is legitimized or justified through ideologies of racism or progress. Rather, colonialism has always, equally importantly and deeply, been a cultural process; its discoveries and trespasses are imagined and energized through signs, metaphors and narratives; even what would seem its purest moments of profit and violence have been mediated and enframed by structures of meaning. Colonial cultures are not simply ideologies that mask, mystify or rationalize forms of oppression that are external to them; they are also expressive and constitutive of colonial relationships in themselves.

This is not, however, to say that colonialism should be seen 'as a cultural system' if that would imply a coherent symbolic order. It is not simply the fundamental division of interest between colonizer and colonized that inevitably differentiates and fractures constructions of colonial projects and relationships. Colonizers have also frequently been divided by strategic interests and differing visions of the civilizing mission; the ways in which such differences are most effectively charted is one of the main concerns of this book. But more fundamentally, colonizing constantly generated obstacles to neat boundaries and hierarchies between populations, exemplified by 'degenerate' half-castes and frontier whites who were anything but civilized. Colonizing projects were, moreover, frequently split between assimilationist and segregationist ways of dealing with indigenous peoples; between impulses to define new lands as vacant spaces for European achievement, and a will to define, collect and map the cultures which already possessed them; and in the definition of colonizers' identities, which had to reconcile the civility and values of home with the raw novelty of sites of settlement. Their coherence, in other words, was prejudiced both by internal contradictions and the intransigence and resistance of the colonized.

This book is primarily a critique of some of the ways of recognizing and interpreting colonialism that are currently available in anthropology, history and literary studies. While I consider the concept of 'discourse' as a necessary element of any adequate way of interpreting colonial representations, I find that a great deal of writing on 'colonial discourse' fails to grasp this field's dispersed and conflicted character. In recent writing an interest in disclosing the heterogeneity and the internal ruptures of colonial discourse is frequently declared. Similarly, recovering or reinstating the subjectivity of the colonized is claimed to be a central aim. However, the modes of analysis that are typically employed often paradoxically characterize 'colonial discourse' in unitary and essentialist terms, and frequently seem to do more to recapitulate than subvert the privileged status and presumed dominance of the discourses that are investigated. Colonial discourse has, too frequently, been evoked as a global and transhistorical logic of denigration, that has remained impervious to active marking or reformulation by the 'Other'; it has figured above all as a coherent imposition, rather than a practically mediated relation.

While this book is driven by an interest in localizing colonialism in encounters, and in the socially-transformative projects of colonizers and colonized, it is also concerned to historicize something that can usefully be referred to as 'colonialism'. Given that this word can, quite properly, refer to a great variety of asymmetrical inter-social relationships, 'colonialism' seems to have been present through most of world history in one form or another; what can be said about it may thus be general to the point of banality or in fact only true of privileged examples. While the Columbus quincentenary has prompted many writers to reflect on the relevance of the conquest of America to our own epoch, I am struck by basic discontinuities between Renaissance colonialism (whether in the Americas, Asia or elsewhere) and a modern paradigm of power. That paradigm itself was never

homogeneous, yet possessed (and possesses) a certain distinctiveness beyond mere difference from what transpired before.

This is the context in which something can be said about the
three terms of my subtitle. Anthropology, travel and government
are not concepts but ambiguous apparatuses, ways of thinking
that are at once enmeshed in the problematic of colonial power
yet available to the analysis and critique of it. These paradoxes
make possible and lie behind the discussion in much of the rest of
this book, but can be signalled in a preliminary way here, taking
the three terms in reverse order.

In cultural theory since Foucault, the idea of government is
central to the critique of language, knowledge and narrative,
because it presupposes their constitution in and through power
relations. What might otherwise have been understood as neutral
media, or as a cultural heritage possessing universal value, is
instead grounded in specific interests and a project of dominance.
Further, the practice of governing can conversely be understood
as a discursively complex exercise, entailing an ethnographically
specific knowledge of particular populations, enabled by various
methods of documentation, accounts of disorder or backwardness and conceptions of reform and advancement. For Foucault,
the 'governmentality' that these knowledges and programmes
amount to is not a transhistorical feature of all polities, but a
distinctively modern development that displaced other modes of
political power and state dominance. The prison, welfare systems,
town planning and political economy can all be seen as expressions of this order of governmentality, which is manifested both in
colonial administration and in changes in metropolitan policies
and institutions. In effect, modernity itself can be understood as a
colonialist project in the special sense that both the societies
internal to Western nations, and those they possessed, administered and reformed elsewhere, were understood as objects to be
surveyed, regulated and sanitized. If these interests in government
are therefore rewarding in the scope created for exploring various
kinds of discursive legislation, it is essential at the same time to
recognize that government is not a unitary work but heteroge-
neous and partial, and moreover that the meanings engendered
by hegemonic codes and narratives do not exist in hermetic domains but are placed at risk, revalued and distorted, through
being enacted and experienced. In colonial encounters, marked

not only by struggle but also by misrecognition and by disingenuous compliance, the risks are very real indeed. It is vital, then, to make explicit the efforts to govern that are present in particular fields of colonial representation, without ever assuming that this government is stable and secure.

Travel, like government, can be thought of as a universal in human societies, but may be more powerfully conceived as a peculiarly modern activity, in so far as it entails expansive steps away from 'traditional' ties, and – more crucially and distinctively – an attitude of extension and displacement towards those traditions. As Ian Watt points out with respect to *Robinson Crusoe*, 'the hero has a home and family, and leaves them for the classic reason of *homo economicus* – that it is necessary to better his economic condition . . . Crusoe's "original sin" is really the dynamic tendency of capitalism itself, whose aim is never merely to maintain the status quo, but to transform it incessantly.'[1] This is partly why travel is much more than movement across space; activities as diverse as fighting tigers and savages, collecting Egyptian mummies and drawing crusader castles, are frequently self-fashioning exercises that discompose and recompose the traveller, sometimes with absurd or degraded rather than refined and accomplished results. Though this is a very familiar point with respect say to the Grand Tour, it does alert us to a broader sense in which colonizing as well as travelling is fundamentally reflexive: it may be society as home that is 'discovered' or newly explicated, as travellers purport to discover or remake a colonized space. In recent critical literature, the imperialist dimension of travel writing has been extensively discussed; understanding it as a kind of spying would only seem too crude if travel writers such as Mungo Park had not themselves been so preoccupied with the perilous proximity of their projects to commercial and political espionage. While the devices which travel writers used to denigrate the 'natives' they visited have often been rehearsed and censured, travel has also been widely regarded – not least by anti- and postcolonial critics – as an enlarging and liberating process that unsettles the confidence of authority. Witness Edward Said's juxtaposition of two models of scholarly practice, one based on surveying a specialist domain with detachment and mastery, the other more fluid and transgressive:

we can be there in order to reign and hold sway. Here, in such a conception of academic space, the academic professional is king and potentate ... The other model is considerably more mobile, more playful, although no less serious. The image of traveler depends not on power, but on motion, on a willingness to go into different worlds, use different idioms, and understand a variety of disguises, masks, and rhetorics. Travelers must suspend the claim of customary routine in order to live in new rhythms and rituals ... the traveler *crosses over*, traverses territory, and abandons fixed positions all the time. To do this with dedication and love as well as a realistic sense of the terrain is, I believe, a kind of academic freedom at its highest.[2]

What is remarkable here is not only that a renowned critic of Orientalism – a discourse in which travel-writing figures prominently – can find, in travel, the figure for an idealized, honourable academic freedom, but moreover that his imaging of travel in terms of movement beyond one's customary assumptions is so familiar, particularly to readers of anthropology. Those obliged to suffer both a good deal of posturing about the intellectual virtues of ethnographic displacement from within that discipline, and the surfeit of recent critique from outside it that takes this crossing over as a duplicitous tactic of imperial authority, might be puzzled or irritated. What is contradictory, however, is not so much the statement as the project of travel itself, which has indeed frequently affirmed the values and precedence of the centre, under the guise of taking a 'genuine', critical interest in the different spaces of the exotic. What Said calls 'a realistic sense of terrain' is no doubt crucial, if the figure of the traveller is to be salvaged or rescued.

Travel has already brought me to anthropology. Again, all societies have had their ways of perceiving and thinking about others, which have no doubt often prompted comparative reflection upon their own customs, and innovation. Anthropology, however, is not merely a disciplined expression of a universal human curiosity, but a modern discourse that has subsumed humanity to the grand narratives and analogies of natural history. Even when anthropology has apparently been a project of hermeneutics rather than the science of man, particular peoples (or races, or cultures) have been seen, like species, as the bearers of particular characters, physiques, dispositions, systems of meaning and forms of social and political organization. The interest in the characterization of others' natures and others' cultures that this leads to is quite different from a self–other dynamic that must be universal. Sometimes a relativist project, this has also been articulated with evolutionary hierarchization, and has implicated anthropology deeply in the practical work of colonialism: if ethnology was in fact often of little practical value for administration, it can be understood at least to reinforce an imperial sense of epistemic superiority. The prosecution, in the case of anthropology and imperialism, can bring forward an enormous range of evidence; but it is important to recall that anthropology has never been just this or entirely this. What is most neglected at present in the chorus of criticism is the fact that a great deal of contemporary anthropology not only responds to, but is motivated by, the work of 'postcolonial' critics such as Edward Said. Some of the criticism has, moreover, been generated within the discipline; as Johannes Fabian has pointed out, it is precisely the intersubjective space of ethnographic encounters that prompts and demands such questioning of objectifying scientistic discourses.[3] In this restless and critical mode, historical anthropology offers a localized vision, not of communities imagined outside global relationships, but of moments, transactions and events in the constitution and reconstitution of colonial power. If the discipline was long predicated on the elision of the colonial processes to which 'cold societies' in fact owed their distinctiveness, the oxymoronic contortion of an 'anthropology of colonialism' may provide an effective alternative to the weakly contextualized analyses that abound in colonial studies at present.

This amounts to saying that travel, modernity, anthropology and colonialism are constitutive of each other, and since postcolonial critique is necessarily deeply engaged with colonialism, it is not surprising that the deconstruction of the imperial museum of anthropological knowledge is supervised by a reinvented anthropology (which can also take J. W. Lindt's studio as one of its sites for fieldwork). Nor that for the critique of travel writing, travel paradoxically is privileged as a metaphor for intellectual liberty. Postcolonialism is distinguished, not by a clean leap into another discourse, but by its critical reaccentuation of colonial and anti-colonial languages. This may seem a compromised and partial step, but it is one which expresses the impossibility of simply transcending or forgetting the anxious violence of colonial power.

This book has two parts, but is not divided into 'Part I' and 'Part II' because they overlap and interpenetrate. The first is a discussion of theoretical questions and influential texts, and the second pursues the issues through case studies. I begin with Edward Said's *Orientalism*, a book which has inspired many of those who have written more recently on colonial discourse. While the book is deservedly widely read, it has been treated as an exemplary critique of Western discourse concerning non-Western populations; this textbook status is problematic, simply because responses to the Middle East leave us unprepared for the singularity of representations of other regions, such as east Asia and the Pacific (which are not only different culturally and historically, but figure in global politics and strategic contests in an entirely different way). Even if a critic's sole interest was in emulating *Orientalism*, that would not be done effectively by generalizing its account, but only by beginning with the same broad assumptions and investigating what discourses on a particular region presumed, and how they had evolved. And it is hardly uncharitable to Said, whose subsequent writings have been equally distinctive and compelling, to suggest that *Orientalism* cannot, in any case, serve as a theoretical charter for colonial cultural studies. While some of the issues it raised remain central, there were also basic weaknesses, such as a relatively simplistic approach to the gendering and sexualization of colonial relationships; some of these shortcomings are further discussed below.

Developments of colonial discourse theory can be found in influential essays by Homi Bhabha, Gayatri Chakravorty Spivak and Abdul JanMohamed, but despite their many stimulating propositions these exemplify deficiencies of the kind mentioned above; in place of this 'critical Fanonism' I advocate an understanding of a pluralized field of colonial narratives, which are seen less as signs than as practices, or as signifying practices rather than elements of a code. In this emphasis I am inspired by, if not rigorously following, the work of Pierre Bourdieu; his interest in located subjectivities informs an analytic strategy which situates colonial representations and narratives in terms of agents, locations and periods; these terms are conducive to a far more differentiated vision – of colonialisms rather than colonialism. At the same time, however, these located projects must be seen in the context of larger shifts, and I develop the questions referred to earlier concerning the distinctiveness of modern representations of others within a paradigm of anthropologically informed government.

In the second part of this book, I illustrate the value of this historicized, ethnographic approach through discussion of a number of colonial projects and discourses from the late nineteenth and early twentieth centuries. The first of these exhibits the peculiar modernity of 'governmentality', the second and third illustrate rival colonizing projects which offered other models of difference and narratives of settlement, and the fourth displays the failures of colonial representation as well as its triumphs. I should note here that all these examples are drawn from British empire histories, not only because of the limits of my own scholarly competence, but also because I wish to focus on differences between competing models of colonization rather than what might appear to be differing national styles.

Why focus on that period, rather than on that of the conquest of America, or the eighteenth century? While stimulating reinterpretations are being offered of colonial histories and imaginings of almost every conceivable epoch and region, the late nineteenth century has, I suggest, a special importance, not just because it was the period in which the largest proportion of the world was under direct colonial rule. Somewhat more important, for my purposes, is the fact that the epoch is the one with which colonialism is most associated, in a broad, cultural sense: by virtue of a muddle of texts, histories and names – the Scramble for Africa, Stanley, Conrad and Kipling – Empire and the late nineteenth century connote one another. While there is clearly some justification for defining imperialism, as a political ideology and a form of expansive capitalism, in historically specific terms, it is another thing to assume that colonialism in general is somehow typified by this period. One of my arguments is that colonial culture is conceived both in theoretical circles and in at least some wider public usage in unsatisfactorily narrow terms; my sense is that these restrictive conceptions are best undermined by establishing that even examples drawn from the Victorian period cannot be contained by the model of racial denigration and

domination that is frequently proposed or presupposed. The
point of breaking from this unitary idea is not some perverse
argument that colonialism was not really as vicious or unpleasant
as has previously been thought, nor is it mainly intended to lead
to a more empirically particular understanding of colonialism's
innumerable localized manifestations. What I want to establish,
rather, is that a wider and more plural formulation changes the
way we perceive the present: in particular, I hope that it equips us
better to contest contemporary forms of colonial culture which
tend not to be recognized as such.

My concluding chapter, therefore, moves from the early twentieth century to contemporary representations, and particularly to
the primitivism which is conspicuous in constructions of native
peoples in Australasia and north America. While this might be
seen as a perpetuation of an earlier kind of colonial discourse – as
it indeed resonates with a succession of older representations – I
suggest that it needs to be accounted for as a historically situated
expression, in the same way that I earlier account for the administrative culture of the British in Fiji, the imaginations of
evangelical missionaries, the fantasies of 'constructive Imperialism' in South Africa and a number of other discourses. The
suggestion that contemporary primitivism exemplifies a further
kind of colonial culture may place left–liberal culture as the most
recent expression in a series; this way of situating the present
should suggest that relations of cultural colonialism are no more
easily shrugged off than the economic entanglements that continue to structure a deeply asymmetrical world economy. But at
the same time I do not wish to construct colonialism as an unlimited or entirely inescapable system. A further reason for dealing with contemporary primitivisms is that they are in the process
of being challenged and undone through a variety of creolized
and subversive indigenous performances. My consideration of the
senses in which these interventions are postcolonial constitutes
not only this book's ending, but a limit of colonialism's culture
itself.

1

From Present to Past: the Politics of Colonial Studies

The scene: a Canberra kitchen. The voices: a radio breakfast programme. We have just heard the BBC world roundup and a brief discussion of the latest AIDS figures from Thailand; now, a well-known political journalist, a white woman, is interviewing an Australian writer, a white man, about his recently published history of an Aboriginal massacre in New South Wales in the early nineteenth century – a massacre of Aborigines, of course, rather than one perpetrated by them. After he gives a summary account of the tragic events, both parties to the conversation lament the brutality and racism common to the perpetrators and the settler society of the time. She opines: 'It seems to me that all the colonizers last century were like that. They thought that the native peoples were simply inferior, that the right thing to do was go in and take their land, never mind how many you killed.' 'Absolutely right,' he agrees, 'they knew in their hearts it was wrong, but they all acted that way.' 'Not just the British either,' she adds, 'but the Germans, French, and Belgians as well – horrible!' This exclamation seems to exorcize the spectre of past savagery; a few remarks more, and the slice of history is displaced by chat about new movies, and then a news update – the AIDS figures again.

The listener, washing coffee cups, has mixed feelings about this, as he does about the book he is attempting to write about forms of colonial culture. Of course, it is a good thing that the invasive character of the white nation's history can be discussed and confronted, and important that this can take place on national radio rather than in small-circulation left-wing magazines or among minority dissidents; and since this has not always been the case, the conversation marks a kind of progress. But what was said also manifests a popular perception of colonialism that is absolutely misleading, not 'absolutely right'. In this understanding, colonialism was monolithic, uncontested and efficacious. It is also an understanding which fails to speak of what colonialism *is*; instead, it *was* this and that, and is evoked most frequently as a late nineteenth-century phenomenon, here Australian settler violence, elsewhere through the names of Livingstone and Stanley. Its aggression was licensed by a racism common to Europeans, although this is seen, at least by the writer of Aboriginal history, to have been at odds with an underlying or universal moral feeling; there was an implicit sense, even at the time, that colonialism was a negative or shameful venture. This repressed truth can now be recovered and paraded, by a historian-analyst emulating Auden's Freud:

> he merely told
> The unhappy Present to recite the Past
>   Like a poetry lesson till sooner
>   or later it faltered at the line where
>
> Long ago the accusations had begun . . .
>   'In Memory of Sigmund Freud'

If the Victorian epoch is seen as the colonial age *par excellence* (as, notwithstanding Foucault, it is associated especially with sexual repression), there may be a sense in which the period figures as an other against which an open liberal modernity has defined itself, with respect both to sexuality and racism: those bad old ideas no longer have a hold on us, no longer sustain a false morality or a false hierarchy of colour. It is all too evident that this kind of progressive self-fashioning would stereotype the era in something like the same way that geographically removed societies or peoples have been stereotyped (as has been far more frequently noted) for the purposes of self-definition and self-affirmation. Of course, dead people can hardly be troubled by being 'othered'; the problem is to do with the extent to which we may be fooling ourselves.

If an image of colonialism as nineteenth-century racist oppression really does have some currency in the nebulous spaces of public discourse, conflicting notions are no doubt equally alive:

on the reactionary side, attitudes to empire may be frankly nostalgic; on the other, radicals are hardly alone in seeing racist ideas,
practices and social structures as possessing continuing power,
not being merely unfortunate relics of a superseded ideology that
once legitimized plantation slavery in America and white conquest in societies such as Australia, South Africa and New Zealand.
If, in evoking this idea that colonialism has been seen basically as
a homogeneous thing of the past, I am caricaturing public culture
to the same extent that I accuse it of caricaturing history, it is
notable that much the same understanding, or misunderstanding,
has recently been attributed to anthropology. Reflecting in a 1989
essay on the shortcomings of a discourse that is of course im-
measurably more elaborate and sophisticated than the chat show
banter I have recalled, Ann Stoler suggested that the attention
bestowed by ethnographers upon cultural complexity among the
colonized has never been matched by interest or sensitivity to
heterogeneity and tension among colonizers:

> even where we have probed the nature of colonial discourse and
> the politics of its language, the texts are often assumed to express
> a shared European mentality, the sentiments of a unified, conquer-
> ing elite . . . even when we have attended to concrete capitalist
> relations of production and exchange, we have taken colonialism
> and its European agents as an abstract force, as a *structure* imposed
> on local *practice*. The terms *colonial state, colonial policy, foreign capi-
> tal,* and *the white enclave* are often used interchangeably . . .
> colonizers and their communities are frequently treated as diverse
> but unproblematic, viewed as unified in a fashion that would dis-
> turb our ethnographic sensibilities if applied to ruling elites of the
> colonized . . . the assumption that colonial political agendas are
> self-evident precludes our examination of the cultural politics of
> the communities in which colonizers lived.[1]

Stoler proceeded to note that racism has long been seen as the
common denominator of colonial cultures, 'as a virtually built in
and natural product of that encounter, essential to the social
construction of an otherwise illegitimate and privileged access to
property and power'. This perception, which she attributes to
writers such as Albert Memmi and Jean-Paul Sartre, among others,
accords with the perception of nineteenth-century settler cultures
as uniformly and unambiguously racist, which I found character-

istic of the debate on Australia's violent conquest history. To question this view of the past is not to deny that colonizers often represented the peoples they encountered and dispossessed through bestializing imagery, and acted accordingly; it is not to deny that colonialism was often marked by an almost incomprehensible excess of violence, by a form of terrorism.[2] But, as Stoler points out, this homogenizing vision 'accords poorly with the fact that the *quality* and *intensity* of racism vary enormously in different colonial contexts and at different historical moments.'[3]

Three further points might be added to Stoler's objections to the ways colonialism has been typically understood. First, a radical anti-essentialist might claim that 'racism' is meaningless as a general category – given, say, the differences between discourses of discrimination associated with slavery in the American South, Pakistanis in Britain and dispossessed indigenous peoples in Australia or Palestine. Certainly, the 'colour prejudice' that might be common to these examples is hardly the most fundamental problem. Perhaps less obviously but still more crucially, it needs to be added that some models of inequality between peoples, that set colonizers above colonized and licensed the former to enslave or wage war upon the latter, were not based on notions of racial difference at all, but (for instance) on religious distinctions and ideas about the appropriate conduct of Christians towards those who rejected the faith. Racism, then, is not a universal feature of inter-ethnic or inter-societal relations;[4] where it is indisputably present, as an element of colonial perception or government, it takes forms that are variable both because they emerge from particular traditions and vocabularies through which human difference is recognized, theorized and aesthetically responded to; and because these conceptions, whether present in elaborate intellectual form or manifested unreflectively and practically, are either sharpened or ameliorated by the dynamics of particular colonial confrontations.

Associated with this homogenization of racism is the prevalent perception of colonialism as a destructive process and one which entailed inexcusable denials of the sovereignty and autonomy of the colonized; this obscures the extent to which colonial projects were in many cases regarded as civilizing, progressive, necessary undertakings. Not merely were particular forms of economic extraction or appropriation rationalized, but the construction of new societies was seen as an advancement upon corrupt and overcrowded regimes in Europe – hence the colonizers might see themselves, as well as the colonized, being uplifted in new lands. As Johannes Fabian has recently suggested, not only 'the crooks and brutal exploiters, but the honest and intelligent agents of colonialism need to be accounted for.'[5]

Second, it is widely assumed that colonialism was pervasively efficacious: natives were extirpated, the impact was fatal, the colonized were dominated and assimilated. The extent to which these perceptions require qualification is variable, and it could not be denied that in some cases colonizers did wipe out or almost wipe out indigenous populations, as they also completely displaced local economies with regimes of plantation slavery or settler pastoralism. A 'fatal impact' has, however, been detected in European historiography far more frequently than it actually occurred, and this is no doubt linked with the appeal of a romantic narrative that nostalgically regrets the destruction of idealized precolonial communities.[6] Though generally sympathetic to the plight of the colonized, such perceptions frequently exaggerate colonial power, diminishing the extent to which colonial histories were shaped by indigenous resistance and accommodation. In many cases what may appear as the exercise of colonial hegemony – the imposition of Christianity, for example – is in fact better understood as the appropriation of introduced institutions, material objects or discourses to strategic effect on the part of colonized peoples, or particular groups within them.[7] Fantasies of conquest were frequently realized only partially or farcically; rituals of colonial administration may have created an appearance of dominance and order, an aura of government, that was matched neither by practical control nor by more than a limited transformation of indigenous life; and the products of assimilation were taken to be subversive as often as they attested to the successes of civilizing missions.[8] It is misleading even to attribute uniformly to colonizers an imagining of, or a will to, total dominance: colonial rule was frequently haunted by a sense of insecurity, terrified by the obscurity of 'the native mentality' and overwhelmed by indigenous societies' apparent intractability in the face of government; even if colonial knowledge often took the form of a panoptical, encyclopedic appropriation of indigenous customs, histories, relics and statistics, such displays of intellectual rapacity were frequently accompanied by a kind of despair, which found the space and social entity of the colony to be intangible, imperceptible and constantly untrue to the representations that might be fashioned of it.[9] In other words, even when colonizers surrounded themselves with the persuasive scenery of possession and rule, the gaps between projection and performance are frequently betrayed by the anxieties of their texts, which reveal the gestural character of efforts to govern, sanitize, convert and reform. And it is not merely a matter of some proportion of success and failure, but also a question of exchange, and the extent to which particular colonizing projects are inflected or altered by the indigenous societies they encounter.

Third, and as was implied above, an assumption that colonialism is primarily a social form of the past entails definitions that are too specific – for example, that it is the formal rule of a dominion by a metropolitan country. Particularly if our interest is in colonial *culture*, it is important to recognize that a variety of colonial representations and encounters both precede and succeed periods of actual possession and rule, and pertain in generalized forms about whole regions or continents at a level detached from particular imperial ventures. Colonial culture thus includes not only official reports and texts related directly to the process of governing colonies and extracting wealth, but also a variety of travellers' accounts, representations produced by other colonial actors such as missionaries and collectors of ethnographic specimens, and fictional, artistic, photographic, cinematic and decorative appropriations. To acknowledge that such a range of cultural products is in some sense inflected by colonial relationships is not to propose some new, highly inclusive definition of colonialism, as if that were a solution. The interest is rather in establishing how productive it is to pose a series of questions about, for example, how differences between colonizers and colonized are postulated in particular texts, and how the temporal development of those relations is imagined through narratives that may project conquest, assimilation, segregated development or some other transformation. These questions are as salient to recent works like the 1991 Oscar-winning film *Dances with Wolves* as they are to obvious examples from nineteenth-century exploratory writing: it is this very challenge to the present that justifies the renewed attention that colonialism is receiving. If there is some disadvantage in undoing 'colonialism' as a coherent object, the compensation lies in the exclusion of a secure progressive narrative that too easily separates a colonial past and a liberal present. If colonial perceptions and relations can take diverse forms – including, say, a gentle exoticism as well as racist settler violence – a stance of comfortable dissociation from what is being analysed and criticized is less available; we may indeed be distant from some colonizing projects, but not necessarily from all. This question of how contemporary critical exercises are motivated and situated with respect to what is analysed will be further addressed below.

This suggestion, that colonial ideologies may have been more variable, complex and ambivalent than has been generally acknowledged, may offend some who are quite appropriately disgusted by the acts of violence and sexual exploitation that were and still are conspicuous elements of colonial relationships; it may appear that an appeal for a more nuanced analysis is likely to rehabilitate projects that were fundamentally invasive and destructive. But an argument that draws attention to positive imaginings of colonialism in the discourses of colonizers should not be mistaken for one that rereads the relationships and projects in positive terms. The aim is not to rehabilitate imperial efforts, but to understand how far and why they were (and are) supported by various classes and interest groups; it is important, for example, to appreciate why Zionism long attracted so much support among organized labour and the left; a diagnosis of the grounds of its original appeal does not so much endorse the movement, as help explain how something that was recognized by a range of those involved at the time as a brutal exercise in dispossession could also be represented as a progressive, collectivist form of pioneering that redressed rather than created a historical injustice. This interest in the cultural construction of particular colonizing projects is thus not a denial of their violations of human rights or of their racism; it is rather an effort to account for their possibility, and for the imaginative and practical specificity of the intrusions that colonized populations had to resist or accommodate.

The sense that there needs to be a new anthropology of colonialism parallels concerns in a range of humanities disciplines: espe-

cially since the mid-1980s, there has been a wave of new analyses
and critiques concerned with race, imperialism, Orientalism and
related topics, in literary studies, art history, cultural studies, political theory, work on film and photography, the histories of
science and medicine and, of course, in history generally. In some
of these areas, such as the history of ideas, there had been long
traditions of writing on ideas of race or the exotic, as in art history
there have been numerous compendia of Western images of Indians or blacks, but such studies tend to have been reinvigorated
or redirected conceptually as a result of the influence of feminism
and various strands of critical theory. Hence, while texts in the
1960s might have been concerned with British 'attitudes' toward
Africans, or 'perceptions' of them (emphasizing individual
prejudices), work in the 1980s and 1990s has often used the term
'colonial discourse' (and dealt rather with collective traditions).[10]

This recent plethora of scholarship has involved efforts of several kinds. Baldly, the project in literature could be seen as the
converse of the anthropological and historical effort, in the sense
that the former has put colonialism into culture while the latter
has put culture into colonialism. Critics have argued that particular texts, and especially canonical works such as *The Tempest* and
Jane Eyre, are to some degree 'about imperialism' (or race or
colonialism) in ways that had previously been ignored or diminished;[11] anthropologists and historians, on the other hand, have
been pointing out that colonial exploration and administration
are not self-evident crudely political operations, but practices perceived and enacted through fields of symbolism and meaning,
that are often densely conflicted and contradictory.[12] In both
cases, there has also been an interest in recovering non-canonical
sources and materials, such as apparently minor works of travel
literature, or colonial postcards, which were previously beneath
any serious critical or historical interpretative vision. Much of this
work has also, of course, been oppositional, in the sense that
dominant versions of colonial histories have been contested, not
just by work on black and non-European literatures, or by populist
histories 'from below' that have challenged elite narratives, but
also in a more fundamental way through critical deconstruction of
the operations and politics of colonialist historiography.[13] This
typifies the way in which the further representation of colonial
subjects, relations and histories is now seen to be implicated – in

either a collaborative or oppositional way – with the dominant discourses of the past. This sense of urgency about the politics of representation has also given writing on the colonial dimension of anthropology itself a different dimension; while the critiques of the late 1960s and early 1970s were mainly concerned with practical collaboration between anthropologists, colonial administrations and military intelligence, and with the fact that anthropologists had largely neglected the incorporation of many 'traditional' societies into the global economy, the new debates explored asymmetries of representation, presumptions of authority and the ways in which anthropological constructions of cultural difference could elide sexual and other differences and fetishize certain kinds of exotic authenticity.[14]

Much of this work has necessarily been interdisciplinary; it has almost created a postdisciplinary humanities field, in which histories, cultural studies, cultural politics, narratives and ethnographies all intersect and are all open to being challenged. If there is something basically enabling and positive in the undoing of disciplinary boundaries, authoritative privileges and canonical sources and modes of presentation, it may nevertheless be too easy to celebrate this new fluidity, this new scope for exhilarating trespasses. It would be a pity if the spectacle of intellectual plurality fostered a relativist permissiveness, that acknowledged the fertility of diverse agendas and refused to discriminate among them. It remains important to argue about the effectiveness of different disciplinary technologies; about the politics of analytical strategies; about priorities among different ways of contextualizing texts and events; about the appropriateness of particular theoretical languages. Where there is such a low level of common or credible agreement about objectives and standards within particular disciplines, any argument is likely to be partial and contentious, but nevertheless in this book I espouse a historicization of colonialism (but not a historicism that imagines some progress or teleology); and I argue against certain deconstructive and psychoanalytical approaches. I emphasize that this is not an argument against deconstruction, but against some expressions of it and for the kind of deconstructive history that Gyan Prakash has recently called 'postfoundationalist';[15] it is not about disciplines such as anthropology and history that might be opposed to literary scholarship and cultural studies; it depends less on discipline-based criteria of adequacy than, first, on the importance of a nuanced understanding of the plurality of colonizing endeavours and their continuing effects, and second, on what I would claim is the overarching value of political relevance. My adjudications, like any other critical arguments, are both limited and enabled by their particular geographic, social and cultural locations, and though their blindnesses and weaknesses are no doubt more obvious to others than they ever can be to me, I attempt below to say where I stand.

In referring to political relevance, I do not mean any narrow relevance to a programme, interest group or struggle, but that some intellectual projects address the circumstances of scholars and their audiences in the world far more directly than others, in aspiring to help both parties to account for the cultural and political predicaments that surround us. It is this sense of intellectual and cultural worldliness, conspicuous in the works of Raymond Williams and Edward Said, that I seek to argue for here, not an index of political correctness or a false assumption of militancy on the part of academics who, after all, are engaged in privileged work at some remove from the most consequential theatres of political debate and action.

This is to presuppose a relationship between present scenes of writing and reading and the analyses of past discourses and encounters that constitute colonial cultural studies. At some level, the reason for exploring histories and representations is a sense that despite their remoteness in time, they have some resonance and bearing upon our continuing arguments with contemporary imperialism and racism; this sense is particularly conspicuous in feminist critique. The urgency that runs through much writing on colonialism could surely not be accounted for if all that mattered was a better knowledge of the past, if there was not also an interest in what Foucault called a critique of the present, an effort to use history to impose a new perception of sexuality, political economy, welfare, and modernity – or, what bell hooks has called a yearning for change.[16] But the intensity of this wish to be critically effective is not matched by self-evident or unproblematic links between a historical and geographical 'elsewhere' of analysis and a 'here' of living and writing. It is not obvious, for example, that current writing on colonialism has emulated Foucault's style of using histories to subvert the present: the past does not show up the contingency of modern conceptions and arrangements; it is not used to deform a progressivist understanding of where we have arrived.[17] This is not to say that Foucault's work offers a good model or the only model, or to accuse those whose writing exhibits political motivation of mere posturing and self-validation (even if there is much more oppositional style than real opposition).[18] It is rather to suggest that if the political worldliness of certain historical and textual inquiries is not to be merely a matter of wishful thinking, or of gestures stemming from desires that are 'unclarified and unreconciled',[19] it is necessary to address more directly how former colonial discourses and the present might be related.

One operation discloses conformity between the colonial past and the locations in which critics read and write.[20] While the sort of popular understanding that I alluded to earlier would see colonial practices and ideas as a past ensemble, one sort of analysis exposes continuities between former colonialist ideologies and those that retain currency and dynamism in the present. This could be seen as an inversion of the strategy of relativizing displacement which has long been employed in critical or sceptical European writing. When Michel de Certeau declared that 'Other regions give us back what our culture has excluded from its discourse,' he was referring particularly to the efforts of Pierre Bourdieu and Foucault to expose the peculiar 'tactics' of modern Western society via the 'different spaces' of Algeria and the French ancien régime,[21] but the comment holds for a much broader field within and beyond anthropology: the *difference* of another cultural or discursive regime has consistently been used to disclose the specificity and contingency of the present. In the case of anti-colonial critique, it is the *similarity* of past and present that defamiliarizes the here and now and subverts the sense of historical progress. That sense, that permits the radio announcer to take comfort in the distance between a colonial massacre and the presence of our speech and writing, is undone, the distance effaced or blurred, by a detemporalization of colonialism.

In its overall rhetoric, Edward Said's *Orientalism* exemplifies this argument for continuity or conformity. Said's book has of course been extensively discussed, but often in ways that have been either uncritical (on the part of followers) or hypercritical (on the part of defensive practitioners of Asian studies, among others); for some, it is 'three hundred pages of twisted, obscure, incoherent, ill-informed, and badly written diatribe';[22] for others, it effects the radical step of shifting 'the locus of contemporary theory from the Left Bank to the West Bank and beyond.'[23] While *Orientalism* has still not received a balanced assessment, despite the surfeit of comment, I do not attempt to provide a comprehensive critique here, but instead draw attention to differences between Edward Said's project in that book and projects that seem necessary now, from my own perspective.

While critical interest in colonial representation appears to be a recent phenomenon, there were many earlier studies of 'images of' non-European peoples. An array of stereotypes were identified, from the monsters at the edges of maps and women with sagging breasts of medieval and Renaissance accounts, to the noble and ignoble savages of the Enlightenment voyages and the nineteenth century; from the simian cannibals of primitive tribes and effete despots of Asiatic civilizations, to representations prevalent today, such as the fanatical Arabs of terrorist journalism and the passive and beguiling women of tourism's Asia. Some are debased, some are picturesque, some are seductive, others are threatening; all are evidently distortions that reveal more about the interests and motivations of observers than they do about whoever is notionally represented. Figures of this kind indeed abound in the media, and in colonial literature and art, but the idea of the stereotype is at once too static and too free-floating to have much enduring critical value. On one side, the stability of a figure such as the 'noble savage' distracts us from the differing values which idealized natives might bear in various narratives; on the other, the type is not linked with any particular colonizing or imaginative venture, but is generally present or available to certain cultural traditions.

It would have to be said, as well, that much work on European images has been documentary rather than critical or analytical: this has been especially true of the exhibition catalogues and compendia in which visual materials have often been reproduced. The result is that an intriguing plethora of sources have been presented, while their discursive affiliations and underlying epistemologies were frequently passed over. Edward Said's studies undoubtedly drew on some of this kind of work, but completely transformed the field by drawing attention to the ways in which a whole series of European writers and scholars created a texted Orient through persistent images and metaphors, some of which were numbingly familiar.

> It is utterly impossible to induce the natives to build their boats after any improved system. Year after year, though they have beautiful European models before their eyes, the obstinate fools persist in turning out hundreds of these execrably-devised boats . . . and why? because their fathers, and their grandfathers, and their fathers before them, from time immemorial, have continued to build their boats so.[24]

Notions such as the idea that Oriental customs had remained unchanged for thousands and thousands of years were not merely stereotypes current in certain circles or traditions, or instances of some simple individual bias, but expressions of an evolving and enduring discourse of Orientalism. Through repetition and claims to authority, this tradition created a reality that it appeared merely to describe, and thus acquired 'material presence or weight';[25] it placed a tremendous burden upon a geographic distinction between East and West, and bestowed truth upon the characteristics of an eternalized totality evoked as 'the East'; it was possible for statements to be made about 'the' Oriental mind, Oriental manners, personality, and so on; a field was defined through which societies, people and events were represented, not on the basis of their own statements, but by European experts, whose writing presumed the silence and absence of Orientals themselves. Hence Said appropriated Marx's famous – or notorious – claim concerning the inability of the peasantry to speak or act on their own behalf: 'They cannot represent themselves; they must be represented.'[26] Some critics claimed Marx's reference to a more literal kind of political representation was being distorted,[27] but the very resonance of the sentence marks the extent to which Said's book had shifted the issue from the bias of particular depictions to one of the politics of discursive representation.

> How does one represent another culture? What is another culture? Is the notion of a distinct culture (or race, or religion, or civilization) a useful one, or does it always get involved either in self-congratulation (when one discusses one's own) or hostility and

aggression (when one discusses the 'other')? ... How do ideas
acquire authority, 'normality,' and even the status of 'natural'
truth?[28]

These concerns stem in part from Foucault's insistence upon
the political character of knowledge: the emergent task is not
the separation of a true knowledge of the Orient from the ideological constructs of Orientalism, but a dissection of the kind
of truth that Orientalist discourse produces. While the anger of
Said's account arose partly from the sheer distortions of Western
representation, what was singular in his analysis was not a familiar
critique of its 'prejudices' and 'biases', but its production of authority and essentialized collectivities: propositions were not true
of individual Arabs, or of some Arabs, but of an abstracted singular figure, 'the' Arab. Against these typifications, Said often ap-
peals to ideas of shared humanity. James Clifford has pointed out
that this rests upon a humanism entirely at odds with Said's
chief theoretical debt to Foucault, and reference to a common
underlying nature that is not culturally differentiated is certainly
unwelcome and problematic from the perspective of anthropological relativism.[29] Clifford however neglects the political question of the extent to which claims about human sameness have
often been far more powerful (in anti-slavery and civil rights
movements, for example) than expressions of native difference.
But the issue is not crucial for the adequacy of Said's critique,
since Orientalist (and anthropological) preoccupations with racial, ethnic and cultural differences can be displaced, not by a
universalism, but by an interest in a plethora of differences that
would crosscut ethnic–cultural totalities and subvert the language
that specifies the natures of 'the' Balinese or 'the' Fulani. The
argument, then, would not be that colonial and anthropological
accounts of the exotic and different Balinese are false because the
people concerned are really the same as everyone else, but that
differences of gender, religion, social strata, historical experience,
and so on pluralize Balinese culture as deeply as they do any
other. The fact that a universalist argument might be of more
political value for a particular group is a problematic but somewhat distinct issue.
 Said's work has been enormously challenging in the specifically
academic context because it established the extent to which os-

tensibly scholarly accounts of Islam and the Middle East have consistently resorted to reification, mystification and distortion, in a manner that must be traced to the perception of the Arab nationalist movements and states as threatening enemies needing to be controlled and contained. In separate publications Said had documented the representation of the Palestine question and Islam in the media and in the writings of 'experts';[30] if his critiques seemed crude and repetitive, they were no more so than the works in Middle Eastern studies that he discussed, which were situated largely within the agendas of American foreign policy, and for the most part reflected the extremely negative views of Arabs and Arab perspectives then prevalent. Said did note in 1978 that greater revision and dissent had characterized academic work on other regions, such as Africa and east Asia,[31] and by now this is also true of Middle Eastern studies, even though, more than a decade later, it is still possible for absurd racist generalizations concerning, for instance, the Arab mentality and propensity for violence, to be dressed up in quasi-scholarly guise; David Pryce-Jones' *The Closed Circle: an Interpretation of the Arabs* is a bestselling example (see discussion in chapter 3). The authority of Orientalist texts may have diminished, but their proliferation has not.

The progressive and optimistic liberal idea that former stereotypes have been superseded by a more scientific or objective way of seeing, or by the close and sympathetic vision of anthropology, is thus undermined. If we discover hidden harmonies between the kinds of authority appealed to in modern scholarship and in older colonial discourses, it becomes difficult to avoid a dogged and continuing interrogation of the motives implicit in academic descriptions and commentaries, even those that are just being invented in various kinds of experimental ethnography. That might seem like a sort of nagging, a tedious interruption of the proper business of well-defined scholarly work – but just as nagging typically arises from the logic of kinship and domesticity, this disrespectful heckling is founded in the kinship and ancestry of anthropological representation.

The general point that emerges is that academic disciplines cannot be distanced from imperial relationships through some separation between political and non-political representation. On the contrary: the questions must always arise of what claims are being made by particular texts, how and why they employ notions of national, racial or cultural difference and what political concerns are embodied in, or furthered by, particular descriptions. However, Said's imputation that discourses of cultural difference – whether manifested in fiction, travel-writing, anthropology or other scholarly work – always ultimately involve 'hostility and aggression' is unproductive. There are too many forms of colonial representation which are, at least at one level, sympathetic, idealizing, relativistic and critical of the producers' home societies. If the critic assumes that the problem with Orientalist and kindred discourses is that they are negative, he or she is distracted from representations which are manifestly not aggressive, but which may through exoticism or primitivism nevertheless become legislative, by privileging certain identities and stigmatizing others as inauthentic.

However, Said's over-emphasis on the negative dimensions of Orientalism needs to be placed in its context. While black Africans and Australian Aborigines are often portrayed in sympathetic or humanistic ways at present, in contrast to the highly racist images typical of the nineteenth and early twentieth centuries,[32] the trajectory with respect to the Middle East is virtually the reverse: there was a distinct 'arabophile' strand in nineteenth-century views, that continues to be conspicuous up to say the 1950s in books such as those of Charles Doughty and Wilfred Thesiger, and in films like Frank Hurley's 1948 *Cradle of Creation*,[33] that sentimentally idealized the biblical lifestyle of marsh-dwellers, pastoralists and Jerusalem potters. While these texts mostly failed to question the privilege of Western perception, and often rendered Middle Eastern societies as archaic, picturesque and decaying, they frequently dealt with individuals rather than types, and oscillated between approbation and denigration. But the circumstances of the Arab–Israeli conflict from 1948 on led to a consolidation of the most negative of prior images, which were later augmented by deeply dehumanizing constructions of the terrorists who, it was explicitly suggested, took up where Hitler had left off. These images were (and still are), circulated like other cultural products in a diverse and uncoordinated way through feature films, novels, journalistic commentary and many other means, but the specifically political effectiveness of such representations was ensured by the efforts of the pro-Israel lobby in the United States to silence and discredit pro-Palestinian voices

– efforts which were remarkably successful up until the invasion of Lebanon in 1982. What must still be considered one of the most effective public relations operations of modern politics created a climate in which any advocacy of an Arab perspective, and even merely scholarly interests in more balanced accounts of events that had been profoundly distorted, was stigmatized and ident-ified with anti-Semitism. Even though Israel is now more widely perceived as a colonial-settler state – unique in its genesis and strategic location, but not in the political contradictions its exist-ence engenders – and as a racist society that presents problems not wholly alien to those belatedly being addressed in South Africa, the climate of opinion is still such that Said can be de-scribed as a 'Professor of Terror'.[34] In these circumstances, it is not surprising at all that the work he did in the 1970s was lar-gely preoccupied with the ways in which colonial discourses, even in their more complex and apparently sympathetic manifesta-tions, resorted to traditional denigrations that were ultimately aggressive.

In situating Said's work in this way, I endeavour to make it clear that the account he offered was appropriate (as it regrettably still is, to a large extent) to discourse about one part of the world, from the vantage point of a moment (a long, agonized and very costly moment) in political history; but it follows also that this will be incomplete and inadequate so far as other strands of colonial representation are concerned. A full, balanced or comprehensive account of colonialism's culture is indeed lacking in his work – as it must be lacking in any other, including this book. While an account may aspire to offer a global theory, or may, like Said's book, be referred to and read as though it did, any text on colonialism will be deeply shaped both by the positions from which we speak, and by the particular kinds of texts and histories we feel compelled to address. Hence Said's work is motivated, energized and limited by the fact of his being a Palestinian in the United States; in the same way the Subaltern Studies project is conditioned by its primary point of reference in the critique of south Asian nationalism, and by its ambiguous bases in both India and an academic diaspora; equally, the tone and orientation of less politically ambitious studies are inevitably deeply inflected by the particular representations that they work upon; these may be deeply racist (pornographic postcards from colonial Africa), or ennobling and romanticizing (the hardy Eskimos of the frozen wastes epitomize man's struggle with nature).[35]

The particular site and interest of this book was signalled by my opening anecdote. No white Australian can avoid taking one stance or another towards Aboriginal culture and to the history of invasion that permitted the establishment of the settler nation. My aim, though, is not to 'sympathize with' Aborigines, as though they should be grateful recipients of such intellectual charity; still less is it to attempt to rewrite colonialism from the other side, on their behalf, as it were; that has been done often enough. My departure point is not the 'problems' or 'experiences' of blacks, but the problematic ways in which contemporary white culture deals with Aboriginality.

In Australia, Aboriginal culture is now cherished rather than denigrated; what is indigenous is identified with the mythological Dreamtime, with the Rainbow Serpent, with spirituality, with caring for your relatives, with respect for the Land; with everything that is primordial, metaphysical and natural. In the environmental movement, and in the Green consciousness that has spread well beyond lobby and activist groups, Aboriginal uses of land and resources are idealized as non-destructive and caring, in contrast with white society's inability to restrain its extractive rapacity. Being Aboriginal is about not being greedy; it is about things that are elemental and ancestral; forces of the landscape and nature rather than artifices of the city and the self. The same is true of constructions of other indigenous peoples such as the New Zealand Maori and native North Americans; the 1991 Oscar-winning film, *Dances with Wolves*, ennobles Sioux in opposition to the wholly brutal and degenerate frontier whites, and moreover sentimentally establishes their form of sociality as one in which the white protagonist, alienated from his own society, can discover an identity, a name, a wholeness, even love, that seemed impossible elsewhere (see discussion in chapter 6). Similarly, a plaque commemorating a particular people in what is now British Columbia proclaims nostalgically that the band 'traditionally lived in harmony with nature, respecting and nurturing their world which provided food and shelter.'[36] Given how much in common there is between these accounts of different peoples, it is not surprising that primitive spirituality is frequently evoked as a homogeneous essence, that Africans, native Americans and Australians share.

'The tribal look is the hottest interior design trend in years' announces an article on two furniture-makers in a weekend newspaper's colour supplement.

> Jessner spent eight years with far-flung tribes in South Africa, especially the Ndebele people. Other influences include Navajo Indian and Aboriginal designs, and patterns from nature.
>
> Rogowski, who used to run Melbourne's Soda Sisters restaurant in Chapel Street, says, 'People are growing more aware of the environment. Primitive people are more in harmony with the earth. Their designs represent that, and the symbols are thought to have power in themselves. Perhaps people are intuitively responding to it.'[37]

It is apparent here that one tribal culture is interchangeable with others, that all are closer to nature and that even in the contrivance of their art, these natives operate at a natural,

Plate 1   *Furniture from Artikeln*

almost non-linguistic level; in the bourgeois living room, this culture evidently offers a spiritual palliative to our overheated, overconsuming, unnatural, postindustrial world. Primitivism has always inverted rather than subverted the hierarchies of civility and modernity, and there is nothing novel or surprising here, even if the commoditization of Green sentiment is more pronounced than would have been the case a decade ago. What needs to be noted, though, is that this essentialism has a negative side: the celebration of authentic Aborigines or Navajo fixes the proper identity of those peoples in their preservation and display of a folkloric and primitivized culture and denigrates and marginalizes urbanized or apparently acculturated members of these populations who speak English, lack ethnic dress, do not obviously conduct ceremonies and do not count as real natives to the same extent as those who continue to live in the bush and practise something closer to traditional subsistence. 'Compared with, and at times comparing themselves with, the "real Aborigines", Aboriginal people are caught between the attribution of unchanging essences (with the implication of an inability to change) and the reproach of inauthenticity.'[38] In fact, it could be argued that the persisting violence against Aborigines, manifested particularly in the willingness of the police in outback areas to imprison and brutalize large numbers for very minor alcohol-related offences, leading to a scandalous number of deaths in custody, is not separate from the primitivism of the sentimental conservationist, but is licensed by a similar underlying notion of what correct Aboriginality is: a drunk black can be an object of hatred in a way that a drunk white cannot, because the former is degenerate in the specific sense of being untrue to his or her racial and cultural nature.

What is striking, then, is the persistence of primitivist constructions of Aboriginality in a liberal culture that likes to think that its colonial and racist roots have been rejected. Does this mean that the perception of the present as a 'postcolonial' epoch is a fraudulent mystification? Are representations and narratives that could legitimately be seen to constitute a postcolonial culture inaccessible or inevitably marginal? And what kinds of anthropology and cultural critique might disrupt the complacency of one 'postcolonial' sense while creating spaces for the other? These predicaments amount to the situation from which this book is written, but do not constitute its subject-matter; I do not enter into an extensive discussion of cultural politics in Australia, but seek to develop a way of writing about colonial culture which is adequate to this kind of case and this political moment. A more direct address to my own scene of writing could have employed the same master rhetoric that empowered Said's *Orientalism*: in that case, as I have noted, the shock arises from the conformity between contemporary perceptions of the Middle East and long traditions of Orientalist denigration; in the case of attitudes toward indigenous Australians, Maori or native North Americans, the argument I have suggested in the preceding few paragraphs is that the apparently sympathetic representations of the present have a great deal in common with earlier, manifestly primitivist, discourses. This is evident particularly in the notion that indigenous sociality may be simpler than 'ours', but is marked by greater mutual respect, generosity and civility: a number of eighteenth-century voyagers in the Pacific found the warmth and 'Charity' of South Sea islanders preferable to the shallow Christianity of their countrymen,[39] while the author of a polemical fiction of the same period had his character despise the American Indians 'till I found them my equals in knowledge of many things of which I believed them ignorant; and my superiors in the virtues of friendship, hospitality, and integrity.'[40]

While it is important to show that contemporary representations such as *Dances with Wolves* lack the novelty that they claim, there are two reasons why this strategy of revealing the parallels between new and old discourses must be qualified and complemented by other critical operations. One reason is that an interpretation that discovers conformity is inevitably double-edged: it makes the conceptual advance of identifying a certain enduring discourse or rhetorical form, but inhibits analysis to the extent that the specificity of the constituent texts and projects must be understated. Hence, while contemporary primitivisms in North America and Australasia indeed have much in common with various antecedents, an argument that is primarily interested in establishing the common ground cannot avoid distorting and decontextualizing each case. Certainly, there is a sense that moral worth is found where material progress is not, which is common both to modern celebrations of indigenous life and to eighteenth-century polemic, but the critic can only be in shallow water if the particular meanings of associated terms, such as progress (in the eighteenth century) and environment and spirituality (in the twentieth), are neglected, and if the differences between contemporary enunciations of this sort of counter-modernism in societies with and without indigenous minorities are overlooked.

The second reason is that an argument for the conformity of contemporary Orientalism or contemporary primitivism with antecedent cultural stereotypes not only decontextualizes particular expressions of these discourses but risks treating them as historically continuous and pervasive. Stereotyping 'the Other' can be seen to accompany social asymmetries in any epoch, and in some form or another it no doubt does. This suggests, though, that colonial discourse has not been sufficiently specified, that it is not understood as something with particular cultural and political determinations. If more specific forms of colonial representation are defined, and situated within a field that is differentiated and fissured, continuities may indeed be postulated between certain discourses, but at the same time ruptures are identified that mark the emergence and the displacement of particular ways of constructing others and relating to them. Some colonial discourses may, then, be specifically modern, not codes for denigrating that people have always deployed against their neighbours and enemies. Some, also, have much longer lives than others; if these characters are to be stripped of their weapons and their authority, it is important that the opposition can discriminate between those whose past violence reverberates and those who continue to pursue their business methodically, quietly and efficiently.

2

Culture and Rule: Theories of Colonial Discourse

... anti-imperialist discourse has proved a last bastion for the project, and dream, of global theory.

Henry Louis Gates, Jr.

A commonsense understanding of colonial ideology, that might privilege the harsh racism conspicuous in the late nineteenth century, could be expected to fix upon representations such as Thomas Andrew's staged photograph of a cannibal feast, one of a series from the mid-1890s.[1] This is immediately recognizable as an image of primitive barbarity, but the categorical and exhaustive way in which it constructs the Fijian in these terms is worth elaborating upon.

First of all, Fijians are men, and Fiji is an undomesticated space, a jungle, in which male predatory aggression is the emblematic activity. Fijians are also homogenized as warriors with clubs: neither this photograph nor others in the series accord any emphasis to faces or individuals; instead we are shown examples of the anonymous, generic 'Fijian'. This type is unmarked by any civilizing influence whatsoever, even of a negative corrupting kind that might be manifested in guns or pipe-smoking. There is no trace of trade goods, of European clothes or even of contact; the photographer is merely an unseen witness to savagery's radically strange, yet wholly knowable practice of cannibalism. Given that the prominent weapons saturate the image with the Fijian propensity for violence, the photograph can also be seen as effecting an enormous historical displacement of aggression from Europeans, whose colonization of the Pacific depended upon military superiority and the deployment of force at innumerable moments, onto the native, whose complexity collapses into a personification of violence. Fijians are thus not only typed as cannibals, but also radically detemporalized, in that the history of their engagement

Plate 2 *Thomas Andrew, 'The Vanquished', c. 1894*

with Europeans, which in fact is the precondition for the representation, is erased. Although what I am concerned with here is the construction, not the misconstruction, of this sort of islander for this particular imagination, it is relevant that by the time the photograph was taken, Fijians, like most other Christian Pacific islanders, would routinely have worn garments of imported fabric, not the portrayed barkcloth that became reserved for ceremonial occasions. Just as the composition avoids the socialized spaces of the village and the garden, this contrivance suppresses the fact that – from the perspective, say, of evangelists or the British administration in Fiji – the Fijians had already been removed from their state of savagery and heathenism for decades. The elision of the colonial transformation of Fijian life denies any mutability or adaptability in the Fijian character, and excludes the scope for its assimilation to civilized norms (let alone any possibility of its legitimacy on its own terms). Instead, the radical difference and distance of Fijian life is stressed; the invisibility of any form of indigenous domesticity, however flawed, underlines this remoteness from recognizable sociality.

This essentialism has a counterpart in Andrew's photographs of islander women – generally Samoans rather than Fijians – who are dusky maidens sexualized in studio poses. In this case, and in some others, the relative 'advancement' of societies was encoded through gender: the Polynesian Samoans were imaged in feminine rather than masculine terms, as seductive rather than repugnant and threatening (and when Andrew photographed Samoan men, his subjects were mostly chiefs, often vaguely classicized as Polynesians had been since the Cook voyages). Peoples considered more barbarous, or as 'lower races', such as the Fijians and Lindt's Aborigines, were never dignified in this way. Without discussing the permutations that might be traced through a corpus of kindred images, it is clear that the women are similarly detached from any field of social existence, from kinship, domesticity and routines of daily life that make common humanity visible. Of course, any contemporary viewer with the most cursory knowledge of Fiji in the 1890s would have been aware that these pictures were misleading in an empirical sense, in that they did not depict scenes which someone walking around native villages would encounter; even anyone lacking such local knowledge would not take the evocation of a race of male cannibals literally.

There is scope for a good deal of speculative argument about the extent to which a viewer might have accepted or qualified the typifying implications of the islander imaged as masculine warrior or as dusky maiden, but what is important is rather the extent to which the discourse produces a canonical and essential figure, which may then constitute the truth behind any observed or contingent complexities. Hence colonial discourse could compare the appearance of the native, who might be an acculturated Christian, with his savage or cannibal essence; discrepancies did not establish that the European construct of the native's nature might be false, but that his hybridized being was somehow inauthentic.

It seems almost too obvious to add that this imaging of a nature is an operation of power; those photographed do not look at the camera, do not cast their own expressions of censure, mockery or even pathos back at the viewer, but are only unseeing objects of the Western viewer's gaze – of our gaze. To see the picture this 'obvious' way, however, is to be complicit in the result of the photographic process and to pass over the fact that this enactment of cannibalism must have been the outcome of some sort of deal or negotiation. Even if the capacities of the European photographer and the Fijian actors to shape the terms of the arrangement were unequal, the Fijians were possessed of a kind of agency and willed involvement which the photograph effaces, and they may well have been familiar with the kind of image that Andrew sought to produce.[2] In other words, what is true of the representation that reached a public in New Zealand, Australia and Europe is not true of the colonial encounter from which it derived.

Leaving aside the question of the pragmatic preconditions of particular representations, and the extent to which those conditions were disguised or expressed in the resulting texts and images, it is apparent that a very wide range of material might be seen to distance, denigrate and essentialize particular peoples. This is true not just of the 1890s, not just of those who could be labelled cannibals, and not just of photographic images, even if their indexical relation to an external world was ideally adapted to the objectifying fictions that seem to epitomize colonial regimes of truth. Peoples conventionally categorized by Europeans as civilized, such as south Asians, Chinese and Arabs, have similarly been construed as types, belittled and ridiculed. And, just as I regard the foregoing comments as an appropriate (and almost unavoid-able) interpretation of Andrew's photography, it seems necessary to read racist archives from other areas or periods in similar terms. The problem about such analyses is that they leave us unprepared for the kinds of colonial representation that, at least superficially, do not stigmatize or overtly distance the other as a type, as a primitive or Asiatic savage.

I am not denying that 'the forging of racial stereotypes and confirmation of the notions of savagery were vital to the colonialist world view.'[3] But it seems important to go beyond such observations. Though critics such as Abdul JanMohamed have pointed that stereotypes are employed in an erratic and contradic-tory fashion, and are thus insufficient as objects for analysis,[4] and a number of contemporary writers have developed arguments that go well beyond my cursory discussion of Andrew's Fijian cannibals, and moved from stereotypes to such issues as the logic of mimicry and the relations between emancipated white and degraded black subjectivities, I suggest that their approaches fix on negativity and the effacement of native agency to the same disabling extent.[5] In this chapter I review some of this writing, in relation particularly to the work of Foucault and Bourdieu, and the general issue of how 'government' in discourse is understood. My strategies for redressing the problems of this literature include a pluralization and historicization of 'colonial discourse', and a shift from the logic of signification to the narration of colonialism – or rather, to a contest of colonial narratives.

As was noted earlier, Said's *Orientalism* made the crucial and powerful step of moving from the figure of the 'image' to the object of discourse, which is seen to construct a world, geographic domain, or ethnic grouping in a comprehensive way, rather than merely express a particular perception of something that already existed.[6] The general premise has been echoed by other writers such as Peter Hulme: 'large parts of the non-European world were *produced* for Europe through a discourse that imbricated sets of questions and assumptions, methods of procedure and analysis, and kinds of writing and imagery, normally separated out into the discrete areas of military strategy, political order, social reform, imaginative literature, personal memoir, and so on.'[7] Apprehen-sion, definition and subordination are caught up together in a process of representation that can be traced through works that might be conventionally split up into different genres, which contribute to the workings of imperial power in various imaginative and practical ways.

The strongest expression of such kinds of colonial discourse is perhaps the total register of the census; census-like knowledge is also implied by Said when he writes that 'Eurocentric culture relentlessly codified and observed everything about the non-European or presumably peripheral world, in so thorough and detailed a manner as to leave no item untouched, no culture unstudied.'[8] A subject nation is encompassed in a book, in a document that enumerates, classifies, hierarchizes and locates a range of tribes, races, faiths and occupations, according to an array of grids that are objectified and naturalized in the vision of the state. These collations did not only express the colonizers' omniscience, but also addressed more specific problems of classification and administration. As Bernard Cohn explains, British officials in India felt that

> caste and religion were the sociological keys to understanding the Indian people. If they were to be governed well, then it was natural that information should be systematically collected about caste and religion. At the same time as the census operations were beginning to collect information about caste, the army was beginning to be reorganized on assumptions about the nature of 'martial races', questions were being raised about the balance between Hindus and Muslims in the public services, about whether certain castes or 'races' were monopolizing access to new educational opportunities, and a political theory was beginning to emerge about the conspiracy which certain castes were organizing to supplant British rule.[9]

Hence censuses, together with related statistics and reports, partitioned the population and envisaged its fractions in a particular manner – divisions based on religious adherence, codification of caste or imagined 'race'. These distinctions then became the means for allocating resources and responsibilities, for characterizing groups in terms of their proclivities for compliance or hostility toward the regime, and in their suitability for warrior service or other specific occupations.

In a complementary essay on another dimension of official colonial knowledge, Cohn explored the British acquisition of competence in Persian, Sanskrit and Urdu, among other Indian languages, arguing that 'the conquest of India was a conquest of knowledge . . . The vast social world that was India had to be classified, categorized and bounded before it could be hierarchized.'[10] While Said merely alluded to the functioning of this sort of codification, Cohn presents a nuanced and fascinating account of both the rhetoric of appropriation and the actual uses of south Asian languages by British administrators in the subcontinent. For example, John Gilchrist's *East India Guide* of 1825 cautioned that those lacking precise knowledge of grammatical distinctions between polite and familiar forms were open to being addressed disrespectfully by their servants and menials, diminishing not just themselves but risking a wider lapse of British dignity.[11] Linguistic competence, then, was not merely an instrument of effective diplomacy and instruction, or something that helped foster a generalized ethos of appropriation and command, but also a technique of self- and status-fashioning that permitted a more refined exercise of behavioural control in day-to-day encounters, and within colonial households. Cohn might have added that this kind of investment on the part of colonizers in knowledge of indigenous culture, etiquette and language was restricted to populations distinguished by progress toward civilization, such as Arabs and some southeast Asians, as well as Indians. In other words, like the masculinizing and feminizing modes of imaging islanders referred to earlier, it was mediated by social evolutionary notions, and not elaborated by the British who colonized peoples such as Australian Aborigines.

Cohn's essay is, of course, influenced by Foucault's arguments concerning the role of discourses – and particularly classificatory discourses – in the differentiation and government of populations. For him, Foucault's interests seem to license a wide-ranging inquiry rather than constitute a particular model of colonial discourse; on this point a distinction can be drawn between Cohn's historicism, and the concerns of a number of other writers concerned with theorizing colonial discourse in a more general way. In a programmatic statement that provides a useful reference point here, Homi Bhabha proposes that

> colonial discourse . . . is an apparatus that turns on the recognition and disavowal of racial/cultural/historical differences. Its pre-

dominant strategic function is the creation of a space for 'subject peoples' through the production of knowledges in terms of which surveillance is exercised and a complex form of pleasure/ unpleasure is incited. It seeks authorization for its strategies by the production of knowledges of colonizer and colonized which are stereotypical but antithetically evaluated. The objective of colonial discourse is to construe the colonized as a population of degenerate types on the basis of racial origin, in order to justify conquest and to establish systems of administration and instruction. Despite the play of power within colonial discourse and the shifting positionalities of its subjects . . . I am referring to a form of governmentality that in marking out a 'subject nation', appropriates, directs, and dominates its various spheres of activity.[12]

There is something of a discrepancy between this statement, and the key arguments of some of Bhabha's influential essays, which emphasize a doubleness in colonial enunciation that arises from conflicting demands for stable identity and historical reform. The civilizing mission is problematized and partly undone by an excess or slippage inherent in replication: 'almost the same, *but not quite . . . Almost the same but not white . . .* to be Anglicized is *emphatically* not to be English.'[13] Colonial authority thus produces ironic, split identifications; these threatening expressions of hybridity disrupt and subvert colonial hegemony, in the sense that they exclude the possibility of total epistemic mastery, and because they constitute 'a variously positioned native who by (mis)appropriating the terms of the dominant ideology' is able to resist colonial typification.[14] What I will suggest below, however, is that the shortcomings of Bhabha's general formulation match weaknesses in what at first appears to be a more stimulating thesis concerning the dynamics of colonial mimicry; in particular, I will suggest that the allowance made for subversion on the part of the colonized is distinctly gestural, and that this style of theorizing reifies a general structure of colonial dominance in a manner that is curiously at odds with its pluralizing and disarticulating intentions.

A pivotal feature, which is common to both Bhabha's formulation and Cohn's analysis, is a preoccupation with the mutual permeation of culture and government: knowledge and 'governmentality' are almost mutually constitutive. While Bhabha may owe more to Lacan and Fanon than Foucault,[15] his appropriation of the legislative metaphor is directly relevant to the most general problem addressed in this chapter – namely, how analysis can establish that 'culture' and 'colonial dominance' are deeply mutually implicated without reducing one to the other. Bhabha's strategy, I suggest, is poignantly enabling and disabling. As we have already seen, the ideas of differentiating and normalizing discourses certainly address texts and images that are directly linked with colonial rule, such as those dealing with the administration of education and health. These would long have been interpreted by conventional historians as innocent and pragmatic reports and plans, but can alternatively be read as efforts that produce scope for surveillance as they describe and identify particular populations and social problems; that create charters for intervention as they express the omniscience of the colonial state. Behind these shifts, and paralleling the rejection of the notion that colonial ideology is an assemblage of negative distortions, is the displacement of the idea that the work of the state is merely repressive; the common point of inspiration is the central theme of Foucault's later work, namely the productive mutual constitution of knowledge and power: 'we must cease once and for all to describe the effects of power in negative terms: it "excludes", it "represses", it "censors", it "abstracts", it "masks", it "conceals". In fact, power produces; it produces reality; it produces domains of objects and rituals of truth.'[16]

The regime of discipline characteristic of the modern prison was thus not simply a system of punishment or mere constraint, but 'a procedure . . . aimed at knowing, mastering, and using.'[17] The observer, or observing colonizer, commands a knowledge of groups such as institutional inmates, welfare recipients, and the colonized, that is intimately linked with a classification and diagnosis of the inferiority or inadequacy of the latter, that establishes the need for management.

If the bringing-together of questions about representation and questions about government derives from Foucault, the directionality of conceptual extension seems however to have been reversed. Foucault's interest was in establishing the ways in which state power was not simply a matter of repression, but had an epistemological and discursive character. In opposition, no doubt, to narrower instrumental and Marxist views of the state as an organizing mechanism in the interests of the ruling class, which were being expressed by structural theorists such as Nicos Poulantzas over the period that *Birth of the Clinic* and *Discipline and Punish* appeared,[18] Foucault argued that 'governmentality' was a complex assemblage of 'institutions, procedures, analyses and reflections' that allowed power to be exercised over populations through political-economic knowledge, that is, a kind of economic management that had earlier been intelligible in relation to the model of the family rather than society as a whole. Once the unit of population became the significant object of government, the family immediately became secondary, no more than a privileged segment of the larger entity. Foucault claimed that there was a long-term trend throughout the West toward the sovereignty of this particular kind of informed and technical power – in opposition, presumably, to the ritualistic violence against exemplary victims typified by the execution of the regicide Damiens, described in unpleasant detail at the beginning of *Discipline and Punish*. This evolution made the reductive totalization of state power still more inappropriate: 'the State, probably no more today than at any other time in its history, does not have this unity, this individuality, this rigorous functionality nor, to speak frankly, this importance . . . Maybe what it is really important for our modern times . . . is not so much the State-domination of society, but the "governmentalisation" of the State.'[19]

Foucault's argument thus does three particular things: it shifts an investigation of the object of rule from the state onto techniques of control that are clearly at once discursive, practical and localized rather than socially pervasive; they entail the representation of (for instance) criminality and insanity, and institutions and procedures that give effect to certain social diagnoses. Secondly, it is historically contextualized: governmentality is not a universal object, which the anthropologist of politics could discover in any Western or non-Western society; rather, it emerged in European society, at a specific time, replacing other political modes, and has become progressively more important since – but will no doubt be displaced in its turn at some point in the future. Finally, the interest is not in state power as a unitary function, but in a proliferation of operations that have a logic or episteme but not a point of institutional cohesion in common.

Rather than recasting the state in terms of economic knowledge, colonial discourse theory seems to recast culture as a whole in terms of government. Irrespective of whether Foucault's moves – concerning for instance the periodization of different discourses – are defensible, the three conceptual displacements are appealing in principle, because they allow for a historically specific, non-functionalist analysis of political knowledge. The theory that characterizes colonial representation as governmentality, however, seems to pick up Foucault's vocabulary without effecting any one of these three theoretical shifts. Ironically, the terms of analysis that Bhabha puts forward seem best adapted to the critique of official imperial culture – which is in a direct sense engaged in government, and which Cohn does analyse creatively and effectively – yet he says little about the specific fields of education, welfare, policing and so on, while instead attributing general characteristics (such as 'ambivalence') to the singular totality of colonial discourse; among the authors and works included in the exhibit are Conrad, Naipaul, Edward Long's pro-slavery *History of Jamaica*, the propaganda organ of the Church Missionary Society and even the Orson Welles film *Touch of Evil*.[20] Distinctions between the locations and political projects of these cultural products might be acknowledged, but evidently need not be theorized.

To object to this generalizing strategy is not to object to an inclusive approach to colonial discourse; we should be indeed concerned with the ways in which a range of literary and 'unofficial' colonial representations are entangled in various ways with imperialism, but the question arises of the sense in which these are engaged in 'government'. Even though the term 'discourse' rather than 'ideology' is used, analysis seems prone to lapse into a reifying functionalism more reminiscent of some Marxist theory than Foucault; the way 'it' (colonial discourse) plays a role in the totality of imperialism is frequently evoked by reference to an 'apparatus' being deployed, to the operations it performs, to its 'strategic function' in Bhabha's words.[21] Just as classic functional argument in anthropology saw institutions or magic as resolving social structural problems or the psychological tensions of life's uncertainty, JanMohamed – who has his own brand of Lacanian theory – finds that colonial literature responds to the need of the colonizer to manage diversity that is otherwise unintelligible; the texts which he categorizes as 'imaginary' (as opposed to 'symbolic'), that are structured by objectification and identification, and particularly by violent hatred of the native, are 'like fantasies which provide naive solutions to the subjects' basic problems, [they] tend to center themselves on plots that end with the elimination of the offending natives.'[22] A simple dichotomy might be made between interpretations that take the text as a solution to a problem in managing social or cultural relations, or regard it as an instrument of that management, and those that would instead read it as an expression of tensions and conflicts that, so far from being necessarily resolved or ameliorated through being rendered in literature, may be produced, exacerbated, or at least exhibited through the text; if Bhabha's definition of colonial discourse is clearly trapped within the functionalism of the first position, as are JanMohamed's analyses, his argument concerning the disruptive effect of mimicry seems more consistent with the second, more conflicted view; but in that case what is divided and pluralized is the effect of colonial enunciation rather than its source. There is a point here about the coherence and expression of governmentality that might be recast more broadly.

In many ways, and in diverse theoretical traditions, representation has become problematic precisely because language has ceased to be understood as a neutral medium for the transmission of information; the ways in which it – and by extension, narrative codes – is suffused with power relations and encodes structures of control have been critically disclosed and deconstructed, often through the introduction of metaphors concerning government, policing, military rule and similar idioms of dominance. Jacques Derrida, for instance, writes that 'The narratorial voice is the voice of a subject recounting something, remembering an event or a historical sequence, knowing who he is, where he is, and what he is talking about. It responds to some police, a force of order or law . . . In this sense, all organized narration is "a matter for the police".'

Now what can that mean? It would seem to imply that any 'organized' narrative is in effect responding to a tacit interrogation – who? what? when? how? why? etc. That is – narrative in the traditional sense is always acting under the law. We might question at

what point an 'organized' narrative gives way to a dis-organized
one . . . what about a book like *Tristram Shandy*: it certainly has its
own kind of organization – is that a matter for the police?[23]

I take Tony Tanner's remarks on Derrida to allow that there are
indeed necessary and fundamental questions about how representations are licensed, how particular ways of constructing subjects,
their possible actions, the possible moral inflections of their actions, their historical roles and so on may be said to be legislated
discursively, but that there are significant limits to the extent that
one can expect these operations to be visibly policed, or at least
different kinds of policing. To put this in another way, advocates
of a certain political or aesthetic interest are very likely to affirm
and effect certain representations, say of 'pioneering spirit', 'Australian landscape' or 'sisterhood', in whatever genre (novel, journalistic comment, government report, travel book, feminist
essay); at certain times the existence of these objects, and the
appropriate ways of writing about them and using them as vehicles
for stories or characterizations of relations, may be well established. Where a discursive object, and its possible values and uses
in a description or story are secure – such that departure from
these authorized uses is illegible, unintelligible and confusing –
one might say that a discourse is effectively policed; it is organized
in terms of a tacit interrogation that is unitary and dominant. The
shadowy work of these plainclothes policemen certainly warrants
scrutiny, but it needs to be remembered that the 'organized'
or 'traditional' narrative is something of a straw man; like the
'Establishment' that mildly liberal Americans can be anti-, it is as
much a foil for innovative posturing, as a measure of hegemony in
discourse. Isn't a certain degree of incoherence found even in
conventional genres? If this is the case, if narratives are often dis-
organized either because of deliberate experimentation (Sterne's
Tristram Shandy), or because their objects of knowledge are contested or imperfectly recognized, policing may be more conspicuous in its effort than in its effect.

The social theorists Peter Miller and Nikolas Rose aptly distill
the object of inquiry recommended by Foucault's account of
governmentality as an 'intellectual technology', whereby things to
be governed are 'rendered into information – written reports,

drawings, pictures, numbers, charts, graphs, statistics. This information must be of a particular form – stable, mobile, combinable and comparable.'[24] I take the last four adjectives here to be crucial to any government of a literal kind, but it is obvious that unofficial sources – novels and polemical tracts that, far from deploying generally shared criteria and classifications, are often produced to contest them – do not generate information that is 'stable, mobile, combinable and comparable'. At certain basic levels, they may conform to enduring structures and codes, but what is conspicuous in colonial texts is not so much the persistence of elementary structures as superficial similarities of idiom and characterization (Africans as childlike) that belie more significant divergences of purpose, logic and rhetoric. Miller and Rose are, therefore, no doubt doing a good thing to the study of economic policy and accounting systems by drawing attention to the necessary role of language, conceptualization and inscription, but, to reiterate, it is not apparent that what amounts to the converse of this shift, the 'governmentalization' of culture, is equally productive, because colonial discourse cannot be construed as a unitary or stable archive in the fashion of a set of official statistics or reports. Whereas the latter may indeed be a matter for the police – for one organized police force – colonial texts are matters for several corrupt and inefficient forces who disagree about each other's functions and jurisdictions.

If Bhabha fails to theorize heterogeneity in colonial modes of recognition and address, his argument intends, at least, to move beyond what he sees as Said's overstatement of colonial hegemony, the view that 'power and discourse is possessed entirely by the colonizer.'[25] Said's book was, of course, overwhelmingly about Orientalism as a Western discourse, addressed by Western writers, experts and governments to themselves and their domestic constituencies; the question of how this discourse was projected at and received in the Middle Eastern countries, and how it influenced the self-perceptions of their inhabitants – in so far as it did at all – are substantial and somewhat separate problems that Said does not address.[26] If one approach to the issue might have entailed direct engagement with the perceptions of 'the colonized', Bhabha opts instead to identify a contradiction situated within the colonial enunciation, which spawns something camouflaged, necessarily incomplete and uncertain, a menacing kind of mimicry that 'in disclosing the ambivalence of colonial discourse also disrupts its authority'.[27] In a more recent paper, he refers to Veena Das's rejection of essentialist claims concerning the mentalities of south Asian tribes or castes, in favour of circumstances of conflict 'which may provide the characteristics of the historical moment'. Bhabha finds this emblematic of 'the [singular] historical movement of hybridity as camouflage' and asks 'Is this not similar to what Fanon describes as the knowledge of the practice of action? The primitive Manicheanism of the settler – Black and White, Arabs and Christians – breaks down in the struggle for independence and comes to be replaced with truths that are only partial, limited, and unstable.'[28] This could be wrong on both counts: colonial meanings always were partial and unstable (as Bhabha seems to suggest himself elsewhere), while the struggle for independence – the *nationalist* struggle – recapitulates the Manicheanism, authority and essentialism of colonial discourse at least as much as it deconstructs those terms. It is ironic that Bhabha makes this claim in reference to the Subaltern Studies scholars, since one of the central arguments of that project has been precisely that Indian nationalism was and is a 'derivative discourse', that failed to transcend the very power structures and forms of thought that it overtly aimed to repudiate.[29] The incongruity here may arise from the fact that Bhabha is attempting to parade a theoretical and political genealogy, or array of affiliations, while his project is in fact entirely different to the historicized critique advanced by the Subaltern Studies group. Though mainly diasporic academics, their arguments have been deeply and consistently grounded in Indian history and politics, and at a considerable remove from the 'Fanon etc.' category which Bhabha frequently evokes.

The weakness of the argument arises particularly from its construction in universalized psychoanalytic terms: 'cultural norms and classifications' such as the figure of 'the Lying Asiatic' are reduced to 'strategies of desire in discourse' and 'nonrepressive productions of contradictory and multiple belief'.[30] What could not be counted as a strategy of desire? What beliefs, or at least what beliefs of any complex and politically significant kind, are not contradictory and multiple? And the question is not *whether* a classification such as 'the Lying Asiatic' can be seen in these terms, but for what gain and at what cost?

The generality of the terms is matched by the inclusiveness of the cases I alluded to earlier; Jamaica, India, Fanon, Conrad, Naipaul. I would not dispute that the texts referred to evince apparently parodic or ironic distortions of dominant enunciations; but I suspect then that the identification of this singular logic, common to such diverse histories, conveys a truth about discourse as such, rather than one about colonialism. I suggest that mimicry has a different logic, and hybridity a variety of threatening and unthreatening effects, under different colonial regimes such as the Renaissance discourse of conquest and conversion, modern assimilationist and segregationist projects and nineteenth- and twentieth-century evangelical imaginings. In particular, it makes an important difference if, as in much nineteenth- and twentieth-century British discourse and practice, there was an interest in specifying the essential character of the native, and positioning that in a distinct and separate domain that was governed rather than converted or otherwise subjected to a civilizing transformation. In Fiji in the early twentieth century, the menace of mimicry is conspicuous in white responses to indigenous resistance; the latter took the form of millennial protests, some fuelled by rumours suggesting that the British had lost the First World War. The *Fiji Times* speculated that these emanated 'from natives who read English in a parrot-like fashion and do not quite understand its purport'; the literate native, then, was something of an anomaly. Reports concerning one leader named Sailosi were replete with attributions of inauthentic, disputed and confounded identities: the 'alleged' prophet was 'deposed as an imposter' and not even the origin himself of the sedition, 'but the mouthpiece of a German white Fijian', a man who had gone native and was living in a Fijian village; this inverted assimilation on the part of itinerant or marginal whites was of course always an object of official disapprobation. White writing around the affair was pervaded by anxieties directly arising from false conversions, 'sly civility' and parodic dissimulation; as the same newspaper editorialized, 'the native is becoming educated to the fact that it is possible to use religion as a cloak to hide a multitude of sins and ulterior motives.'[31] While this case would seem entirely compatible with Bhabha's analysis, there can be no doubt that this threat of mimicry is largely attributable to the specificity of the British regime, which devoted a tremendous amount of energy to documenting and characterizing the nature of the Fijian people, establishing a correct form of quasi-feudal communal sociality, a framework that could be sealed off from commerce and modernity and ordered through the machinery of indirect rule (see chapter 4). This particular administration, and similar segregationist projects, had a singular investment in the establishment of a fixed indigenous nature, which was threatened by the partially assimilated native to an extent that other constructions of the colonial process could never be; the Government Ethnologist in South Africa, G. P. Lestrade, claimed that the culturally assimilated or missionary-educated native was 'about as original as a glass of skimmed milk'.[32]

The underlying problem here is simply that it is thought necessary to take 'colonial discourse' as a singular and definable entity at all. Even a writer who otherwise champions Bhabha's interventions poses the question of whether colonialism 'always demonstrate[s] the ambivalence which he claims or do his examples constitute particular privileged moments?'[33] Though Bhabha's earliest source is Edward Long's *History of Jamaica* (1774), most of his other references are to nineteenth-century texts. This suggests either that colonial discourse is understood to be peculiarly modern – and hence did not exist, for example, in the period of the conquest of America – or that it is assumed that the logic identified is equally applicable in that case, and in others. This is to say that the limits and conditions of possibility of colonial discourse remain unspecified; it is as though the brute fact of the significance of imperialism in modern history exempts the critic from the need to locate its enunciations and reiterations – a paradoxical blindness, given the current preoccupation with the positions from which critics, historians, anthropologists and their interlocutors speak. In fact, there are strong arguments for the distinctiveness of modern colonialism, and, as I argue in the next chapter, for a coherently 'anthropological' mode of typifying natives that is manifested in varying ways from the late eighteenth century onward. But if colonial discourse is described through the psychic dynamics of self-other relations, or in a logic of camouflage or mimicry, it cannot be accorded this historic peculiarity.

The global condition of the object of analysis is also directly at odds with the fact that not only Bhabha's work, but writing on colonial discourse generally, is perceived to be seeking to pluralize its object of analysis, 'to dislodge the construct of a monolithic and deliberative colonial authority by demonstrating the dispersed space of power and a disseminated apparatus.'[34] If this really is an aim, the concepts that have been employed can only be seen as singularly poorly adapted to the objective. Unlike governmentality, 'colonial discourse' is not a specific modality of a general entity (power), but a generalized, transhistorical thing, that becomes difficult to distinguish from discourse as such.[35]

A more genealogical inquiry, concerned with the displacements of discursive and practical modes rather than the attributes of a total and generalized mode, can only proceed if there are colonial discourses in a plural sense that (like Foucault's governmentality) did not exist at one time, and are emergent, hegemonic or highly contested at others. Nor should it be supposed that there is only one salient discourse at a particular period. Given the extent to which colonial representations could in fact be highly diverse in their genres, social contexts and conflicting theoretical positions, concerning such fundamental questions as the nature of human diversity, the significance of race, the scope for elevating or ameliorating the conditions of other races and so on, it would here seem productive to adopt something like Peter de Bolla's notion of discourses, despite its being developed in quite a different investigation: 'at any specific historical ... juncture a discursive network articulates the 'real', it allows and controls the possibilities for representation. This network is made up of a number of discrete discourses, which interact, sometimes without hostility, at other times with considerable violence, with each other. The distance and lines of force between specific discourses vary to a great extent ...'[36] The different discourses that de Bolla has in mind are exemplified in the eighteenth century by discrete discourses such as those of ethics, politics, aesthetics, gaming and cookery: some are proximate to, others remote from, each other. What is at issue here is not the value of these terms as such, but rather what can be done with them; de Bolla takes specific areas of debate (among them public credit and finance, oratory and pictorial perspective) and attempts to trace common shifts in the formulation of the subject in these diverse fields. Needless to say, the kinds of arrays of texts that I construe as discrete discourses are different; I am concerned specifically to locate those of particular colonial agencies, such as scientific explorers, missionaries, and official administrators. This implies also a more socially and historically grounded kind of characterization, than I believe either Bhabha or de Bolla is interested in; but the value of the latter's terms are that they permit discourses to interact violently, and that is what I want to emphasize. Colonialism is not a unitary project but a fractured one, riddled with contradictions and exhausted as much by its own internal debates as by the resistance of the colonized.

My argument here is not simply for a plural rather than a unitary construction of colonial discourse. There are other shortcomings in the recent literature on colonial discourse to which I draw attention here, in the interests of specifying a more adequate approach. Despite the important way in which Bhabha identifies the failures and ruptures of colonial discourse, and its necessary proliferation of inappropriate identities, there are three main points that seem problematic in his general formulation of colonial discourse, that I quoted earlier; despite their theoretical differences, these emerge also in the texts of other critics such as Spivak and JanMohamed.

First, differences are said to be 'recognized and disavowed' in colonial discourse; it is not clear from Bhabha's somewhat involved usage what specifically is meant by either of these terms, and presumably the implication is not simply that actual differences are perceived, and then suppressed, since reference is made elsewhere to the codified character of 'rules of recognition' that 'cohere' in the voice of colonial authority.[37] Of course, actual historical and cultural differences, as well as similarities, do precede colonial encounters and the European project to recognize and construct particular subject races; these conditions, together with the array of notions available to particular writers, and the practical and discursive imperatives, presumably contribute to the way difference is constructed in any particular text. What is unsatisfactory in Bhabha's account is the implication that the work of colonial discourse is essentially to diminish or deny difference, whereas it might be argued that in many contexts it is equally concerned to deny similarity. JanMohamed has also suggested that the European can respond to 'an incomprehensible and multifaceted alterity' either in terms of identity (where divergences are ignored) or difference (which is rendered absolute); though in either case the colonizer refuses to suspend 'his own cultural values'.[38] The problem here is that the situations and peoples that Europeans encounter are *not* entirely incomprehensible: many aspects of daily life, political relationships, sexuality and so on witnessed by colonizers or visitors in other societies are entirely understandable as versions of familiar practices or as exemplifications of the behaviour and characteristics already attributed to ancients or non-European people. Of course, this recognition may frequently entail various degrees of misunderstanding, but the important point is that in the experience of contact, unfamiliarity is not necessarily overwhelming. By presuming that this is an actual condition that the European must respond to, JanMohamed seems to take as a fact what is itself a familiar cry of colonial representation: the unintelligible, indescribable, inscrutable and unknown character of other places and peoples.[39] Ironically, JanMohamed's observations seem more valid for cases other than those that he actually deals with; while the degree of established prior knowledge and familiarity was considerable in, say, most African encounters from the early nineteenth century onward,[40] a problem of recognition was more fundamental in the literature from the discovery and conquest of America, where, as Tzvetan Todorov has shown, entirely unanticipated human difference was simultaneously 'revealed and rejected'. Columbus, at different moments, stressed identity in seeing the Indians as human beings to be assimilated, and difference in the inferiority of their being, but he was never able to acknowledge non-hierarchical difference, 'the existence of a human substrate truly other, something capable of being not merely an imperfect state of oneself'.[41]

This double movement of recognition and denial that JanMohamed generalizes seems related not only to the fact of surprise and novelty of the New World, but also to the relative lack of 'anthropological' vision in this period. While the nature of the Indian came to be debated by Acosta, Las Casas and others, these discussions were concerned more with theoretical questions concerning the application of Aristotelian concepts of 'natural man' than empirical information concerning the behaviour of natives.

Even if Foucault's arguments concerning the birth of the human sciences overstate the novelty of 'Man' as an object of knowledge, there is certainly a striking contrast between inquiry into human diversity in the seventeenth and eighteenth centuries and the virtual lack of interest in other peoples in fifteenth- and sixteenth-century works of travel and exploration (a shift that is discussed in the next chapter).[42]

Once an ethnological interest in discerning and accounting for diversity in manners and customs assumes more significance, the question of the recognition and non-recognition of difference emerges in another fashion. To the two gestures noted by Todorov and JanMohamed – the alternatives of denying difference through assimilation and affirming difference hierarchically – must be added at least a third: the restricted affirmation of authenticated difference constitutive of exoticism and primitivism. I do not want to be schematic about these alternatives, or categorical about any periodization of them, but it is crucial to note, as a general tenet, that texts and images often *create* differences that do not exist, which are maintained and exaggerated, and not disavowed or suppressed. Allusions to the 'normalizing' projects of colonial discourse may suggest that the ideology responds to dissimilarity by enforcing some degree of conformity; yet, in the case of India for instance, Orientalist scholarship and many other genres have persistently neglected the features of Indian polities that are comprehensible in general terms, or similar to European models, and rendered Indian society as pervaded by religiosity and caste. In short, India is the opposite of the West.[43] Any travel account is likely to embody both exoticizing and familiarizing gestures, but the frequent tendency to set other places up as picturesque exhibits, as things to be seen rather than as locations in which action occurs, effects a displacement into the domain of the aesthetic and the ornamental.

Secondly, Bhabha suggests that racial origin is the basis for attributions of degeneracy to particular peoples, and it could not be disputed that racial classifications have been enormously powerful, especially since the early nineteenth century, but race is not the only basis for representing others or representing them negatively; in medieval and Renaissance accounts, monsters and pagans, rather than other races, occupy the periphery; in other contexts, a series of religious, linguistic and societal differences

may figure in the stigmatization of particular populations, which
may be energized as much by analogies with subaltern domestic
classes as by their race, or by their feminization. Race may be the
key differentiating category of much nineteenth- and twentieth-
century discourse, but the characterization of others as heathens
rather than blacks or Asiatics has obviously persisted in evangelical representations, which have hardly been marginal or inconsequential in large parts of Africa, among other regions. It might be
added that various other differentiations constructed primarily
around lack – of civility, industrial goods, economic development
and so on – are not reducible to ideologies of racial difference;
and while environmental understandings of human diversity have
a complex relationship with racial ideas, the theory that indolence
and mental inactivity are induced by tropical climates can be
invoked to establish the degeneration of creoles and settlers as
well as natives.[44] Disparaging observations along such lines were,
for example, standard features of British anti-Dutch (and anti-
Portuguese) propaganda in southern Africa from the beginning
of the nineteenth century, if not earlier. A theory that privileges
race as sovereign hierarchical operator remains within the categories of nineteenth-century imperialist thought; what needs instead
to be done is to diagnose those terms and expose the awkward
relationships between constructions of race and the other forms
of classification that it never completely displaced.

Thirdly, it is generally presumed that colonial discourses depict
colonized people pejoratively; yet, just as some sexist imagery can,
at least superficially, exalt and celebrate women, attractive and
even sympathetic constructions of colonized peoples may admire
or uphold them in a narrow or restrictive way. There are, for
instance, whole traditions of appreciative Orientalist images of
India, which privileged Islamic architectural styles and reproduced them faithfully, thus making them available for quotation
and imitation;[45] or which took an interest in the luxuriant decay of
Hindu temples, some of which were awesome, subterranean exca-
vations; or which feminized rather than bestialized Asiatic bodies
(as Andrew feminized the Samoans). In the expensive but popular acquatints of William Hodges, the Daniells, Henry Salt and
James Fraser,[46] India is not a place, but a series of views and scenes;
the sense that a building is not a functional structure of some
kind, but a monument or sight does not arise merely from the fact

Plate 3   *Henry Salt, 'Mosque at Lucknow', 1809*

that the landscape or edifice is represented, but is further emphasized by the frequent presence of small groups of Indians in and
around the structures, who are entirely idle – seemingly present
just as tourists.[47] Indian labour and the complexity of Indian social
life may well be elided in these images for aesthetic reasons rather
than consciously political ones, yet the picturesque apprehension
of the subcontinent catered for a colonial imaging by making the
place archaic, decayed and available to antiquaries. This kind of
representation made sense within the larger archive of orientalist
representation of the subcontinent, yet was a kind of colonial
ideology that worked through elision rather than denigration,
and was thus quite different from the evocation of savagery
exemplified in Andrew's Fijian photographs.

Benita Parry has pointed out that while Bhabha aims to discover
the subterfuges through which natives could destabilize 'the
effectivity of the English book' he 'declines to engage' with any
alternative or autonomous text they may have produced.[48] She
adds that while Gayatri Spivak's arguments are basically different,
their effect is the same, in that it is presumed that the impact of
colonialism was such that the colonized were left 'without the

Plate 4   *Thomas and William Daniell, detail from 'The
great bull, a Hindoo Idol, at Tanjore', 1798*

ground from which they could utter confrontational words'
('There is no space from which the sexed subaltern subject can
speak').[49] This is the point at which these critics' anti-imperialist
intentions would seem most puzzlingly and ironically deflected by
their analytical strategies. In the case of Spivak's argument, imperialism's own sense of its pervasive efficacy is reproduced in the
assumption of its consequence of effacement; while, with respect
to Bhabha, however radically subversive an instance of colonial
mimicry might be, it would necessarily arise from colonial enunciation, and necessarily be deeply conditioned by it. 'Sly civility',
however sly, entails some acknowledgement of a reigning model

of civility, and is a form of resistance that is expressed on the ground defined by the oppressor. To see responses of the colonized in these terms is to presume that colonizers do in fact impose codes (which may then be subverted); this excludes the possibility that 'natives' often had relatively autonomous representations and agendas, that might have been deaf to the enunciations of colonialism, or not so captive to them that mimicry seemed a necessary capitulation.[50] This view is radically different from that of most of the Subaltern Studies scholars, who inaugurated their project with the following account of subaltern politics.

> This was an *autonomous* domain . . . it neither originated in elite politics nor did its existence depend upon the latter. It was traditional in so far as its roots could be traced back to precolonial times, but it was by no means archaic . . . Far from being destroyed or rendered virtually ineffective, as was elite politics of the traditional type by the intrusion of colonialism, it continued to operate vigorously in spite of the latter, adjusting itself to the conditions prevailing under the Raj and in many respects developing entirely new strains in both form and content.[51]

While Guha in fact provided brilliant illustrations of resistant inversions of dominant codes, of peasants' efforts to turn things upside down by appropriating elite artefacts and signs, the general argument is not that their actions were contained within or specified by the dominant culture. Subaltern resistance is seen, in any case, to contest not one dominant culture, but an interpenetration of colonial and indigenous hierarchies; though precolonial elements and syncretic forms are almost invariably found to be significant by historians of various anti-colonial movements, it is not clear how, if at all, they are recognized in theories of colonial discourse.

This underlines again, the limitations of the assumption that 'colonial discourse' is automatically apparent to the colonized in the first place. Given that much of what we refer to by that term was addressed not at colonized populations, but at public opinion within colonizing nations,[52] it needs to be acknowledged that the discourse may not have impinged upon indigenous consciousness at all, or was at best indirectly related to discourses that were expressed at the site of colonization; to presume imposition is to overstate the importance and effectiveness of imperialism, to forget that imperialists were often arguing with each other or speaking narcissistically to themselves. An alternate theory, equally extreme, could be constructed on the basis of Aguirre's extravagant declarations of possession, that resonated only in the delirious and afflicted mind of the colonizer, as his drifting, fragile raft spun slowly through the Amazonian rainforest.[53]

The tortuous fashion in which these theorists approach or evade the expressions and representations of the colonized echoes broader difficulties that poststructuralism, like structuralism, has with agency. If we are concerned to deal more adequately with the presence of 'the colonized' in colonialism, with the autonomy of their enunciations and strategies, we need to adopt a theoretical perspective that accords more importance to competence without lapsing into an uncritical, subject-centred humanism. Pierre Bourdieu has not written at all extensively on colonialism, but his work is useful in this context because its interest in practice can counterbalance the evacuation of wilful innovation and subversion from 'discourse' in Foucault's account. I will suggest later that the concept of a colonial *project* can draw together interests in discourse and interests in agency, not with the objective of creating a coherent or harmonious theory, but in order to establish a productive analytical tension, a reading that is stretched between regimes of truth and their moments of mediation, reformulation and contestation in practice. It is this reference to the practical expression of discourse that crystallizes the differences between my stance and not only colonial discourse theory, but a good deal of other conventional and radical writing about imperialism and imperial culture. While the only substantiation of these differences can be in my case studies (particularly in chapter 4), it is worth being explicit about what is attempted.

Aspects of Bourdieu's argument were directed against anthropological knowledge in general and structuralist anthropology in particular; in the eloquent critique of Lévi-Strauss which opened *Outline of a Theory of Practice* (1977), he argued that the celebrated theories of marriage and reciprocity were preoccupied with the 'mechanics of the model' and suppressed the temporality and necessary strategic dimensions of gift-giving. His objection, essentially, was that a variety of normative social theories suppressed something crucial: the competence of the actors. 'The language of rules and models, which seems tolerable when applied to "alien" practices, ceases to convince as soon as one considers the practical mastery of the symbolism of social interaction – tact, dexterity, or savoir-faire – presupposed by the most everyday games of sociability and accompanied by the application of a spontaneous semiology, i.e. a mass of precepts, formulae, and codified cues.'[54] While Bhabha's suggestions concerning the subversive effect of mimicry do something to reinstall a kind of agency on the part of the colonized, this perspective, rooted in more conventional social theory, seems to provide scope for a better appreciation of the heterogeneity of empowered practice among both colonizers and colonized. It is important to add that Bourdieu's rejection of reified models or structures, and the insistence upon the complexity and the wilfulness of action, did not mark a return to voluntarism or humanism, and certainly has nothing in common with the interest in individual character, action and motivation that so constrains conventional history. Bourdieu stated forcefully in a different theoretical discussion, which set out the foundations of his brilliant analysis of taste and consumption, that he was not concerned to privilege subjectivity, choice or the personal.

> The aim is not, of course, to reintroduce any form of what is called 'lived experience', which is mostly often merely a thinly disguised projection of the researcher's 'lived experience'; but to move beyond the abstract relationship between consumers with interchangeable tastes and products with uniformly perceived and appreciated properties to the relationship between tastes which vary in a necessary way according to their social and economic conditions of production, and the products on which they confer their different social identities. One only has to ask the question, which economists strangely ignore, of the economic conditions of the production of the dispositions demanded by the economy, i.e., in this case, the question of the economic and social determinants of tastes . . . [The experiences of consumers] do not have to be felt in order to be understood with an understanding which may owe nothing to lived experience, still less to sympathy.[55]

Bourdieu's object here, is, of course, quite remote from those being investigated in this book, but there are aspects of his method that are highly relevant. Neither colonial social relations nor their representational codes can be seen as structures that are simply reproduced; rather, their persistence depends upon performance, upon practical mastery. Although Bourdieu's own accounts sometimes suggest a rather circular and non-dynamic form of social reproduction, by means of which structuring structures are structured, strategic action in colonial contexts is almost necessarily transformative, because the field for action and representation is not a unitary society but a social division, marked both by the cleavage between colonizers and colonized and by the partial or transposed character of both groups; the one is incomplete because it represents a mutation or extension of what may be perceived as a complete social entity at home, the other truncated to a varying degree by displacements and intrusions. Just as the world of modern consumerism cannot be effectively understood if it is assumed that the mass of objects for sale cannot be manipulated and reconstructed according to the tastes fashioned within particular class fractions and subcultures, the dynamics of colonialism cannot be understood if it is assumed that some unitary representation is extended from the metropole and cast across passive spaces, unmediated by perceptions or encounters. Colonial projects are construed, misconstrued, adapted and enacted by actors whose subjectivities are fractured – half here, half there, sometimes disloyal, sometimes almost 'on the side' of the people they patronize and dominate, and against the interests of some metropolitan office. Between the Scylla of mindlessly particular conventional colonial history, which fails to move beyond the perceptions of whichever administrators or missionaries are being documented, and the Charybdis of colonial discourse theory, which totalizes a hegemonic global ideology, neither much tainted by its conditions of production nor transformed by the pragmatics of colonial encounters and struggles, lies another path, which amounts to an ethnography of colonial projects: that presupposes the effect of larger objective ideologies, yet notes their adaptation in practice, their moments of effective implementation and confidence as well as those of failure and wishful thinking.

Bourdieu's observations about the analyst's attitude to the perceptions of his bourgeois consumers are also relevant; his insistence that their dispositions and schemes of appreciation be taken into account is not necessarily based in shared experience or a politics of identification. This would exclude both the dishonesty entailed in 'speaking for' a subaltern group and the conventional historian's often unreflective identification with past characters, which can often lead to rationalization of the actions of figures such as colonial governors, who are 'understood in their own terms'.[56] Following Bourdieu, I would argue that if the effect and singularity of colonial missionary work is to be better understood, the criteria of degradation and progress, the techniques of salvation and reform, the grand narrative of conversion, the place of industry and other features of the evangelical imagination, must all be grasped; but even if that apprehension entails some sense of the conditions of mission life, and the perceptions that missionaries male and female had of their work and its worth, this act of understanding cannot be a sympathetic one that forgets how intrusive and sometimes destructive missionaries were, how their benevolence and will to control were indissociable. But why deny complexity and agency to those accused of denying them to others?

Consider another photograph of staged savagery: one taken, not a century ago, but in 1975, and published in 1991. In *Identity through History*, his account of constructions of past and present identities among Cheke Holo speakers in the Solomon Islands, Geoffrey White describes a visit to a ritual site that had long been abandoned by his Christian hosts.

> The Togasalo men hacked away at the underbrush to clear vines and dense growth, gradually exposing two stone structures – a pyramidal (once rectangular?) shrine and a low bed of flat stones. When finished, they had exposed a sacrificial altar said to have been used to make offerings to the spirits of powerful ancestors ... With the shrine as a visual reminder of the past, Forest and Josepa launched into a story about the site's most dramatic purpose: human sacrifice. Adding immediacy to the account, Fr. Hudson [the man photographed] assumed the posture of a sacrificial victim to demonstrate the procedure for ritual decapitation (up to a point). He sat down with his back against one end of the shrine, leaning his head back, and stared upward with neck exposed. He and the others then described the scenario for human sacrifice,

Plate 5   *Hudson Lagusu demonstrates use of the sacrificial altar*

carried out to enhance the strength of Knabu warriors. About forty
men would assemble in a line extending away from the altar. Once
the victim was decapitated, the severed head would be handed
down the line 'like a coconut' so that the warriors could drink its
blood.[57]

In another context, in which school pupils from the same
region were invited to write essays on the time before the church
came, typical responses 'formulated their image of the past by
inverting ideals of the present': 'our ancestors, our fathers and
mothers, did not understand the love that we know today. And
they did not know about the togetherness of the present time
either. They did know about killing people, about eating people
and about fighting . . .'[58] Does this simply attest to the extent to
which certain 'natives' may swallow the message of particular
colonizing 'fishers of men' – here Anglican missionaries – hook,
line and sinker? To the extent that these Solomon Islanders other
their ancestors in the same way and to the same extent that those
ancestors were othered by a variety of Europeans? It is difficult to

avoid seeing a colonization of consciousness here, but such a view needs to be balanced against an understanding of local Christianity. In Santa Isabel, as in many other parts of the Pacific, Christianity cannot be regarded as a unitary Western imposition that has displaced indigenous tradition; rather, as is a commonplace among historians and anthropologists of both the Pacific and Africa, it has been indigenized in a great variety of localized variants. Among the manifestations of this are the interpenetration of specifically religious ideas, such as the Christian blessing of gardens in a manner reminiscent of indigenous agricultural fertility ritual, and the mutual reinforcement of indigenous chiefly leadership and church roles. Indigenous understandings also often deflect the notion that Christianity was a missionary import by positing a latent or implicit Christianity in ancestral religion and sociality, which evangelists merely brought into the light.[59] It would no doubt be overstating the case to argue that indigenous culture has 'incorporated' or 'assimilated' Christianity if this implied that the first term had itself resisted transformation; but there is no need to make a choice between one model (whereby imperialism introduces ideas that efface local culture) and aother (where imports are merely assimilated within a prior cultural structure). The space between these hypothetical alternatives is the space of colonial politics at the local level, the space of practical resistance, acceptance and appropriation. The significant feature of these dynamics in the Solomons has perhaps been that, while the colonial state – the British Solomon Islands Protectorate – was certainly oppressive (in its imposition of a head tax, for example), the indigenized or semi-indigenized churches frequently provided institutional bases for expressions of resistance and regional autonomy (as has frequently been the case elsewhere).[60]

White's photograph differs from Andrew's 1890s image. The man depicted is not a pure heathen victim seen by an unseen camera, but evidently a modern Melanesian dressed in shorts, whose amusement is manifest – as is perforce the fact of re-enactment. He is not a generic Solomon Islander, a warrior type, but a man who is named, and marked as an Anglican priest, in the photograph's caption; and as it happens Father Lagusu is also the author of an article describing the sacrifice he was playfully performing, not a voiceless subaltern.[61] While the 1890s photograph invited the viewer to be titillated by a spectacle of savagery's naked truth, White's photograph makes a number of cultural transpositions explicit, and displaces a standard critical response to the tropes of cannibalism and human sacrifice; if, in general, we would want to reject the denigration of natives by whites that such images implied, that proper critique is unavailable here, because the 'natives' appear to impose the trope of savagism upon themselves, yet in an unserious fashion that makes the term 'denigration' inappropriate. If the 1890s image might threaten the colonized in so far as it degrades their humanity and licenses their subjection, what the recent photograph prejudices is rather the coherence of *our* categories and moral schemes: 'colonialist' typification becomes less easy to specify as something 'the colonizers' do to 'the colonized'.

To draw attention to the transposition of Christianity, together with its stigmatizing discourse on heathenism, is not to suggest that the colonial history of this particular area has not entailed the dominance of colonizing states and agencies, such as the Anglican church. It is rather to draw attention to the complexity of exchange in the colonial process, to the lack of harmony in the projection and functioning of colonizing efforts, and to suggest that expressions of colonial discourses in metropolitan contexts need to be separated from their transpositions in colonized regions. While metropolitan colonial discourses are often marked in various ways by the irruption of indigenous resistance, irony, or mistranslation, the cultural and political dynamics of the dispersed process of colonization can involve a much deeper interpenetration of indigenous and colonial meanings, and may be conditioned, in a profound way, by singular features of indigenous cultural structures and power relations.[62] However colonial projects and artefacts – the gun, the Bible, currency, literacy and so on – are offered or imposed, it is likely that they will be subjected to some appropriation and redefinition. And this is no less true of the stuff of colonial discourse itself: 'representations of the other' are transposed, deployed in debates within indigenous society concerning its affirmation, reform and refashioning; they are projected back at Europeans with a variety of serious and parodic intentions, and enter into discourses of tribal, customary and national identities. Our interest in charting colonialism's points of incoherence is thus largely anticipated by a succession of appropriations that not only generate internal ironies, but disrupt it from spaces beyond its limits.

3

From Past to Present: Colonial Epochs, Agents, and Locations

If there can be no global theory of colonial culture, it remains the case that colonial cultures are global phenomena; they are, at least, extralocal and transregional, in the sense that particular metropolitan powers have usually attempted to project discourses and control in a number of remote regions at once, confronting colonized peoples with alien institutions, practices and representations. These extensions and displacements that constitute colonial relationships strain an analytical vision struggling to focus at once on large- and small-scale maps, but this effort of perception is further prejudiced by the often striking parallels between civilizing missions in colonies and those at home. Identifications could be proffered between geographically remote and internal others, such as the late medieval religious deviants within Europe who were represented in the same terms as the anthropophagi of the New World, and the eighteenth-century Englishmen contesting a rule of property who were called 'arabs and banditti'.[1] More fundamentally, with respect to modes of socialization and government, it seems that, in the nineteenth century especially, both underclasses at home and natives in the colonies were being subjected to the same kinds of surveillance, reform, and economic redefinition.[2] In the face of these parallels, colonialism itself threatens to vanish as a distinctive and visible object.

Given that colonial discourses should be seen to include a great variety of specialized and popular representations, yet must also be understood as a pluralized and dispersed field, often overlapping with or reflecting various 'internal' colonialisms, the question must arise of exactly how the specificity of particular constructions is described and accounted for. Or rather: how can this be done without lapsing from analysis into mere empirical particularity? Is it possible to map the endlessly variable localized expressions of colonialism while remaining aware of the continuities among these manifestations, their longer-term development, and their (perhaps limited) degree of systemic global coherence?

Those writing about colonialism often make distinctions on the basis of familiar tools for differentiating historical and cultural phenomena, such as periodization, agency, modes of production, national origin and geographic location. That is, a colonial effort might be situated in an epoch; as the work of a particular kind of colonizer, such as a trader, a missionary or an explorer; in a context of mercantilism or plantation capitalism; as a French, British or Belgian venture in India, west Africa or Australia. Some of these terms imply merely descriptive attributions; others might lend themselves to more powerful analytic characterization; I suggest that all are ambiguous instruments, which tend to homogenize whatever contextualizing category is privileged. That is, if differences between national styles of colonial government are privileged, useful contrasts between French and British models may indeed be identified, but only at the same time as diversity within French and within British practice is disguised; if, alternatively, a study is primarily concerned with the evolution of British constructions of south Asians, privileging the differences between 1780 and 1850, the conflict of voices at each of those dates is likely to be muted. If these necessary blindnesses are ameliorated by a strategy that aims to deploy and jeopardize several, rather than only one, of these analytical instruments, there may, in addition, be quite different ways in which colonialism's complex continuities and differences can be imagined. In particular, I will argue that perceptions of gender frequently encode ideas of racial difference, and that it is often these overlaid constructions that display the complexity and distinctiveness of particular modes of colonial representation.

Bernard McGrane has set out constructions of the other that reigned in the Renaissance, the Enlightenment and the nineteenth century. For him, the historical contingency of these models makes them conceivable, not as counterparts to modern anthropology, still less as actual visions of real others, but instead as discursive forms that are distinctive to epochs and epistemes. In the Renaissance the inhabitants of remote parts of the world are not monsters, as they had been in Pliny's *Natural History* and on the fringes of medieval maps; they are non-Christians and more particularly potential Christians of the kind sought by Columbus. In the early eighteenth century, according to McGrane, what becomes crucial is not religious lack but rather the ignorance of the Other: 'Anthropology did not exist; there was rather the negativity of a psychology of error and an epistemology of all the forms and causes of untruth.'³ This master trope is in turn displaced by evolutionism, by 'the positive and positivist form of a *comparison* between past and present'.⁴

Of course, an analysis that proceeds by identifying epistemological breaks and ruptures, that valorizes terms by establishing their distinctiveness, can only suppress continuity across periods and ways of perceiving alterity that remain salient and available, if in varying forms, over time. The level of generality also blurs more immediate historical changes; it is as if 'the Enlightenment's' discourse on society and the other is the same before and after events such as the American War of Independence, the French Revolution, and Toussaint L'Ouverture's slave uprising. McGrane's sequence of constructions of the Other is thus unsatisfyingly crude; on the other hand, there are important and fundamental contrasts between the ways of conceiving difference available to the conquerors of the New World and those expressed in the eighteenth and nineteenth centuries and subsequently. Curiously, relatively few writers have attempted to chart systematically these long-term shifts: most studies have been situated *within* one epoch or another, and may deal in a subtle way with shorter-term changes in European perceptions, but have tended not to address directly either the issue of the extent to which the constructions that are identified are distinctive to the period described, or the problem of what the fundamental differences might be between, say, seventeenth-century discourses and later colonial imaginations. For instance, Tzvetan Todorov, Stephen Greenblatt and Anthony Pagden have all written fine studies of European responses to the New World, while Bernard Smith and Philip Curtin have engaged in what might seem comparable exercises for a later period, tracing mainly British representations of the Pacific and Africa from the late eighteenth century to 1850, but very few writers have attempted to relate the earlier period to the later. Todorov uses the 'extreme, and exemplary, encounter' of the Conquest to discover generalities about the relations of Self and Other; Greenblatt pursues a succession of questions – of cross-cultural communication, of the ambiguities of possessiveness and wonder, of the straining of European codes – in relation to what can now be seen as mainstream literary texts as well as travel narratives and other works; Pagden traces the development of early ethnological thought with enormous erudition and subtlety.[5] The topics explored by Smith and Curtin are strikingly different – evolutionism, environmentalism, noble and ignoble savages – and both authors, along with many others tracing shifts over the same period, discern during the first half of the nineteenth century a hardening of racist attitudes and a withering of what is seen as a genuine curiosity and empathy for other cultures, characteristic of Enlightenment explorers and natural philosophers.[6]

It would only be surprising if the issues privileged by scholars of these periods were not radically different, but the question then arises of *how*: of what in fact is distinctive about the colonialism and colonialist imaginings of one period as opposed to those of others. This is a large and crude question, but unless it is addressed, a cruder operation can proceed: that is, any history or case study can be taken to be emblematic of colonialism, or imperialism, or self–other relations, or the magic of cultural contact and misunderstanding. An archaeological differentiation of forms of colonialism may undermine a generalizing moral discourse of the sort offered by Todorov, but perhaps more positively enables us to chart our own locations.

One answer to the question of how the colonialisms of different epochs differ from one another could extend the kind of history that Pagden writes, arriving at a genealogy on the basis of inspection. This might be the most scholarly strategy, but its sheer accumulation of interconnections would also, perhaps, disable rather than enable a cruder sense of what is modern about modern colonialism, of what distinguishes the histories and geographies of the recent past and present. At this heuristic level, an analytical fiction that postulates distinctions between colonial epochs is more valuable than a history of colonialism, though it needs to be understood that such a fiction is a rhetorical device; it is constructed in order to subvert easy totalities or progressive histories, but like any other intellectual device carries its own conceptual liabilities, and must be subverted in turn. This is to suggest that a Foucaultian 'history of the present' of the kind imitated by McGrane has a strategic value, even though, as was noted in the previous chapter, its preferred terrain of discourse offers an inhospitable environment for the living agents who elsewhere seem to make and change colonizing projects. In the following discussion, I bracket off the significance of agency, in the interests of an argument about the singularity of modern colonial projects, but find in the end that the latter cannot be described adequately, unless there is a turn back to the struggle to document the complexities of located histories and empirical changes.

Unlike McGrane's sequence of society's others, an equally schematic periodization put forward by Johannes Fabian emerges directly from an anthropological autocritique. It may be this closer articulation with the arguments of the present that makes Fabian's typification more useful for my purposes, even though I extend it and adapt it in ways that go beyond his purposes.

In *Time and the Other*, Fabian proposes that there is a basic distinction between modern and premodern constructions of time and space.

> Enlightenment thought marks a break with an essentially medieval, Christian (or Judeo-Christian) vision of Time. That break was one from a conception of time/space in terms of a history of salvation to one that ultimately resulted in the secularization of Time as natural history ... this not only entailed a change in the quality of time (sacred vs. secular) but also an important transformation as regards the nature of temporal *relations*. In the medieval paradigm, the Time of Salvation was conceived as inclusive or incorporative: The Others, pagans and infidels (rather than savages and primitives), were viewed as candidates for salvation ... The naturalization of Time which succeeded to that view defines temporal relations as exclusive and expansive. The pagan was always *already* marked for Salvation, the savage is *not yet* ready for civilization ... One [model] consists of concentric circles of proximity to a center in real space and mythical Time, symbol-

ized by the cities of Jerusalem and Rome. The other is constructed as a system of coordinates (emanating of course also from a real center – the Western metropolis) in which given societies of all times and places may be plotted in terms of relative distance from the present.[7]

What I seek to extrapolate from this is an argument that in premodern European discourses, non-Western peoples tend to be characterized not in any anthropologically specific terms, but as a lack or poorer form of the values of the centre. From this perspective, discussion of representations of 'the Other' is almost misleading in so far as it implies recognition of a distinctive type; what I suggest is that pagans were conceivable primarily as incomplete or imperfect forms, rather than as 'peoples' of a comprehensibly distinct kind. To be sure, over the sixteenth and seventeenth centuries, early ethnological texts began to describe 'Indians' possessing identities that were more singular than those of generalized pagans or infidels, but it is really not until the mid- to late eighteenth century that figures of inadequacy are subordinated to a distinctively *anthropological* discourse, which registers a variety of human races or peoples, who are mapped and ranked, as Fabian notes, in an evolutionary natural history. My emphasis will not be on this familiar temporalization of variety – that permitted some groups to be situated just above apes, and others as immature civilizations – but on a correlate of this natural-historicization of humanity, namely an analogy between human varieties and animal species. This enabled particular peoples to be seen as distinctive and essentially different (rather than, or as well as, being poorer or less advanced types than the Western exemplars of civilized, Christian humanity). My analytical fiction, then, tells of a shift from an absence of 'the Other' (as a being accorded any singular character) to a worldview that imagines a plurality of different races or peoples. This distinctively modern and anthropological imagining projects natural differences among people that may be rendered at one time as different 'nations', at another as distinct 'races' or 'cultures'. The underlying epistemic operation – of partitioning the human species – makes possible a variety of political and ethnographic projects: particular populations may be visible as objects of government; they may serve as ethnological illustrations or subversive counter-examples in comparative social

argument; and these reified characters may be available for appropriation in anti-colonialist, nationalist narratives.

In Renaissance Europe, the Christian understanding of non-European peoples seems to owe something, at a formal level, to an idea
that was familiar from classical literature: that of the barbarian. As
is well known, this was originally merely the Greeks' word for
foreigner, and was sometimes applied to peoples who were not
regarded as inferiors. What 'barbarian' connoted, however, was
generally *lack*: the absence of the civilized life of the *polis* which
the Greeks regarded as distinctive to their own culture.[8] When
presence was not juxtaposed with absolute absence – as nomadism
could be starkly contrasted to the settled community of the city –
the counterpart to the civilized institution was incomplete, being
'characterized by paucity and confusion.'[9] For example, in
Herodotus Scythian ritual is characterized 'above all . . . by a
number of absences: the absence of a place of sacrifice; the absence of any preparatory phase (fire, first fruits, libations);
the absence of blood.'[10] Given the asymmetry of value that seems
inherent in the distinction between presence and lack, it is
not surprising that the word 'barbarian' acquired strong connotations of inferiority as early as the fourth century BC: barbarians
were not only crude and unrefined, but were also distinguished by
cruel practices such as cannibalism that were absent from culti-
vated life.[11]

There were parallels with later Christian ideology,[12] in the sense
that the Christian community could be seen to displace or incorporate the idea of the *polis* as the collective centre, with religiosity rather than civility its constitutive virtue; neo-Aristotelian
theologians saw the city not just as an urban aggregation or
physical site, but as 'a metonym for the entire human community,
the largest, most perfect unit of society', and in its Christian form
as 'a spiritual community with a quasi-mystical presence.'[13] Again,
the status of those outside could be understood more through
missing elements than any distinctive positive characteristics: according to a French writer in 1582, savages were '*sans roi, sans loi,
sans foi*'.[14] As Todorov has noted, it is highly revealing that
Columbus's first remark – and subsequently one of his most frequent – upon the Indians refers to their lack of clothes, 'which in
their turn symbolize culture.'[15] The apprehension of otherness as

the absence of what is the same of course has great historical generality, but its particular Christian framing gives Renaissance expansionist thought and (to some extent) practice a distinctive character quite different from that, say, of the Hellenic discourse of the other's lack. Given the basic tenets of Christian theology – the unity of creation and the prospect of a Second Coming – humanity had to be regarded as a single population, and one that was prospectively wholly Christian: 'it was . . . crucial that non-Christians should be granted access to the Christian community: and, indeed, cajoled or forced into entering it.'[16] Those who are naked can thus be dressed, if their identity as heathens is not so much a premiss or justification but an enframing metaphor for the whole process of conquest, as it seems to have been for the Spanish in America.

The perceived difference between discoverers and natives, colonizers and colonized, was therefore religious rather than racial or national. In the text referred to as Columbus's journal, the admiral does not call the intruders Spaniards, Europeans or whites, but Christians, and the Indian is not a savage of any particular type but a vacancy that is available to be converted: 'they would easily be made Christians, for it appeared to me that they had no creed.'[17] Because the only aspects of the Indians that are significant are their nakedness and paganism – the behavioural and strictly religious facets of a condition that is merely negative – Columbus describes the Indians in generalities, and actually affirms that there are no differences among those he encounters: the indigenous populations on Cuba 'are of the same character and have the same customs as the others'; they too had no creed, and seemed ready to imitate the sign of the cross and say *Ave Maria*.[18] Of the English in Guiana a century later, it would seem similarly beside the point to speak of their 'representations of the other', since what is striking in Sir Walter Ralegh's account, and in other texts, is the preoccupation with resources ready to be extracted, that almost wholly excludes any comment on the people. While later writers frequently attributed femininity to colonized *peoples*,[19] when Ralegh wrote that '*Guiana* is a Countrey that hath yet Madenheade' he indeed meant the country rather than its inhabitants, though natural resources and the wealth of the people were equivalized as valuables equally ready to be appropriated: 'never sakt, turned, nor wrought, the face of the earth hath not beene ttorne, nor the vertue and salt of the soyle spent by manurance [cultivation], the graves have not beene opened for gold . . .'[20] The few cursory observations on the Indians related specifically to their service to the invaders, or to customs relevant to their rapacious activities: they did not bury their wives with them, 'but their jewels, hoping to injoy them againe . . . In the graves of the Peruvians, the Spanyards founde their greatest abundance of treasure . . .'[21] If the lack of others might figure constructively, in the sense that they were prospective Christians, not essentially different to Europeans, it also took a more radical and sinister form, in the sense that others, as bearers of distinct manners, concerns and polities, were simply not visible, and not to be accounted for, in an imagination of mercantile expansion which merely responded to the riches that it found.

Turning from generalized conceptions and representations to practices, the behaviour in moments of initial contact on the part of the conquistadores in America and Spanish explorers elsewhere in the world can be seen to accord with a unitary model: peoples encountered on the beach, whose prior natures were of no special interest, were baptized and dressed, while indigenous place names were effaced by Christian names: Pentecost, Santa Christina, Madre de Dios, Espritu Santo and so on. Names derived from the holy calendar at once incorporated new lands into a Christian geography, and commemorated the course of discovery.[22] Magellan even warned the chiefs in the Philippines that his men could not enter into sexual relations with unbaptized native women,[23] implying that what tended to be deplored as inter-racial prostitution by later naval captains was regarded rather as a proper element of the encounter, to be contained within its proselytizing logic.

Of course, the vacancy of otherness tended to be adumbrated as colonial administrations developed: it was necessary to represent and manage both converted populations and those who were more intransigent; it is in this context that the more negative dimension of the discourse becomes increasingly conspicuous. Prospectively Christian populations were not always responsive to the faith; given that its propagation tended to be accompanied by expropriations and violence, it is not surprising that it was often vigorously resisted. From the viewpoint of the colonizers, there was thus a trend for the distinction between Christian and prospectively Christian to evolve, in any particular situation, into a differentiated relationship between Christians and those who seemed receptive, on one side, and those who rejected the faith on the other; non-Christians, in other words, could be divided into heathens and heretics.[24] The latter, who included Muslims and various schismatics, were regarded as enemies of Christ, who could be justly enslaved or massacred. Where native Americans failed to respond to Christian teaching, they could be assimilated into the second category, and this is exactly what took place in one of the most fateful incidents in the conquest of Peru, which is still commemorated in folk theatre.[25] In 1532 Atahuallpa visited Pizarro at Cajamarca, in order apparently to negotiate with him; Father Valverde, Pizarro's chaplain, offered the Inca a Bible, and explained that the pope had commissioned the emperor of Spain to conquer and covert the peoples of America, and that this was Pizarro's mission. According to W. H. Prescott's classic narration, Atahuallpa retorted that he would be no man's subordinate, and threw the Bible to the ground; moments later, Pizarro gave a signal, and a massacre followed which left between two and ten thousand Peruvians dead; the Inca himself was captured and later executed.[26]

The dominance of the religious frame is apparent not just from initial perceptions, justifications for conquest or the explanations of violence, but also in more extended and systematic 'ethnological' writings. Though José de Acosta's *Historia natural y moral de las Indias* (1588) was, in many ways, an innovative work in its extent, its thoroughness and its emphasis on knowledge gained through experience, Indian practices are apprehended primarily as false versions of Christian ones, and the religious activities and institutions that were described are explained as the work of the devil, who seeks constantly to counterfeit and imitate God.

[H]e hath not onely counterfaited in idolatry and sacrifices but also in certaine ceremonies our sacraments, which Iesus Christ our Lord hath instituted and the Holy Church doth use, having especially pretended to imitate in some sort the Sacrament of the Communion . . . The Mamaconas of the Sunne, which were a kind of Nunnes of the Sunne, made little loaves of the flower of Mays, died and mingled with the bloud of white sheepe, which they did sacrifice that day; then presently they commanded that all stran-

gers should enter, who set themselves in order; and the Priests,
which were of a certaine lineage, discending from Liuquiyupangui,
gave to every one a morcell of these small loaves, saying vnto them
that they gave these peeces to the end they should be vnited and
confederate with the Ynca, and that they advised them not to
speake nor thinke any ill against the Ynca . . .[27]

While the extent to which indigenous customs are perceived
and diversity appreciated in Acosta's work offers a sharp contrast
to the blank uniformity of Columbus's account, and the even
hazier presence of the Indian in some of those who wrote after
him, such as Ralegh, this text displaces lack merely by falsity and
error and refrains from according otherness any original distinctiveness. Although the expansion of Hispanic settlement and
problems of policy and legitimation prompted more extensive
accounts of native American societies, the idolatrous usages and
superstitions that came to be represented in greater detail are not
explained by the particular character of the people, by responses
to environmental circumstances or by the degree to which their
society was evolved. The governing notion is rather that of slavery
to Satan: religious manners, in particular, can only figure as the
signs of 'foolish illusion' and service to false gods.[28] While the
comparative 'natural history of man' later detected parallels between the customs of savages and those of antiquity, in the model
of time and space that Fabian describes as essentially secular,
comparison here explained particular rites as false versions of
Christian usage; native practices were thus derivative effects of the
cosmic struggle.

Of course, the fact that the ideologies of the conquest were
religious and incorporative rather than racist did nothing to
ameliorate the violence of invasion: as has been noted, the total
suspension of humane treatment could be rationalized by resistance to the faith. Although the management of colonial relationships, once established, can proceed in some cases through
subtle mechanisms that produce co-operation or collaboration on
the part of the dominated, conquest always entails moments of
terror, and often protracted terrorist campaigns. The nature of
violence was determined in part by indigenous resistance, partly
by the pragmatic circumstances of colonial encounters, and only
partly by the character of the colonizers' ideology. It must be
apparent, also, that while Christian assimilationism would theo-

retically have placed converted natives and Christian colonists on an equal plane, the generalized doctrine was not necessarily taken to have particular social content. As Todorov has pointed out, if Jew and Greek, bond and free, male and female, 'are all one in Jesus Christ' (Galatians 3:28), Christian egalitarianism applies at a universal and asocial level: 'Christianity does not combat inequalities (the master will remain a master, the slave a slave, as if this were a difference quite as natural as that between man and woman); but it declares them irrelevant with regard to the unity of all in Christ.'[29]

Johann Reinhold Forster, describing Frobisher's visit to Greenland in 1577 in his *History of the Voyages and Discoveries made in the North* (1786), wrote:

> Of two women whom they found there, they took one along with them, together with her wounded child; the other was left on the spot, on account of her extreme ugliness. The sailors, moreover, suspected this woman to have a cloven foot; but her buskins being taken off her legs, her feet were found to be exactly like those of other human beings . . . Here again we meet with an instance of that cruelty which has ever marked the discoveries of the Europeans.

The incident demonstrates how the shift away from a religiously framed colonialism entailed new models for constructing otherness; these were couched in a narrative of natural history rather than salvation and privileged distinctiveness in character and physique rather than faith. What is most visible in these transitions is perhaps not however their epistemic and conceptual features, but their temper, their turn toward virulence.

In retrospect, the most striking feature of colonialism in the nineteenth century seems to be its overt, pervasive, and extraordinarily confident racism, which was manifested in military operations such as the wave of terror that made Australia a place of white settlement; in apartheid laws regulating marriage, residence, and education; in phrenology and similar forms of physical anthropology that made natural inferiority recognizable; in stray jokes and judgements in travel books; and in the stereotypes of mass-circulation juvenile literature.[30] In representations of many specific populations, a shift is apparent from the late Enlightenment onwards, that saw an ambivalent array of attitudes, including humanitarian and appreciative assessments as well as more negative judgements, displaced by a more uniform, intolerant, and less subtle denigration of those whose physical inferiority and moral faults were unmistakable.[31] While the ideas put forward by Edward Long in his pro-slavery *History of Jamaica* in 1774 were much harsher than those found in most geographical descriptions or travel narratives of the time, whether from Africa, Asia, or the Pacific, by 1850 they would be echoed in accounts from all of these regions.

Critical historians of race have emphasized that colour prejudice has not been an eternal or universal social fact, but have turned to times as remote as the medieval period and antiquity to find a pre-racist European culture. Frank Snowden, for instance, argues that

> the ancient world did not make color the focus of irrational sentiments or the basis for uncritical evaluations. The ancients did accept the institution of slavery as a fact of life; they made ethnocentric judgements of other societies; they had narcissistic canons of physical beauty; the Egyptians distinguished between themselves, 'the people,' and outsiders; and the Greeks called foreign cultures barbarian. Yet nothing comparable to the virulent color prejudice of modern times existed in the ancient world.[32]

Nancy Stepan suggests that racism was inconsequential in antiquity and the Middle Ages, and relates its emergence to the slave trade: though a general prejudice against darkness had spread widely by the sixteenth century, she suggests that because slaves were almost exclusively black by the late eighteenth century, connections between mental and moral inferiority, and black skins, were naturalized.[33] So far as modern history is concerned, this suggestion might diminish the sense that there was anything particularly distinctive about the aesthetic which categorical racists such as Henry Stanley and Thomas Andrew expressed in their images of African darkness and Fijian cannibalism: racial prejudice existed previously, except in remote antiquity, was manifested for instance in the attitudes of some Portuguese in Goa, and was simply consolidated in a more extreme form in the second half of the nineteenth century.[34] We would thus not regard the powerful hierarchizing device of racism as an ideology novel to a particular modern period, but rather as something that had developed gradually; the implication of the association with the slave trade would be that racist constructions of non-negro populations, such as Asians and Pacific islanders, were extrapolated logically from this specific race hatred, in the sense that if African blacks were regarded as the lowest form of humanity, then brown-skinned peoples would be assigned intermediate statuses.

The weakness of this view arises from the commonsense idea that racism is merely a kind of xenophobic distaste directed against those of darker skin. The model thus generalizes an individual's attitude or psychological disposition to the level of a set of concepts or an ideology. Racial theory is, however, much more than a textual version of an emotion such as hatred: it presumably postulates races that have a certain unity and origin, that are meaningful as entities and that can thus be ranked; it ought to be seen as a *discourse* that engages in conceptual and perceptual government, in its apprehension and legislation of types, distinctions, criteria for assessing proximity and distance, and in its more technical applications – in, for instance, notions stipulating that certain forms of labour are appropriate to one race but not another. Racist discourse may often indeed be manifested personally, in responses of displeasure, fear or antipathy, but these should be understood as subjective internalizations of non-subjective ideologies, rather than the emotional springs from which the latter flow. In any case, though the discourses are manifested in personal attitudes, they also embody theoretical codifications, disquisitions and justifications that objectify these personal responses by grounding them in a condition of the negro or the savage that is inferior and contemptible in its nature, rather than merely something different that a white person instinctively despises.

From this point of view – that seeks to specify the conceptual distinctiveness of modern racism – the shift referred to earlier, from the range of relatively benevolent eighteenth-century attitudes to the more deeply negative racism of the nineteenth century, may be of less consequence than the more basic development that separates much modern discourse from the religious construction of otherness described earlier, the reinterpretation of human variety in natural terms, meaning that 'peoples' defined on some basis or another are understood to differ in essential ways. Of course, there is nothing intrinsically racist about the presumably universal process of dividing known populations: what is important, rather, are the various conceptions of difference, and the clarity and fixity of the borders that they mark. Social boundaries may be based on contingent matters of cult practices, etiquette, faith or language, which may be permeable if people can adopt one regime as they dissociate themselves from another. On the other hand, difference of a more fundamental kind may be postulated.

European colonial discourses have often dehumanized others and thus made brutal treatment seem more intelligible, less shameful, even appropriate, but a less conspicuously violent but perhaps more crucial ideological operation perhaps requires greater scrutiny. In effect, this makes differences among human populations analogous to differences between animal species: the types are essentialized, and seen to have the same manifest coherence and distinctness. There is a striking contrast between the relatively untenable character of such a model in the sixteenth and seventeenth centuries and its security in the nineteenth. While the earlier polygenetic writers were struggling to make discrete kinds of humans or humanlike beings visible through distortions and evasions of the biblical narrative, a writer such as Henry Stanley was able, in contrast, to apprehend distinct human types quite effortlessly, in his quasi-diffusionist account of human variation in Africa.

> The Wahuma are true descendants of the Semitic tribes, or communities, which emigrated from Asia across the Red Sea, and settled on the coast, and in the uplands of Abyssinia, once known as Ethiopia. From this great centre more than a third of the inhabitants of Inner Africa have had their origin. As they pressed southward and conquered the negro tribes, miscegenation produced a mixture of races; the Semitic became tainted with negro blood, the half-caste tribes intermarried again with the primitive race, and became still more degraded in feature and form ... From among the Kaffirs, Zulus, Matabeles, Basutos, Bechuanas, or any other of the fierce South African tribes, select an ordinary specimen ... and plant him near a West African, or Congoese, or Gabonese type, and place a Hindu between them, and having been once started on the right trail of discovery, you

will at once perceive that the features of the Kaffir are a subtle amalgamation of the Hindu and West African types . . . Advancing across the Zambezi towards the watershed of the Congo and Loangwa, we observe among the tribes a confusion of types, which may be classed indifferently as being an intermediate family between the West African and the Kaffir; an improvement on the former, but not quite up to the standard of the latter.[35]

Passages of this expository ethnological kind are not especially numerous in Stanley's writing, which features many less systematic racist observations in the course of an adventure narrative, but they nevertheless represent a significant aspect of his project; works such as *Through the Dark Continent* and *In Darkest Africa* did not merely provide influential models for imperialist aggression and pioneer masculinity; they also displayed the comprehensive aspect of European power. Stanley did not only penetrate thick vegetation, illuminate darkness and accomplish particular military and exploratory objectives – that had, among other effects, the result of exposing the Congo to some of the most brutal colonial exploitation in world history; he could also see, travel across and represent the colonized spaces and races, and their underlying history, their formation and differentiation. The mechanism of miscegenation among prior stock is not hypothesized, but perceived, and it goes without saying that this grasp of the totality expresses a knowledge that members of these populations could not have possessed of themselves. The constitutive elements of this peculiarly and profoundly modern discourse are thus epistemic as well as stereotypic; particular races constitute definite entities that can be known; and while Stanley merely asserts his truths, the fidelity and exhaustiveness of physical differentiation was elsewhere demonstrated statistically and photographically.[36]

In seeking an answer to the problem of where this authority, and its objects, come from, we should turn, I suggest, not to the obvious antecedents of physical and racial anthropology in cranial studies,[37] but to a descriptive vocabulary emergent in the second half of the eighteenth century, that was initially concerned with animals rather than human beings. Buffon's *Natural History* offered a general theory of the formation of the earth and of various topographic and environmental features, as well as an account of life cycles and other phenomena, but also provided characterizations of a very large number of animals, which were finely depicted in coloured engravings in many later editions of the work. These accounts had a standard form in that they began with certain generic markers, such as horns and the number of teeth, and then proceeded to a more evocative sketch of the character of the beast, and its relation to man, in which philosophical speculations were frequently interspersed.

> The dog has six cutting teeth and two canine in each jaw: he has five toes on the fore feet and four, and often five, on the hind feet. His tail bends toward the left, a character common to the whole, and first observed by Linnaeus.
>
> The dog, independent of the beauty of his figure, his strength, vivacity, and nimbleness, possesses every internal excellence which can attract the regard of man. A passionate, and even a ferocious and sanguinary temper, renders the wild dog formidable to all animals. But in the domestic dog, these hostile dispositions vanish, and are succeeded by the softer sentiments of attachment, and the desire of pleasing. He runs with chearfulness and alacrity to his master's foot, where he lays down his courage, his strength, and his talents. He attends for orders, which he is always solicitous to execute . . . He assumes the very tone of the family in which he lives. Like other servants, he is haughty with the great, and rustic with the peasant. Always eager to please his master, or his friends, he pays no attention to strangers, and furiously repels beggars, whom he distinguishes by their dress, their voice, and their gestures.[38]

In virtually every case, the animal is not treated as a collectivity, but reduced to a singular standard specimen: 'The ape . . . is as untractable as he is extravagant. His nature, in every point, is equally stubborn.'[39] 'The badger is an indolent, diffident, solitary animal . . . He seems to fly society, and even the light, and spends three fourths of his life in his dark abode, from which he never departs but in quest of subsistence.'[40]

The singularization of the species permits an account that is remarkably fresh and vivid; rather than being given a dry and abstract description of what might be statistically correct of an entire population, the reader imagines the particular animal, whose actions and character are evoked in an immediate fashion; he is here, running, biting, barking. But this singularization also of course permits a more complex conceptual operation, since the description shifts from the concrete and observable facts of the dog's teeth and tail, to the generalized disquisition upon species character, that would seem far less coherent or plausible, were it not for the attachment of these attributes to a single dog, that is here now, running and barking. Despite the fact that Buffon's environmentalism made him sensitive to variability and mutability of species, and despite the fact that the modifications of the dog's nature arising from domestication are of interest, there is still a discursively fundamental sense in which the dog has a nature; this nature is the object of the description. Yet a species is an entirely different entity to a particular creature, and it might be thought that the characters of species could only be appreciated in a partial way, just as travellers could only have opinions that were limited by their restricted knowledge of a place visited; but such qualifications evaporate if it possible to speak of the dog's intelligence and the ape's stubbornness. What the species has is the same as what the person or singular animal has, namely a character and personality that can be recognized through behaviour and dispositions. It is evident that a dog's master knows the dog, and the evocation of the particular animal elides all the differences between this kind of knowledge and any possible knowledge of the whole variety.

Buffon's history is also suggestively and avowedly anthropocentric, yet it scarcely acknowledges partiality on this account. It is rather taken for granted that the actions of a dog, in relation to man, are not merely to be understood circumstantially, but manifest the nature of the animal. This understanding privileges the experience of a socially-located knowing subject in a radical way: it is his sense of the behaviour of the creature to be known that serves as an index for the attributes of the latter. In the case of the dog, it goes without saying that the perspective of the master rather than that of the beggar affords comprehension of the nature of the animal; and just as the dog's positive service marks a character that can be assessed favourably, the deficiencies of other animals are discernible in the human response to them. Animal character is objectified, yet apprehended in a rigorously subjective fashion.

There are many parallels between this way of knowing and evaluating and the modes of recognition and assessment present in explorers' and travellers' accounts of other peoples in the decades around Buffon's great publication; such parallels do not exist in the literature of the early to mid-eighteenth century (although writers on Europe, such as the widely-read jurist and encyclopaedist Samuel Pufendorf, had been constructing similarly naturalized typifications of the characters of the various European nations since the late seventeenth century).[41] On one side, for instance, Kolben's *Description of the Cape of Good Hope* (1731) is interested largely in the people, but makes no effort to construct any stable account of their natures or national character; on the other, works dedicated to natural history, such as Adanson's *Voyage to Senegal* (1759), do describe and characterize plants, but fail to assimilate humanity to their botanical and zoological subject-matter.[42] In contrast, the object of man and the technology of natural history are integrated in Johann Reinhold Forster's *Observations made during a Voyage round the World*, a publication based on participation in Cook's second voyage to the Pacific of 1772–5. One of Forster's key sections dealt with 'the VARIETIES of the HUMAN SPECIES, relative to COLOUR, SIZE, FORM, HABIT, and NATURAL TURN of MIND in the NATIVES of the SOUTH-SEA ISLES.' Forster opened this discussion by parading the sort of characterization he would proceed to engage in.

> The varieties of the human species are, as everyone knows, very numerous. The small size, the tawny colour, the mistrustful temper, are as peculiar to the Esquimaux; as the noble and beautiful figure, and outline of the body, the fair complexion, and the treacherous turn of mind, to the inhabitant of Tcherkassia. The native of Senegal is characterized by a timorous disposition, by his jetty black skin, and crisped wooly hair.[43]

Despite their compressed character, it is clear from these typifications that an entity was recognizable, consisting both of physical features and a 'natural turn of mind', that had its own singularity; that is, it was unnecessary to qualify the account by saying that *some* Senegalese were timorous, or to consider that you or I, or the inhabitant of any region, might engage in treachery under certain circumstances; these dispositions were instead rendered natural and peculiar to a type of humanity that could be clearly distinguished from its neighbours. The 'variety' of humankind, sometimes a sub-category of a 'nation' or 'race', at other times a loose equivalent, was thus not something that might be stereotyped in an unscientific manner, but a unitary entity which could be known, that stood as the referent for a certain kind of truth.

In the thumbnail sketches just quoted there is a Buffon-like conflation, whereby the experience and perception of the knower are taken not merely to express his response to the other, but her essential nature: like beauty, the 'outline of the body' is something primarily in the mind of a viewer, who takes the other person as something to be seen, rather than as an actor of the same kind as himself. This operation is enlarged in Forster's fuller accounts: of the Tongans, he wrote: 'the character of these people is really amiable; their friendly behaviour to us, who were utter strangers to them, would have done honour to the most civilized nation.'[44] He was less kind to the inhabitants of Tierra del Fuego.

We found them to be a short, squat race, with large heads; their colour yellowish brown; the features harsh, the face broad, the cheek-bones high and prominent, the nose flat, the nostrils and mouth large, and the whole countenance without meaning . . . Their women are much of the same features, colour, and form as the men, and generally have long hanging breasts, and besides the seal-skin on their backs, a small patch of the skin of a bird or seal to cover their privities. All have a countenance announcing nothing but wretchedness. They seem to be good-natured, friendly, and harmless; but remarkably stupid, being incapable of understanding our signs, which, however, were very intelligible to the nations of the South Sea.[45]

The singularity of this sort of account may be more recognizable if we briefly recall Columbus's interest in the fact that the Indians 'all go naked, men and women, as their mothers bore them, although some of the women cover a single place with the leaf of a plant or with a net of cotton which they make for the purpose.'[46] For Columbus and his contemporaries, the presence of rudimentary garments is only a small qualification to the most important fact, which, despite its evident lack of categorical truth, is reiterated and emphasized. Forster's allusion to similar genital coverings, though equally cursory, belongs to an entirely different discourse: what is registered is a presence or fact concerning the specific nature of clothing, rather than a negative state that is incidentally qualified. The reference to the use of the bird or seal skin is a fragment of a much more extensive description that presents tortoiseshell earrings, bone arrowpoints, tattooing, canoe forms and the Terra del Fuegians' 'very long' scrotums and stinking train oil. As physical forms, as characters, as bearers of customs and distinctive material artefacts, others were visible as knowable types.

Typification proceeded most powerfully through the evocation of the singular character: the native of Senegal or the Tongan. Even though this grammatical device is not always employed, the same pattern of characterization proceeds, not just in Forster, but increasingly commonly towards the end of the eighteenth century, in works such as Mungo Park's *Travels in the Interior Districts of Africa* (1799).

> The natives of the countries bordering on the Gambia, though distributed in a great many distinct governments, may, I think, be divided into four great classes...
>
> [The Feloops] are of a gloomy disposition, and are supposed never to forgive an injury... This fierce and unrelenting disposition is, however, counterbalanced by many good qualities: they display the utmost gratitude and affection toward their bene-factors... During the present war they have, more than once, taken up arms to defend our merchant vessels from French privateers.
>
> The Jaloffs (or Yaloffs) are an active, powerful, and warlike race, inhabiting [a] great part of that tract which lies between the river Senegal and the Mandingo States on the Gambia; yet they differ from the Mandingoes, not only in language, but likewise in complexion and features. The noses of the Jaloffs are not so much depressed, nor the lips so protuberant, as among the generality of Africans; and although their skin is of the deepest black, they are considered by the white traders, as the most sightly Negroes in this part of the continent.
>
> The Foulahs (or Pholeys), such of them at least as reside near the Gambia, are chiefly of a tawny complexion, with soft silky hair, and pleasing features. They are much attracted to a pastoral life...
>
> The Mandingoes, generally speaking, are of a mild, sociable, and obliging disposition. The men are commonly above the mid-

dle size, well-shaped, strong, and capable of enduring great labour; the women are good-natured, sprightly, and agreeable.[47]

There are small concessions to variation here: what is said of the Foulahs is not necessarily true of those further from the Gambia, and the Mandingoes are what they are, 'generally speaking'. On the whole, though, this discourse proceeds through confident assertion about the natures of whole populations, and is marked consistently by the slippage noted above, whereby the behaviour of particular peoples towards Europeans, or the responses of the latter to the former, are taken as emanations of the natives' essential characters, rather than facts arising from the circumstances of contact. Park does not acknowledge that he has

Plate 6   *'A Javan of the lower class'. From Raffles,* History of Java, *1817*

a positive attitude toward the Feloops because they defended British vessels against the French; rather the fact that they did so is taken as a manifestation of their internal nature: their commendable 'affection toward their benefactors'. Hence, while this operation of anthropological typification afforded a larger environmental view – manifest in Raffles's comments on the Javanese and Malays – it entered at the same time into more sentimental, less quasi-scientific descriptions, and into narrative as well as exposition. Raffles's Papuan illustrates further that this anthropological model was not the only language through which others could be represented: while 'more advanced' natives tended to be seen as differentiated 'national' types, explicable on the basis of

Plate 7   'A Papuan or native of New Guinea, 10 years old'. From Raffles, History of Java, 1817

their environmental situation, those at the bottom of the ladder were naturalized more immediately through a language of physical anthropology. This is what Raffles's text effects, while the print evokes the abolitionist image of the melancholy slave; both underplay the cultural, as opposed to the physically, singularity of the Papuan. Other constructions and narratives thus always jostled with the anthropological discourse that I have traced.

More than a century later, Franz Boas was writing against evolutionism in anthropology, and against the racism with which it was generally linked. Ironically, however, the analogy that he employed to deny the possibility of any rank ordering echoes the parallel that was fundamental to comparative ethnology after Buffon: 'Cultures differ like so many species, perhaps genera, of animals, and their common basis is lost forever. It seems impossible . . . to bring cultures into any kind of continuous series.'[48]

Race was here displaced by the idea of culture, but 'cultures' have a great deal in common with 'races',[49] as 'races' did with the 'nations' of eighteenth-century representation. Each of these concepts privileged differences – understood at different moments primarily in temperamental, physical and now cultural terms – and rendered the essentialized entities through an array of attributes that are supposedly peculiar to them. Just as Forster had rejected the cruelty and stupidity of the sailors who expected to discover that the other was physiologically different, anthropologists rejected arguments for racial inferiority. Like Forster, however, they remained certain that others possessed specific and knowable natures and guarded the epistemic privilege of colonialism while rejecting its violence. Modern representations of 'others', whether in anthropology or in far less sympathetic genres, such as those of colonial fiction, have been deeply conditioned by the availability of this language of typification. Though expressed in extremely diverse ways, and in forms that may be highly self-conscious and culturally relativist, or deeply racist, nativist or scientific, the notion that others are possessed of specific and distinct natures is of critical importance.

Rather than pursue the complex and often critically conscious usage of Boas and his contemporaries, the current significance and political ambiguity of this discourse can be attested by two more recent examples: one being modern (not postmodern) cultural anthropology, the other being current political commentary on Middle Eastern politics. I suggest that despite the apparently radical differences among these discourses of the present, and between them and those of the eighteenth century, human variety is still primarily available for understanding through natural-historical models that essentialize types in basically the same way as was manifest in Buffon's foundational text. In this sense, modernity has been an epoch of anthropological typification; even when colonial discourses do not purvey or rely on typifications, they must often direct themselves against them. In other words, the dominant status of the concept can be illustrated as much by the way it has been resisted, as by its effective hegemony. Whether the workings of this sort of cultural and ethnic essentialism are finally now being deconstructed by cultural practices under the banner of postcoloniality is a question I take up at the end of this book.

Though the extent to which twentieth-century anthropology has employed the idea of cultural plurality has been variable (French, if not British, structuralism, for instance, operated instead in a universalistic frame) the culturalism of the 1970s and 1980s reproduced some of Boas's crucial assumptions. Although there were obviously diverse and very significant shifts, and although contemporary symbolic anthropology is clearly entirely different to earlier cultural paradigms in its modes of theorizing symbols and metaphors, the fact that the issue of cultural difference has been relatively undiscussed until recently is in itself significant. For instance, a debate about Clifford Geertz's interpretive anthropology could focus almost wholly on the question of the emphasis on the symbolic, and its implications for anthropology's capacity to deal with social conflict and social change, without broaching at all one of the assumptions that is most pervasive in cultural anthropology, that is, the possibility of writing meaningfully as though Javanese, Balinese, Moroccans, and various others were the bearers of distinctive cultures.[50]

Geertz's work (which is as diverse as any other substantial *oeuvre*) occupies a rather curious status in contemporary anthropology; certainly in North America and to some extent elsewhere, it is far more widely read and referred to by historians, art historians and literary critics, than the writing of any other anthropologist;[51] within the discipline, it no longer sets any agenda and differs quite sharply from the perspectives advanced in many subfields, but it nevertheless remains influential in general terms, if rejected in its specifics, and a key reference point, for instance for influential 'postmodernist' works such as George Marcus and Michael Fisher's *Anthropology as Cultural Critique*.[52] There is therefore a sense that despite the somewhat unrepresentative nature of his theoretical orientation, Geertz's work speaks for the discipline: it provides a poor guide to what anthropology is, but a good one to what it can be taken to mean.

This is all the more illuminating once certain contemporary echoes of the old 'national character' discourse are examined: it would seem that Geertz's work is influential not only because it is well written, but because it articulates with ideas that are already in circulation, that stem, in fact, from the naturalized typifications that can be traced through Forster, Buffon and (on European nations) Samuel Pufendorf. Without a history of such characterizations, would we be able to understand this sort of thing, extracted from Geertz's contrast between north African and Indonesian varieties of Islam?

[R]ather than the restless, extroverted sheik husbanding his resources, cultivating his reputation, and awaiting his opportunity, the national archetype [in Java] is the settled, industrious, rather inward plowman of twenty centuries, nursing his terrace, placating his neighbors, and feeding his superiors. In Morocco civilization was built on nerve; in Indonesia, on diligence.[53]

This kind of description is simply not legible without the tradition that we have of taking national varieties as peculiar entities, and of characterizing them in certain summary ways. While the echoes between the content of this passage and Raffles's typification of the Javanese is striking, it is perhaps less crucial than the more basic conformity with the mode of characterization that has been traced through Pufendorf and Forster; it is perhaps closest to the former, in the sense that Forster's interest in the combination of physical and temperamental attributes is purged of the racial element; while Forster's Senegalese had 'jetty black skin' and 'a timorous disposition', Geertz's equivalents carry only cultural temperaments – no skin but a timorous disposition. There is a more significant degree of continuity, since Geertz does not only grammatically singularize his typical 'sheik' and 'plowman' in this passage, but uses two individual personages – a sixteenth-century Javanese prince and a seventeenth-century Morrocan saint – to illustrate his contrast between the southeast Asian and north African 'classical religious styles' – 'two men, two cultures'.[54] His method is thus to 'trace the development and characterize the nature of' these two religious traditions, that are recognizable as distinct entities with different styles in the same way that you and I are.[55]

I contend that there is nothing accidental about his resort to the word 'nature'; the character that is posited is a fixed essence attached to a species, a nation, a people or a culture. In a general way, Geertz acknowledges that this has arisen historically, and would not take it to be immutable, or resistant to further development; but Buffon also took species nature to be susceptible to environmental influences. In neither case does this allowance for history seem to qualify the fact that the people or species *has* a nature, or character, or style, that is available for description.

Of course, it could be suggested that the evocation of 'the national archetype' is a tongue-in-cheek exercise, that what is proferred is patently a generalization or ideal type, and that no one writing or reading about the 'rather inward plowman' seriously expects to encounter him. Such a generous reading of the text would entirely miss the point that what is quoted is not simply a stray passage but a description that replicates the theoretical architecture of the whole of *Islam Observed,* and which moreover has parallels in other well-known studies by Geertz.[56] Like most anthropologists, Geertz is not generally so interested in sketching national characters as he is in the book on Islam, but the same logic operates in the argument that particular peoples or cultures possess distinctive representations and beliefs, that can be referred to as 'the Samoan construction of the person', 'the Malayan conception of kingship', 'the Aboriginal notion of the land', that are all deeply different from 'Western' notions. Geertz has devoted a book to a claim of this kind, that Balinese states reflected 'an alternate conception' of what politics is about, a work which we can take to illustrate the faults of this approach.

Like Louis Dumont's much-criticized construction of the Indian as *Homo hierarchicus*,[57] the Balinese polities that are depicted in Geertz's *Negara* are introduced as an aberration from the perspective of our own order: they were characterized by what is, 'to us, [a] strangely reversed relationship between the substance and the trappings of rule': stupendous rituals were not means to political ends, 'they were the ends themselves, they were what the state was for . . . Power served pomp, not pomp power.'[58] Geertz explores various features of traditional Balinese society in some detail, but the central thesis of his book is remarkably simple: *negara* do not conform to models of the state available in Western political theory because they are orientated above all towards symbolic expression, rather than the mechanics of rule and government. Just as Dumont depoliticized the realm of caste that was contrasted with the nonsymbolic politics of kingship, Geertz situates power in the level of social relations below the state, in what are essentially village politics.

It might thus be complained that while the Balinese furnish a provoking distortion of ourselves, they are at the same time stabilized and reduced to a showcase. In many ways, Bali exists in Geertz's text as the opposite or complement of the West.

> [T]he Balinese conception of their political development does not, like the American, present a picture of the forging of unity out of an original diversity, but the dissolution of an original unity into a growing diversity; not a relentless progress toward the good society, but a gradual fading from view of a classic model of perfection. . . . What our concept of public power obscures, that of Bali exposes; and vice versa.[59]

Negara however offers more than a simple reiteration of these themes. In fact, the message of the concluding section is rather different.

> That Balinese politics, like everyone else's, including ours, was symbolic action does not imply, therefore, that it was all in the mind or consisted entirely of dances and incense. The aspects of that polity here reviewed . . . configured a reality as dense and immediate as the island itself . . . [Men and women] were pursuing the ends they could through the means they had. The dramas of the theater state, mimetic of themselves, were, in the end, neither illusion nor lies, neither sleight of hand nor make-believe. They were what there was.[60]

This would seem a universalizing discourse that overtly disa-
vows any Orientalist characterization of Bali as a place consumed
by scent and ceremony, and instead postulates Balinese rational
actors who did what they could with what was there. But the
words 'does not imply' convey less than what is evoked in image
and aroma by 'dance and incense'; while there might be a wish
to exploit decorative imagery, yet exclude its implications, it is
stereotypes that resonate for the reader, especially since so
much of the rest of the book is dedicated to the painting of
Balinese ritual. What is paradoxical here reflects a deeper tension
in the book's reigning image: the forceful claim that Balinese
political life is theatrical turns upon the difference between
theatrical performance and other kinds of action. The show
does not work if we presume, in the first place, that political action
everywhere is a work of symbolic display: the account of one
particular polity as a theatre state would then be meaningless
and redundant. So it is affirmed at the beginning that what
is displayed is 'strangely reversed', and this strangeness contra-
dicts the claim made later that theatre is nothing other than
'what there was', in other words, what is natural to society and
political life.

Hence, the rhetoric of *Negara* is no more unitary than that of
liberal exoticist texts, and perhaps echoes a broader paradox that
Marianna Torgovnick has identified in Roger Fry's writing on
African sculpture, which attacks colonial prejudice while airing
and reiterating colonialist stereotypes.[61] The effect of *Negara*, in
the end, is to abstract Balinese society as a picturesque,
transhistorical essence,[62] radically different from Western society.
Despite the fact that the kinds and vocabularies of classification
deployed in anthropological knowledge, and specific theoretical
interests, have changed very considerably since the eighteenth
century, there is an illusion of discontinuity in the sense that some
form of essentialist partitioning has been crucial all along. While
modern anthropology has succeeded Buffon and Forster, in the
sense that it has both followed and displaced them, it remains, so
far as constructions of human variety are concerned, a project
after Buffon. Ideas of the distinctiveness of human varieties that
were insecure or unintelligible before the mid-eighteenth century
persist: usually, it is not that the Balinese is like this or habitually
does that; the entity is instead pluralized, and it is Balinese culture

that is analogous to nation or race, that is the bearer of peculiar attributes.

The idea that other peoples have different cultures also enters into current debate in a distinctly sinister form. In his recent book *The Closed Circle: an Interpretation of the Arabs,* David Pryce-Jones suggests that the Arab world has been profoundly misunderstood by ethnocentric Europeans, who have failed to perceive fundamental social and cultural differences between our way of life and theirs. In his view, Arab societies are alien and basically tribal. They are founded on status competition rather than contractual agreements. Culturally, notions of honour and shame are fundamental to individual responses and motivations; politics is therefore a matter of careerism, and is locked into a 'power-challenge dialectic' that proceeds 'in the absence of institutional checks'. This results in a 'drive to violence' that must be seen as a basic and normal element of Arab political behaviour.[63] 'In the West, what is said and done more or less corresponds with the intentions of the speaker and the doer. Liars and cheats abound, of course, but generally they can only go so far before being caught out in the contractual relationships of their society. Lying and cheating in the Arab world is not really a moral matter but a method of safeguarding honour and status . . .'[64] Pryce-Jones is able to see past Eurocentric misunderstandings because he can understand what is distinctive to these other social forms and cultures, such as the principles that 'Tribal society is a closed order'; 'Honour is what makes life worthwhile; shame is a living death, not to be endured, requiring that it be avenged.'[65] His insight enables him to realize that the quest for Arab modernity was always hopeless, and similarly that it is absurd for Europeans to be shocked by Arab violence, terrorism, and corruption; these propensities are so deeply embedded in the social and cultural fabric that no reforms or changes can be anticipated: 'At present, an Arab democrat is not even an idealization but a contradiction in terms.'[66] It is not surprising that Pryce-Jones concludes that if military action must be taken in the Arab world it 'must be undertaken with inflexible determination to use whatever degree of force is required for supreme arbitration'.[67] This dehumanized Arab nature thus licenses precisely what did take place in late March 1991, when mainly American and British forces massacred an unknown number of retreating and comprehensively defeated Iraqi sol-

s; it did not seem necessary to censor or disguise the opera-
, described as 'a turkey shoot' and 'fun' by some of the par-
pants; it provoked little sustained protest or discussion in any
se.

Enough; this is all grimly familiar, and it is not worth detailing
the ways in which Pryce-Jones's essentialist claims might be re-
futed, the ways in which his sources might be discredited or the
alternative ways in which the violence and the postcolonial histories that are indeed sorry stories might be understood. The
important point is that the characterization is merely a cruder
version of what post-Enlightenment anthropology has been built
upon: namely the idea that particular peoples have natures that
may be mainly racial, cultural or social, but, most importantly, are
distinctive to them. This notion is anthropological but not peculiar to anthropology: it emerges under other names in other
scholarly and broader cultural traditions, and is, for instance,
much the same as the idea recently demolished by Geoffrey Lloyd,
that peoples of a particular place or epoch can meaningfully
be said to have a particular 'mentality'.[68] The crucial attribute
of all of these entities – nations, races, societies, cultures – is that
their distinctiveness is naturalized; it is equivalent to species difference. Both human attributes that might arguably be universal
(at cognitive or linguistic levels, for instance), and differences
that arise from age, gender and a plethora of other considera-
tions, are marginalized by this privileging and essentialization of
ethnic or cultural difference. Though anthropologists are not
disposed to regard anything much as 'innate', the virtually innate
possession of culture is marked by the extent to which accultura-
tion or change produces an inauthentic amalgam, something
false to its real nature. The absurdity of simulation observed by
Pufendorf in those who emulated French manners has also been
detected by Pryce-Jones, who noted that contemporary consumerism, like colonialism, had failed to alter the Arab collectivity;
'steam launches and false hair and fireworks' at the court of
Sultan Abdul Aziz in Morocco merely decorated and degraded
its external appearance.[69] This rejection of expressions of cultural
hybridity – that count as ersatz borrowings, invented traditions
and so on – amounts to the legislative wing of the project
of 'anthropological' characterization that stipulates the nature of
the other.

What I have put forward is an argument that places some modern anthropological writing, and much other public commentary on 'others' and indigenous peoples, in conformity with an enduring conceptual form in modern colonial discourse. I have argued that this cannot be read as a global essence of colonialism, which might be identified with something that all colonizing societies have done to others, but must be seen as a possibility and product of ways of thinking that were distinctive to Europe and to a historical period. Within this epochal frame, the logic of typification that I have described clearly has extremely diverse manifestations, yet is appropriately understood as a form that has long provided colonial representations with considerable force and authority. This discursive technology is moreover one that remains available and powerful, and is thus something that should be contested, and is being contested, through a variety of contemporary indigenous practices and postcolonial critical efforts, that seek to subvert enduring forms of colonial authority. These issues are explored further in subsequent chapters.

Here, however, it is necessary to qualify, if not undermine, the argument that has been put forward locating colonial discourses in terms of generalized periods. This genealogy needs to be placed into tension with an alternative, perhaps primarily synchronic, way of situating colonial discourses and representations. As was noted earlier, much writing on colonialism homogenizes 'the colonizers', and although a historical or archaeological differentiation of representational epistemes establishes that colonialism cannot be seen as a historical unity, such periodization leaves the apparent homogeneity of colonizing actors at particular times intact. In fact, as has already been noted, colonizing was an array of religious, commercial, administrative and exploratory projects that sometimes proceeded in relative harmony but were at other times in tension or outright contradiction. These exercises were not of course necessarily separate: missionaries and explorers engaged in trade, and settlers who were no doubt mainly preoccupied with running plantations or trading might also have been correspondents of the Royal Geographical Society, who occasionally dabbled in ethnology or geology. Of course, categories such as 'administrators' and 'missionaries' cannot serve as fixed, transhistorical points of reference; this difference is cut across by shifts over time of the sort referred to above, and by geographic differences: in breaking up a global theory of colonialism one has not only to pose the question of *who* was colonizing, but also to ask *where*. Colonists formed entirely different conceptions of different places, different civilizations and different uncivilized peoples, and moreover quite different ideas about how these societies might be dealt with and governed. A traveller who went to China, the Malayan archipelago and India was likely to employ quite distinct metaphors and judgements in representing the diverse peoples encountered on such a voyage, which would presumably refract prior representations and actual differences in a complex fashion. At a more restricted level, what were taken to be distinct tribes within colonial states were often constructed antithetically, one group being advanced immigrants, the others conservative and belligerent primitives. Contradictory interests in familiarizing and exoticizing the foreign are thus worked out in quite singular ways with respect to particular peoples. This is entirely predictable, and not especially informative at a general level, but does reflect a further field of colonial vision and adjudication in which constructs of alterity, as well as particular differences, may call for analytical discrimination.

These differentiations of colonial discourse are pursued in the next chapter; here, I turn to another form of difference that may fracture both the progressive unities of historiography and the non-narratives of Foucaultian archaeology. How are colonial discourses gendered? How does the difference of gender refract the unity that 'the' discourse of a period might be thought to possess?

In chapter 4, with respect to evangelical propaganda, I suggest that understandings of the relations between missionaries and indigenous peoples were informed not simply by a code of gender difference but by a hierachical model of familial relationships. Idioms of age seniority and kinship, as well as sexual difference, thus entered into the iconography of paternalistic relationships. Here, I pose the question of the importance of gender more briefly in relation to certain Enlightenment visions of South Pacific islanders, which are frequently thought to typify the romanticization of the 'noble savage'. Bernard Smith's study, *European Vision and the South Pacific*, which in many ways anticipated Edward Said's work, lent some support to this view, while establishing that the concerns of artists and scientists, and the factors which shaped their representations of Pacific islanders and Australian Aborigines, were also influenced in many ways by more specific features of European representational traditions and intellectual preoccupations. The accomplishment of Smith's book derives from the sheer range of its documentation of visual and textual responses to the south Pacific, and the nuanced way in which variations between sketches, paintings and engravings are traced to tensions between neo-classical idealization and ethnographic specificity, between expectations arising from conventional taste and the emerging naturalistic and scientific demand for what was exotic yet geographically distinctive in human beings, landscapes and atmospheres. Smith consistently draws attention to the range of pictorial debts present in particular images, while situating them in debates concerning the moral worth or natural virtue of South Sea islanders. He emphasizes particularly that the 'soft primitivism' that ennobled the Tahitians and delighted in their liberty was contested and by the last decade of the eighteenth century largely displaced by evangelical views, that deplored promiscuity, cannibalism and infanticide, and stressed what was base and deceitful in the native temperament. This trend arose not only from the changing English political and ideological climate, but also from the growth of particularized knowledge of various islanders, which qualified and specified the generalized primitive types and was fuelled by the increasing incidence of violence between islanders and Europeans. The death of Cook in Hawaii in 1779, initially represented largely as a classically tragic confrontation between noble beings, or at least as the work of individual villains among a largely virtuous population, came to be seen, along with other killings, more as an atrocity perpetrated by naturally vicious natives. One of the larger developments that Smith charts is thus 'the transition from the European concept of the noble savage to its opposing concept, the ignoble savage'.[70] The latter figure appears to be displaced in turn by an objectivistic ethic associated with photography from the mid-nineteenth century on: the title of the book's last chapter is 'The rise of science', and its emphasis is upon the longer transition from the neo-classical view of the mid- to late eighteenth century, which sought to exclude nature's specificity from the purview of the artist, to the entirely opposed position of a hundred years later, that equated artistic perfection with empirical fidelity: 'So far had the artist, in the course of a century's collaboration in the business of recording the appearance of man and nature, subjected his own vision of reality to the service of science.'[71]

Smith's nuanced history is remote from any crude progressivism. Its emphasis upon historical developments can, however, be seen to marginalize the sense in which the figures of the noble and ignoble savage were often co-present, and the ways in which rhetorical idealization could persist well into the period notionally distinguished by 'the rise of science'. In particular, the representation of western Pacific islanders in ignoble terms from the 1770s onwards can be seen not merely as an exception to the wider currency of 'soft primitivism', but as the initiation of an ethnological project that ranked islanders in evolutionary terms. Smith notes in passing that the inhabitants of the western Pacific and Australia were interpreted in terms of a 'hard' rather than a 'soft' primitivism, but does not pursue the issue. Since responses to women, and assessments concerning the position of women in the various Pacific societies, were pivotal to the comparative judgements made in the late eighteenth century, it might be suggested that gender is not simply a 'factor' that might usefully be integrated into analysis, but a crucial dimension of difference that often encodes or valorizes other differences such as those based in 'race' or geographic location.

The importance of the Cook voyages arises not only from the elevation of the navigator to the historical pantheon of the British Empire, but also from the fact that a remarkably wide range of Pacific islands peoples were encountered over the three voyages. The result was a dramatic expansion of detailed European knowledge of a variety of related and unrelated Oceanic and Pacific rim peoples, which at first was not articulated with any significantly interventionist colonial project. In other words, the voyages produced an extraordinary range of new ethnographic information, that addressed the developing interests of comparative ethnology rather than any immediate justifications for conquest or colonialist reform.

The distinctive feature of Cook's second voyage was that, for the first time, extensive contact took place with people later termed 'Melanesians'. While, as is well known, Tahiti, and to some extent other parts of the eastern Pacific, were regarded almost as a paradise by many voyage participants, and were largely represented in idyllic terms, the response to the islands Cook called the New Hebrides and New Caledonia was very different. The people, and especially the women, were found to be physically repugnant; they were either ambivalent about the European presence or hostile to it (in contrast to Polynesians, who were mostly welcoming); their technology, artefacts and dwellings were considered crude; and in so far as their political and social forms were recognized, these appeared to be of a more rudimentary character than those of the Polynesians.[72] The British employed bestializing language ('an Apish nation') which they never used in relation to Tahitians; a hierarchization on the basis of colour was conveyed by references to 'fair' Tahitians, 'tawny' New Zealanders, 'swarthy' New Caledonians and 'black' Malekulans. What was distinctive in this racism, then, was not so much the broad assumption of white European superiority, but the capacity to differentiate a whole range of non-European peoples. To use labels applied from the 1830s on, the idea that 'Melanesians' were more primitive than 'Polynesians' was restated frequently in travel accounts, voyage observations and encyclopaedic surveys of Pacific peoples, and entered into twentieth-century anthropology, especially in studies of 'cultural evolution'.[73] This sort of ranking also entered sporadically into colonial administration, in the sense that the British regarded peoples such as the Fijians as far more advanced than Papuans or Solomon Islanders: the former were suited to indirect rule (see next chapter), while the latter were manifestly not. Even within Fiji, the 'Melanesian' people of the western interior were considered to be more primitive than other Fijians and were administered differently. Hence from the nineteenth century on, evolutionary ranking was a central device both for the imperial classification of diverse populations and for adjudications about their appropriate treatment.

While, as was noted, negative assessments of western Pacific islanders referred to a variety of corporeal, artefactual and social attributes, the treatment of women was the key issue, as it was virtually axiomatic for Scottish Enlightenment writers such as Millar, Kames and Ferguson: 'the more debased the situation of a nation is . . . the more harshly we found the women treated.'[74] 'Debasement' refers primarily to agricultural labour, which women in the eastern Pacific did not engage in. The notion that

the women of the more savage societies were distinctly ugly can
be seen as a kind of aesthetic reflex of this principle: the character of the women internalized the brutality of their social environment (which was itself sometimes taken as a reflection of
the dark, harsh and rugged natural environment attributed to the
Melanesian islands) and made them unappealing to European
eyes.

The point of this example is not simply that the ignoble understanding of western Pacific islanders amounts to an exception to
the generally romanticized and positive construction of South Sea
islanders as noble savages which prevailed in the 1770s. Rather,
the way in which the difference was figured makes it clear that
perceptions of women and women's 'status' encoded other forms
of geographic and racial difference. The degradation of women
was a measure for the degradation of a society and enabled it to be
mapped against others in a region. Gender was thus central to the
evolutionary ranking of societies, which was a more significant
project in this period than the usual associations between evolutionism and Darwinian thought would allow. However, the criteria
that were crucial for determining particular peoples' situations on
the scale of advancement only partially overlapped with the in-
dices that were important subsequently. Technology, in particular, played a surprisingly weak and minor role in assessments of
advancement or lack thereof;[75] while perceptions of colour and
supposedly simian physique certainly entered into eighteenth-
century views in much the same way as they did into later 'ill-
natured comparisons',[76] responses to the body were less important
than the work of a gendered vision upon women and upon the
relations of debasement or sexual equality that women's bodies
exhibited. A historian such as Smith, who is not especially concerned with gender, is thus not merely passing over an aspect of
indigenous society to which Europeans responded to one way or
another, but is neglecting an issue which was central to European
interests in discrimination. And while these statements – that one
people were more advanced towards civilization than another –
were of little consequence in the eighteenth century, it was precisely this kind of assessment that later enabled some indigenous
populations to be hunted down and dispossessed, while others
were treated paternalistically.

A historical narrative that imagines a succession of European conceptions of particular populations can be problematic not only because it diminishes variation at a particular time, but also because it implies a progression. Smith's concluding chapter title, 'The Rise of Science', implies a far more teleological argument than his text in fact puts forward: he is not claiming so much that the stereotypes which earlier inflected attitudes toward indigenous peoples were marginalized by a singularly modern objectivity, but is rather referring to a specifically art-historical development, namely the extent to which a classicizing and idealizing aesthetic was eclipsed by scientific concerns with accuracy and with physiological, botanical and zoological detail. However, it is certainly possible to draw from his work a broader developmental argument. In the conclusion to her discussion of representations of Samoans, Jocelyn Linnekin writes:

> Like the noble savage vision that preceded it, the ignoble savage had to give way during the course of Western expansion to a more differentiated understanding of Pacific Islanders. On the latter approach could be founded an anthropology that would compare and contrast peoples on the basis of their customs, beliefs, and character. The progression is prefigured in the retellings of the La Pérouse affair, in which the Samoans eventually emerge not as 'Indians', nor as 'savages', but as Samoans.[77]

If Linnekin does not explicitly value anthropological particularism as a sympathetic advance upon the eighteenth- and early nineteenth-century representations, it is nevertheless strongly implied that anthropology is a more sophisticated form of knowledge. If modern anthropology is certainly more refined than its antecedents in various ways, its interest in what was distinctive to particular populations was not unprecedented: not only Forster but a number eighteenth-century observers, including of course other participants in the Cook voyages, were concerned precisely with the specific characters of localized peoples: with those of the cold far south of New Zealand as opposed to those of the north, with New Zealanders as opposed to Tannese, Tahitians, Marquesans, Easter Islanders and others. So, far from being a nineteenth-century novelty, this mode of typification

could be traced, as was noted earlier, back to encyclopaedists such
as Pufendorf who were defining European 'national characters' in
the late seventeenth century. On the other hand, more recent
discourses on islanders have entailed not only anthropologically
particular constructions, but also highly generalized images,
which continue to be conspicuous in tourist culture and popular
genres. Where would Linnekin place Margaret Mead, who was in
one sense studying 'Samoans', yet quite overtly characterizing
them in opposition to Americans, as bearers of sexual freedom to
be juxtaposed with American constraint? Would not her largely
discredited ethnographic portrait have been equally true of other,
generic 'happy Pacific islanders'? This suggests that a particular
historiographic mode prompts scholars to define a temporal sequence of 'stereotypes' or 'visions', but that over the periods they
select, notionally succeeding discourses are in fact often co-
present for the whole history under consideration. Smith and
Linnekin are entirely justified in identifying various trends and
configurations of these ideas, but from the perspective of a longer
history that compares the discourses they discuss with those of
premodern and early modern colonialism, two things are striking:
first, the relative unity of modern ideas, which are in the broadest
terms natural-historical, anthropological and evolutionary; and
secondly, the basic discontinuity between the colonialism of
Columbus and this reluctant inheritance of ours.

4

Colonial Governmentality and Colonial Conversion

Colonial discourse theory can homogenize colonizing actors, as it arguably effaces the agency of the colonized. In reaction to this elision of subjectivity, analysis could privilege the agency of colonial actors such as missionaries and administrators; but it might end up resembling a great deal of conventional colonial history, and fail to deal with the texted character of these agents and histories, and the discursively complex nature of their endeavours. 'Discourse' and 'agency' can however be reconciled – no doubt with healthy mutual suspicion – in an investigation of colonial projects. 'Project' may be a deceptively simple word, but it has theoretical implications that differ significantly from the terms of reference commonly employed in historical, sociological or anthropological inquiry. It draws attention not towards a totality such as a culture, nor to a period that can be defined independently of people's perceptions and strategies, but rather to a socially transformative endeavour that is localized, politicized and partial, yet also engendered by longer historical developments and ways of narrating them. If the idea of a project were elevated to the status of an anthropological concept, it might imply that people are always orientated toward innovation, or to some kind of political transformation; this may be misleading as a universal tenet, but in colonial circumstances the interest in creating something new, on the part of settlers or a colonized population or both, is widespread; and even if resistance on the part of the colonized seems to entail merely a return to former circumstances, of indigenous sovereignty and cultural autonomy, the struggle to recreate such conditions nevertheless engenders novel perceptions of identity, action and history; even what appears to be simply reactive or retrogressive thus amounts to a project, to a whole transformative endeavour.

This notion aims also to avoid any polarization of material and ideal aspects of colonial (and anti-colonial) endeavours. A project is neither a strictly discursive entity nor an exclusively practical one: because it is a willed creation of historically situated actors it cannot be dissociated from their interests and objectives, even if it also has roots and ramifications which were not or are not apparent to those involved. And a project is not narrowly instrumental: the actors no doubt have intentions, aims and aspirations, but these presuppose a particular imagination of the social situation, with its history and projected future, and a diagnosis of what is lacking, that can be rectified by intervention, by conservation, by bullets or by welfare. This imagination exists in relation to something to be acted upon – an indigenous population, a subordinate class, a topographic space – and in tension with competing colonial projects, yet is also a self-fashioning exercise, that makes the maker as much as it does the made. And projects are of course often projected rather than realized; because of their confrontations with indigenous interests, alternate civilizing missions and their internal inconsistencies, colonial intentions are frequently deflected, or enacted farcically and incompletely. While the administrator might have wished that governing could be effected as forcefully and simply as a flag could be raised, in practice the business of sustaining colonial control is often more like repairing an old car: the cost and energy absorbed into surgery is never reflected in results, parts are replaced, but connections fail, there are inexplicable rattles, and sooner or later the whole effort has to be abandoned – not least (and here it is the analogy that breaks down) because government and its conceptual categories are resisted.

Colonial projects are culturally and strategically complex; they entail a whole worldview that imagined metropolitan society, rival powers and colonized places and peoples in certain terms, which of course articulated with projected action, but these worldviews are not bounded by or wholly different from rival visions. That is, it is possible to identify the distinct projects of colonial states, settlers and evangelists, which represent appropriate relations with natives and social transformation in distinctive and conflicting ways – in a fashion that this chapter aims to exemplify – but it becomes apparent that these share certain models or images, even if these are motivated by quite different narratives. From this perspective, Johannes Fabian's interest in the 'common ground' of religious and secular colonialism is suggestive, but the terms may be broadened, to bring other kinds of distinctiveness and shared ground into view. The case studies in this chapter and the next are drawn from the British colonies in the period central to E. J. Hobsbawm's *Age of Empire* – the decades immediately before and after 1900 – and so raise questions of the divergences and conflicts between contemporaneous projects, rather than differences that might be ascribed to period or the policy orientations of different European powers.

British rule in the former Crown Colony of Fiji[1] was an elaborate and paradoxical affair, characterized by intense interest in indigenous society and a singularly paternalistic and protective attitude towards it. Though the apparent level of respect for the native order as it existed was unusual and atypical, the Fijian example reveals something of the role of knowledge in the constitution of the colonial state in the empire, and suggests more specifically how information and regulation in a particular policy domain – health and sanitation – was at once a colonizing project in itself and a vehicle for more general surveillance and intervention. I have presumed throughout this book that knowledge does not simply 'have' objects in the world; much of the preceding chapter discussed the ways in which coherent objects of racial science and anthropological knowledge were produced. The colonial knowledge in Fiji that is considered here was no exception to the general principle and might specifically be considered an inheritor and a practical application of the essentialist partitioning of human varieties that was effected in various ways in the eighteenth and nineteenth centuries. The Fijian was not so much the bearer of a singular character or culture, but Fijian society amounted to a distinctive communal order that required anthropological diagnosis; a knowledge of this order was a predicate of policy-fashioning and action.

The first Governor, Sir Arthur Gordon, had been shocked by the dispossession of the New Zealand Maori and was determined to subordinate the interests of a much smaller and economically unsuccessful settler population in Fiji to those of the indigenous population. From the time of cession by a group of paramount chiefs in 1874, administrative policies and structures aimed to defend and institutionalize the traditional Fijian communal system; though much debated, this orientation was perpetuated by the influential Governor Thurston, who ruled the colony between 1888 and 1897, and most of his successors. For instance, what were thought to be traditional chiefly privileges were legally enshrined and articulated with an indirect-rule system of appointed village, district and provincial chiefs. Land was made the inalienable property of clan groups of certain types, which were not found everywhere in Fiji, and which people were obliged to create where they did not exist.[2] The pattern was often that a model derived from the areas with which administrators were most familiar would be imposed with difficulty elsewhere; even where there was some relatively close correspondence between an existing institution or social relationship and its codification, flexibility and reciprocity were often suppressed. Hence the obligations of clanspeople towards their chiefs were codified, but not the obligations of chiefs towards their people; land settlements and succession to chiefly titles often froze situations that had been changing; and in general, what the authorities understood of customary arrangements tended, predictably, to be inflected by the interests of whomever happened to be their informants.

What was being 'preserved' thus had to be made up and represented as administration proceeded, but the British did not do this without indigenous help. Chiefs were often ready with advice, and were very pleased to see government doing things in 'the chiefly way', which became coterminous with 'the way of the land' and Fijian custom. Ordinary Fijians, on the other hand, sometimes had to be told by white men what their customs were. In 1902, for instance, because 'the Custom of Fiji is to live in villages' the family of a man named Waivure could not live off in a yam garden away from village and clan; their garden house was in fact pulled down.[3] This minor incident exemplifies the restrictive force of customs that had only just been recognized and specified: while many earlier visitors had understood that Fijians usually resided in villages, as they had seen that they went on journeys for fishing, ceremonial exchange and warfare, village life was now prescriptively normalized, such that temporary residence elsewhere or short-term migration was an aberration to be policed. (This new understanding had wider ramifications: as in India, the equation of native society as a whole with villages rendered it archaic in comparison with primarily European urban domains.)[4] The concern to restrain the movement of the indigenous population was linked with the need to protect them from being recruited for plantation work, which would surely have undermined village society. The government therefore intransigently resisted the demands of planters, among other capitalists, to make more land alienable and to encourage participation in wage labour. The problem of labour supply was instead addressed through importing indentured Indians, who began to arrive in 1879, and who mainly worked on the sugar plantations upon which the colonial economy depended. Consideration was never given to extending the positive attitude towards native Fijians to the Indian immigrants, and of course the draconian social order of the plantation could never have accommodated any form of indirect rule.

The British approach was also markedly different in the Solomon Islands, which became a protectorate in 1891, in its lack of interest in indigenous authority figures and customs and its tolerance for massive dispossession: Gordon was in fact a director of the company that sought a huge land grant in 1898, while Levers and Burns Philp later extracted copra on a vast scale.[5] A different attitude was called for because of the economic imperatives, but possibly also because indigenous societies in the Solomons appeared to be less advanced; though there were local headmen who might elsewhere have been labelled chiefs, they lacked the pomp and autocratic power that constituted an indigenous aristocracy of the kind that the British respected and empathized with in Fiji (as they also did in Nigeria), and there was no polity worth the name. British policy thus responded to native populations on the basis of social evolutionary criteria: the rights of those near the bottom of the ladder, such as Australian Aborigines, received extremely scant notice, while indirect rule was appropriate for peoples with more developed technologies and recognizable hierarchical social institutions, whose cultures were also more fit for study and preservation.

A kind of evolutionary discrimination was also made within the Fijian population: the tribes of the upland interior of the largest island of Viti Levu not only had less powerful chiefs, but also seemed physically distinct: from the early nineteenth century, the Fijian archipelago had been seen as a zone of transition where the

'Melanesian' or 'Papuan' race merged with lighter-skinned and more hierarchical 'Polynesians'; the coastal and eastern Fijians had intermarried with the latter, while the upland tribes were associated most strongly with the former, and with the kind of cannibalistic savagery depicted in Andrew's photographs. In the administrators' vision, horror stories were of less interest than the belligerence and disorder which inevitably arose from the imposition of institutions designed for one social context in another, but which they considered to manifest the backwardness of the people in these regions. The white officers had the same difficulty as Winterbottom in Chinua Achebe's *Arrow of God*: paramount chiefs had to be made where there were none, among people disposed to lying and perjury.[6] One solution, in the fractious parts of Fiji, was to appoint Fijians from other areas as provincial chiefs, which was of course no solution at all. In the areas mainly considered in this section, the indirect-rule policy was qualified and white resident officers asserted more direct control; the colonial experience had, in general, a more repressive character than it did for the Fijian population as a whole.

The disorder of upland Fiji only rarely took the tangible form of insurrection: after an armed rebellion in 1876 had been suppressed, overt resistance was limited and tended to be manifested in messianic revivals of 'heathen' ritual. For the British also, the relation of domination and resistance existed less on a military or political level than on a symbolic one, or rather, in practices that were at once political and symbolic. While Gordon was concerned about 'preserving' the Fijian communal system he also wanted to assert the absolute character of state authority, expressed through knowledge, vision, and regulation. During his first address to the newly-created Council of Chiefs, the Governor expressed his desire to retain all good native customs, along with his intention not to make sudden changes even with regard to those which were 'improper'; but at the same time, he made it plain that the state would constantly be made aware of all events and that no 'irregularity' would escape appropriate punishment. He instructed the local native officials to commit everything to paper and stressed that the administration would be omniscient and omnipotent.

> As for you, the Bulis [appointed district chiefs], if any sudden evil should arise in your districts, write about it at once; let a true

register of births and deaths be kept, and do not allow one to be unregistered; also write and report on all matters to the Roko Tuis [appointed provincial chiefs]. Now, as for you, the Roko Tuis, do you write to me every month, but, if necessary, write to me at all seasons and at all times . . .[7]

The laws of the country may be compared to a net of very fine meshes, nothing can escape: it will cover over all alike . . . Obey the laws . . .[8]

State power thus turned upon inscription, upon the absorption of events into a prodigiously dispersed writing machine. The emphasis upon the necessity of written communication arose not so much from any particular need for much of the information that would be gathered – the mass of trivia in the National Archives of Fiji attests to that – but rather from the overall effect. Such pronouncements as these aimed particularly at creating a sense that the state transcended ordinary social conflicts and partial interests. Gordon urged the chiefs to 'let playing at cross purposes cease', thus differentiating the state from action by any kind of narrow interest and asserting a more generalized purpose that the government, as a detached knowing and organizing agent, could act towards.[9] The agency of the state was thereby constituted through the paradox of an external vantage point for internal engagement, transcendent vision of the totality of Fijian society, custom and life informing the work of regulation and ordering; this was expressed in a neatly organized and extensive array of Fijian artefacts (or 'curios') in Government House, which paralleled the colonial vision elsewhere and that of bureaucratic surveillance and welfare at home. Some of those who visited Cairo in the early and mid-nineteenth century complained that the narrow and disorderly alleys precluded any overview, any sense of the totality; while later colonial architecture created interiors and exteriors, positioned an observing subject, and thus created 'an appearance of order, an order that work[ed] by appearance'.[10] It is, of course, this sense of society as an objective whole, an object of anthropological knowledge and governmentality, that is constitutive not only of modern colonialism but of modernity.[11]

Depiction and documentation – through such media as colonial reports and artefact collections as well as actual painting, drawing and photography – did not merely create representations that were secondary to practices and realities, but constituted political actualities in themselves. Travellers and colonists could regard a space and another society, not as a geographic tract, nor an array of practices and relations, but as a thing depicted or described, that was immediately subject to their gaze. Other peoples, cultures and cities could thus be subsumed to the form of a picture, and seeing a thing first as a representation and secondly as something beyond a representation created a peculiar sense of power on the side of the viewing colonist, which was of course not necessarily reflected in real control over the populations in any particular place. The tendency to fetishize views, scenes, descriptions and accounts is found in diverse genres such as those produced by tourists and missionaries as well as in official sources, and clearly has different implications and effects in each case; in Fiji the will to seize on a representation of indigenous society found a particular nexus that really did mediate the work of government.

The character of the state's relationship to Fijian society was expressed in the 1896 report of an inquiry into a subject that was of considerable concern: 'the decrease of the native population'. This was motivated partly by definite evidence for substantial depopulation and high mortality amongst Fijians but also from a much wider debate concerning the 'decline' of native races. The perception amongst writers of more definitely racist views was that the inferior were destined to fall before the advance of civilization: there was a good deal of interested wishful thinking, especially on the part of planters who wanted more native land. These views, along with more sentimental and nostalgic attitudes, were sporadically expressed earlier, but continued to be aired in the first decades of the twentieth century and became a focus for scholarly anthropological debate in the 1920s. A later missionary's view of the question in the Solomon Islands reflected opinion in the 1890s as well as at the time of writing: the Methodist John F. Goldie hesitated to single out any particular cause and was reluctant to accept the idea that a weaker race should or would die out, but neither could he categorically reject the then-pervasive racial thinking upon which such views were based.

> One of the saddest things in this sad land is the rapidly decreasing population. Men talk of the survival of the fittest, and the fate of

the black man is to go down before the white man. But *is* this necessary? What is the cause of this racial decay? What can be done to arrest the decline? Of the many theories advanced, none seem to fit all of the facts . . . One thing is certain. The advent of the white man, though a contributing cause, is not the principal cause of the decline, which has been going on for years. Going into a heathen village for the first time, seeing the filthy condition of the people, the wonder is not that they decrease, but that they are not extinct.[12]

The one certain thing was actually the one crucial fallacy. It arose mainly from misunderstanding of the indirect ramifications of introduced disease, such as the impact of sexually transmitted disease on fertility and infant mortality. But this error was highly enabling, in the sense that the assumption that depopulation proceeded prior to the white impact located its causes in native behaviour and customs, which could then be represented and described in relation to the problem. Efforts to deal with population decline would also deal with behaviour and customs. While writers such as Goldie might allude in passing to the dirtiness of heathens, the 1896 report was far more extensive and systematic in its ethnographic inquiry. It drew on earlier government reports and statistical papers and on evidence lodged in response to a circular, almost exclusively from Europeans resident in Fiji. It began by setting out and classifying postulated causes for the population decline, factors influencing health and mortality, and proposals for measures to alleviate the situation. Thirty-six potential causes fell into four general groups, among them the following.

Predisposing causes tending to the degeneracy of the people as a race.
i. Polygamy.
ii. Consanguineous marriage.
iii. Epidemic diseases . . .
v. Communal system, with attendant customs of *lala* (tribute and service to chiefs and communities), *kerekere* (mutual appropriation of property), *bose* (councils), and *solevu* (festivals) . . .
viii. Want of virility.
Causes more immediately affecting the Welfare and Stamina of the People individually.
x. Quality and supply of food and drinking water.
xvi. Abuse of *yaqona* [the narcotic beverage also known as kava] and tobacco.
xviii. Treatment of sick persons.

xix. Irregularity of living.
Causes more immediately affecting the unborn child.
xxiv. Work during pregnancy.
xxv. Fishing by child-bearing women.
Causes affecting the infant.
xxxv. Domestic dirt.
xxxvi. General insouciance of the native mind, heedlessness of mothers, and weakness of maternal instinct.[13]

Several hundred pages are devoted in the report to the presentation of evidence and searching inquiry into the relative significance of these factors and consideration of appropriate recommendations. At certain points, the rigour of investigation seems impressive. The consequences upon fertility of certain forms of marriage thought to produce inbreeding were examined statistically – the large and intricate tables partly printed in red must be seen to be appreciated – and the commissioners were obliged to disconfirm the view there was any link with 'the decadence of the race'.[14] There was even a claim to repudiate ethnocentrism: any imposition of British standards upon Fijian circumstances and institutions was unjustifiable, in part because modern civilization was itself divided and imperfect. Despite the note of relativism and the inquiry's manifest care, it is astonishing that such a limited amount of consideration was paid to what has since been demonstrated to have been the most important factor: the longer-term consequence of introduced disease, and particularly an 1875 measles epidemic.[15] On the other hand, much attention is devoted to vague and extremely speculative connections between Fijian temperament and mortality.

> Mental Apathy, Laziness and Improvidence of the people arise from their climate, their diet, and their communal institutions. The climate alone does not stimulate to exertion, the ordinary food of the people imparts no staying-power, and the conditions of production do not demand that the individual must labour in order to exist, while the communal institutions paralyse the exercise of individual effort and destroy the instinct of accumulation ... We are not sanguine that the disposition of the natives will undergo improvement until they begin to attach importance to a more varied and more nutritive diet, when the impulse of increased wants which can only be satisfied with the acquisition of money will lead to the growth of individual effort...[16]

The preoccupation with hypothetical links between ill-defined attributes of food, social life, stamina and so on, did not however lead merely to racist misconceptions. It is apparent that through the process of description and specification, the report constituted Fijian society as an entity: the communal system had its constitutive features, its 'attendant customs'. More significantly, these existed to be acted upon: the document was always intended to be a charter for intervention (that, of course, made maternal health or rather 'the heedlessness of mothers' in particular a locus for reform).[17] The links between many features of native behaviour and the problem of depopulation potentially sanctioned administrative intervention in numerous aspects of indigenous life, even though the commissioners did not accept all the claims made by those who submitted evidence.

The administration was in a complex position because the commitment to the Fijian customary order precluded wholesale reorganization. Gordon, Thurston and many of their subordinates held a view of native administration which anticipated the sentiments so often expressed later in Nigeria and by Cameron in Tanganyika.

> It is our duty to do everything in our power to develop the native on lines which will not westernise him and turn him into a bad imitation of a European ... We must not ... destroy the African atmosphere, the African mind, the whole foundations of his race, and we shall certainly do this if we sweep away all his tribal organisations.[18]

This was essentially a segregationist rather than an assimilationist vision: the emphasis was on the difference between European and essentialized African or Fijian cultures, which were not to be subsumed to a European model but sustained in their distinctiveness. There was a fear of flawed conversion; just as patois and pidgin languages were seen to bring out the worst features of contact between natives and whites, miscegenation, absorption into a plantation workforce and the breakdown of 'the foundations' of the 'race' were associated both with population decline and moral degeneracy.[19] The indigenous movements of the early twentieth century that often combined elements of the messianic 'cargo cult' with overtly political and revolutionary aims were frequently thought to be organized by detribalized or vagrant natives who had departed from their home villages, or who were otherwise partly assimilated, who, as was mentioned above, would read newspapers 'in a parrot-like fashion'. While mimicry was thus proscribed, order could be sustained and some 'uplifting' effected if the native system persisted in an integrated form. In Fiji, this was manifest in the emphasis upon the village as the unit of residence and upon chiefly leadership of corporate clan groups; hence the essentialism in this case was as much sociological as psychological. Intervention to create orderly village life was sanctioned partly through selective representation: chieftainship was understood to be the core of native society, while certain significant ritual activities, often engaged in especially by younger, rebellious men, were categorized not as 'customary' but as 'seditious cults'.[20] Practices were distanced from 'Custom' in order to be legitimately proscribed.

Social regulation, however, was effected mainly through the project prompted by the depopulation inquiry. The view that population decline had a great variety of social and behavioural causes was enormously enabling: almost anything to do with the organization of custom or village life could potentially be modified in the name of sanitation, since this did not emerge from any interested attempt to impose British or Christian values, but from the state's rational interest in preserving the native race. A constant slippage is evident between interests in reducing mortality and other agendas; political, moral and cultural impositions were justified by their association or conflation with the programme of sanitation.[21]

The project of sanitizing-colonizing Fiji expressed a mode of governmentality that was also exercised through social policy in metropolitan countries. Concern about the degradation of the urban poor had usually been strongly marked by bourgeois morality: disease was associated with vice and disorder, and in English cities and in Sydney sanitizing projects of the 1890s also involved description, regulation and the creation of order; these projects can equally be seen as vehicles of a more generalized desire to make underclasses visible and accessible, and in this respect they seemed to differ from earlier welfare projects, which privileged the predicaments of the poor and the diseased rather than the vision of the state. As in the colonies, photographs often paradoxically suggested what was hidden, dark, unknown or indescribable: they depicted indistinct, cramped, shadowy and crowded quarters which inspectors hoped to transform into cleansed and open spaces.[22] The specificity of Fiji, however, derived from the conjuncture of this kind of interest in pervasive state knowledge and power, and the paternalistic attitude of respect toward the 'customary order', which was not to be tampered with; the work of sanitizing mediated these contradictory projects.

The singularity of this effort emerges from the contrasting approach to sanitary conditions amongst indentured Fiji-Indians – or rather, from the contrast with an absence of interest.[23] It has often been pointed out that Indians were seen as working men and nothing more, as 'labour units'. Thus, while documentation of the Fijian population is full of statistics and observations about birth rates and maternity, the only context in which this figures in the *Annual Reports on Indian immigration* is in lists of working days 'lost'; pregnancy is grouped with such things as 'Bad weather' under the subheading 'Absence for other causes'[24] (a classification which could not have been terribly relevant for the women concerned). The problem with plantations was instead that liberal criticism of poor conditions[25] and brutality had to be deflected. Allusions to sanitary conditions thus convey a defensive attitude, and blame unsatisfactory ill-health upon the labourers themselves, or mention government-sponsored improvements.[26] Sanitation simply did not amount to a project in any marked sense. The most significant point here is that because Fiji-Indians were employed in plantations which were controlled more through violence and highly punitive discipline than welfare, the kind of government with which sanitation was associated in the rural Fijian context was irrelevant. So far from Indians being a specific population that required understanding and definition, administrative attitudes manifested a 'fear of culture' appropriate to a proletarianized population. What were to be governed were labour units, rather than bearers of national peculiarities, and it is no surprise that, while administrators in Fiji often dabbled in anthropology, the Indians failed to attract their attention. Indentured labour and the paternalistic insulation of native society from the market were, in terms of the colony's socioeconomic structure, two sides of the same coin; hence the 'logic' of the shocking gulf between the violent punishment in plantations and coolie lines and the indirect and paternalistic discipline in the villages over which Gordon's net of state power was just being cast.

So far as rural indigenous society was concerned, intervention was manifested in a series of regulations that arose from recommendations of the 1896 report or similar later investigations. In some cases these were highly specific, anthropologically informed and frequently intrusive. For instance, the intoxicating native drink kava was usually prepared by infusing powder from a dried root, but was also occasionally chewed by younger men and then spat into a bowl for mixing, a practice which most whites found highly distasteful. This was banned partly on the grounds that it was not really a 'Fijian custom' but had been imported from the neighbouring Tongan islands: a line could conveniently be drawn between practices which were acceptable, and those which were not really traditional, and happened also to be unpalatable from the British perspective. White officials rather than Fijians thus decided what was and what was not proper native custom. While kava-chewing, and the premastication of infant food, another 'foreign' practice that was proscribed, no doubt did in fact facilitate the transmission of disease, the practices modified by other regulations were often not manifestly unhealthy. The following were among the rules passed by a provincial council in upland Viti Levu in 1913.

    b) That dwelling houses shall have sleeping places raised at least 18 inches from the floor and

    c) That floors shall have shingle, bamboos or other suitable material placed there to the satisfaction of the Commissioner.

    d) That all refuse and rubbish from any village be deposited by those so directed in pits, not less than 200 yards from the boundary of the village, and be kept covered with ashes or earth, excepting grass and leaves which shall be burnt.

    e) That around each village a space of not less than eight yards wide shall be kept free of reeds grass and rubbish by the villagers.

    f) That all owners of pigs shall keep their pigs within proper fences, no such fence to be within 100 yards of a village.

    h) That each house shall have a sufficiency of clean mats to the satisfaction of the Commissioner, and that mats be spread on floors and beds.

j) That each household head have a kitchen or the use of a kitchen, the walls of such kitchens to be unthatched.[27]

The effects of these measures upon indigenous health are by no means self-evident. Although some Europeans were offended by the presence of pigs around house sites, more astute observers elsewhere in the Pacific noted that they actually contributed to maintaining hygiene, or at least tidiness: 'Much of the credit for the cleanliness of the village is due to the tireless scavenging of pigs.'[28]

In any case, legislation of this type was clearly determined to a substantial extent by a paradigm of order that privileged openness, visibility, ventilation, boundaries and a particular spatial differentiation of activities.[29] A house was perceived as being 'crowded' if occupied by any sort of larger extended family; 'crowding' itself seemed to be necessarily unhealthy. Cooking houses had to be differentiated from the main residence, though smoke actually helped to keep the latter free of mosquitoes. Cultivation had to be distanced from village sites, though most methods did not involve digging ditches or otherwise creating disease traps. As was noted, the separation of animals into fenced pens precluded (at least in so far as the regulation was heeded) their constructive scavenging. These stipulations thus seemed motivated more by an interest in creating an orderly and accessible village, rather than because their consequences were known to be beneficial.

Efforts to change the nature of domestic groups had more enduring ramifications. Although by this time all Fijians were at least notionally Christian, many men in the interior districts still slept in segregated men's houses, which had been associated with indigenous ritual and cult activities; it was noted in 1903 that the 'custom is dying hard amongst the older kai Colo.'[30] Since men mostly used these houses, a wife sometimes lived in an extended household with the husband's mother; in any case, there were substantially fewer houses than married couples. In the administration's vision, this was associated with overcrowding, but also simply diverged from Western Christian values. In the early years of the twentieth century great efforts were made specifically to provide one house for each married couple. A problem arose because it was usual for the principal occupants of a house to have a considerable number of guests for a period after the dwelling was initially occupied, and a resolution was passed prohibiting such people from asking 'their friends & relations to share'.[31] Some changes ostensibly of sanitary benefit thus merely brought Fijian behaviour into conformity with British values – presumably at some cost in inconvenience and adaptation.

In many cases, though, the consequences of these trivial yet no doubt bothersome regulations can only be speculated about, because changes were resisted or accepted only very gradually. A number of the resolutions quoted above were identical to those passed some years earlier, and the need to reaffirm them attests to indigenous non-compliance. The pattern of response had been uneven, but reflected in part the attitudes of certain villages and districts towards the British administration. Certain areas, and particularly the upland 'Colo' provinces, were notorious for their resistance and intransigence. A 1902 report from Colo West emphasized that most villages visited were disorderly, unsanitary, and overgrown – the first and second attributes coalesced. A more senior official noted that 'I think we all know that Colo W. is not by any means what it should be. The people as I understand them are difficult to manage, or at all events listen to advice and then do not follow it . . . The idea of concentrating the population more is worthy of serious consideration.'[32]

In Tanganyika in the 1920s and 1930s, the British administration worked to concentrate populations on an extensive scale, an effort that was legitimized partly on health grounds – the eradication of sleeping sickness – and partly through reference to the alleged nature of indigenous society, in which people had generally been concentrated around their chiefs, and occasionally on frankly political grounds – because a less dispersed population would be easier to administer and control.[33] In precisely the same fashion, Fijian villages were relocated, partly on sanitary grounds and partly in the scarcely disguised interest of making them more visible. In various parts of Fiji, but particularly in the discontented areas, a remarkably large number of villages were resettled in the period from the 1876 rebellion up to roughly 1920. They were usually moved only relatively short distances, often so as to bring them within what were regarded as the proper limits of their tribal land.[34] The extent and frequency of these movements is marked by the fact that the minutes of a single provincial council meeting could refer to no fewer than four such relocations and a fifth which was not proceeded with. Their imposed character was manifested by the anticipated need to report non-compliance: 'II. That the Noikoro people living at Saqunu are to move to Matawalu by the 21st of the present month, and that Buli Noikoro is to report the absence of any one of them to the Native Magistrate of that district.'[35] In some cases the Fijians, for unrecorded reasons of their own, did in fact want to move, perhaps even because they recognized or had been persuaded that certain sites were unhealthy. But the administrative perception of the difference seems to have been about as good as the understanding of the causes of population decline in general; officials were constantly bewildered by the fact that the mortality rates for 'insanitary' sites were the same as those for good locations.[36] It is apparent from the highly impressionistic character of specific judgements that they had to work hard even to convince themselves. The Colo resident commissioner thought that one village 'should be considered most unsanitary':

> It is situated in a deep canyon and has gigantic walls of rock in front & behind & the only level space is the bank of the Sigatoka [River] . . . the sun is not seen until half past eight in the morning & disappears after 4 in the afternoon.[37]

It is not apparent here how the precipitous nature of the surrounding terrain affected the health of the occupants; if the number of hours of sunlight was of such importance in itself England would have to be regarded as a 'most unsanitary' place in winter. But the lack of visibility gives the real issue away. Concern was frequently expressed about the 'inaccessible' character of various villages. 'Inaccessibility' was referred to as though it were an intrinsic feature of the natural landscape, rather than a relationship which only existed after certain places had become centres or outposts of government control, and it is clear that the state had a strong interest in bringing 'isolated' villages closer to such centres or to the government roads that were being put through the interior during this period. The relocation programme was connected with a larger political agenda, which was scarcely covert. In the 1896 report it had been suggested that village amalgamation would facilitate not only 'regular medical inspection', and better supervision in matters of cleanliness' but also 'inspection' in general – by the Governor, 'superior officers of the Government', magistrates, missionaries, and others.[38] The problem about any 'outlying' settlement was that it might lie beyond official vision and control, as was made quite clear when a Qaliyalatina man who had 'surreptitiously' build a house in a certain locality was obliged to abandon it and return to his village. The resident commissioner noted that 'Fijians have to be closely watched. On various pretexts they get away secretly and start new villages in inaccessible spots. This house is supposed to be the commencement of a new village & to be connected [with] the "Tuka" superstition.'[39] There was thus a direct connection between this project to sanitize and render visible, and the threat of political millenarianism, which, as in the African colonies, was a significant form of indigenous resistance and, in British eyes, a dangerous kind of irrationality and disorder.

The state of the Fijian population was a central concern of the administration for over half a century after the colony's establishment in 1874, and in that period most of the activities of district officials were, in some sense, connected with the project to improve sanitation. Apart from the process of passing regulations and attempting to enforce them, which has been described, a substantial amount of work was undertaken in such areas as providing piped water to villages, which seems to have been done on a surprisingly wide scale by about 1910. The mortality and fertility figures were nearly always the first items mentioned in district and provincial reports, and writers evidently felt that the main burden of their responsibility lay in attempting to foster population growth. The British officials were genuinely committed to this objective, and some of the measures implemented were probably of benefit.

However, it is clear that the causes of high mortality were poorly understood, and that many of the perceived shortcomings of Fijian hygiene were nebulously represented, but in such a way as to justify regulations which, if effective, did little more than bring Fijian practice into a degree of conformity with British values. While both conventional historians and Fijian nationalists tend to endorse the idea that the Fijian way of life has been preserved in an essentially traditional form, there was thus a good deal of cultural colonialism which attempted to transform what was simply different and unpalatable, and more discontinuity than such a history for the present allows. This was effected in part through the redefinition of practices and especially through the construction of an image of the customary way which narrowly emphasized leadership by chiefs, residence in villages and communal work. Other things which were equally and often more traditional in the historical sense were marginalized or constituted as forms of disorder in such a way as to preclude their customary legitimacy. This repressive reordering of village social life did not, however, proceed smoothly; Fijian resistance, which was mostly in the form of evasion rather than direct opposition, was ubiquitous. Many who attempted to ignore or sidestep the Native Regulations clearly ended up in court, but the extent to which avoidance was detected can only be guessed at.

The relocation and amalgamation of villages was also justified on the basis of the line between the sanitary and the insanitary, even though it was acknowledged that the recognized distinction did not clearly relate to actual health. The principal official interest in these relocations emerged rather from a horror of 'small and scattered' hamlets, of 'inaccessible' populations, of dispersal and 'decentralization'.[40] These terms were associated with a lack of visibility and control which was anathema to the ethos of governmentality. Amalgamation was not simply a policy which made certain populations more accessible to inspection; it was a discursive motif on the side of inscription and government, supplanting the disorder and irregularity of the past.

This is the level at which the remarkable array of regulations, ordinances, resolutions and interventions need to be explained. It is the only level at which their essentially irrational character can be accounted for. Setting aside the fact that most of the prescriptions had very little potential impact on the population's health, they seem equally unwarranted from the viewpoint of political control. Whether newly built houses were shared really made absolutely no difference at all. The effort to regulate was a symbolic as much as a practical effort, which aimed to create in reality Gordon's optimistic claim that state power was a net which covered everything. The underlying rationale of prohibitions and stipulations was not the prevention or imposition of specific practices because these really mattered in particular. Specification and regulation were rather ends in themselves, which constituted the ambit of state control.

The British colonizing effort in Fiji was, despite the occasional crudeness of its intrusions, and what strikes us now as the absurdity of its self-righteous paternalism, a modern and subtle project that proceeded through social engineering rather than violent repression, and appeared essentially as an operation of welfare rather than conquest. 'Implicit in the technologies of governmentality was the notion that it was possible to transform society so that both force and politics became unnecessary.'[41] As such, it resembled Lyautey's modernist project in Morocco but differed from earlier conquest-colonialisms and from the process of 'making Algeria French', which began somewhat earlier but continued through the period discussed here. This was characterized essentially by expropriation of resources and by restructuring the social order and the polity according to the economic interests of settlers and metropolitan investors. 'First, the French occupied the buildings of Bône. Second, they grabbed the land on the plain outside Bône. Third, they took over the cork oak forests. Fourth, they mined the area for minerals. Fifth, they displaced the Algerians and peopled Bône with Europeans.'[42] It differed also from the British invasion of the Australian continent, which created spaces for settlement in lands from which savages could be driven out.

Superficially, discourses of conquest often seem to operate through denigrated stereotypes, through types of 'others' such as the savage or lazy native. Though tourist culture in Fiji, and the settlers who wished that the administration would dispossess the natives, made much of the cannibal warrior, the administration's perception was instead of a collective social entity to be codified and regularized, to be preserved in its distinctness while certain faults and flaws were addressed through planning. Like subsequent sociological thought, which saw the social body in organic terms, systemic coherence was assumed, which went along with a segregationist assumption: native society was as essentially distinct as a species, and while it might be bettered and advanced in a variety of ways, it would not be absorbed into a European model. The approach was possible partly because the Christian missions had done some of the groundwork for the colonial state (and also of course because the Indians provided the labour that the plantation economy required). They had converted the bulk of the people to Christianity, and the remainder were converted and pacified immediately after cession. These conditions enabled the colonizing project to take the form of 'improvement' or constructive government rather than a destructive invasivion: the eradication of savagery became merely a matter of policing its traces – in occasional heathen revivals – while, at the most general level, administration resembled the treatment of backward sectors of metropolitan society, which were domesticated and reformed.

At the same time, however, and in the same region, other colonizing efforts constructed indigenous people quite differently, displayed little interest in a comprehensive ethnological vision and saw the ideal native future in a process of total conversion.

I argued in the last chapter that an 'incorporative' ideology and a religious framework characterized Renaissance colonialism: others were represented as pagans rather than as savages or members of inferior races, and their conversion served at least to legitimize expansion, even when it was not systematically pursued. At a general level this view of difference and history could be seen to be displaced by a secular ideology, which understood human variation in natural rather than religious terms, and which tended to postulate fixed hierarchies rather than mutable categories. The premise of stable racial difference underpinned not only slavery and apartheid, but also apparently more benevolent segregationist policies, such as those of the British in Fiji; though, in that case, as we have seen, essential difference came to be constructed more at the level of custom and society than race. It would follow from these arguments that discourses that were never secularized, such as those of modern evangelical missions, might retain something of the older incorporative ideology: though the context is obviously different, and it would not be expected that missionary thought could develop in some isolated or insulated fashion, it seems worth raising the question of whether differences between missionary and secular projects were manifested at the fundamental level of their conceptions of otherness, as well as in more obvious emphases on religious change and development.

The mission to be examined here was established in the western Solomon Islands in 1902 by the Australian branch of the Methodist church, which had inherited various south Pacific 'fields'[43] from the London-based Wesleyan Methodist Missionary Society, which had also worked extensively in Africa and (with significantly less effect) India.[44] On the islands of New Georgia, Vella Lavella and Choiseul, the mission's opponents were not only initially recalcitrant heathen islanders; Catholics and Seventh-day Adventists also had interests in the region, the latter to such an extent that they were referred to as 'pests', 'freaks' and 'parasites' in private correspondence.[45] The Methodists' representations were thus not motivated exclusively by the projects of knowing the other and projecting change in certain terms, but arose as well from the mission's rivalrous interest in justifying its specific programme and orientation. Because the interest here is in the cultural projection of the missionary endeavour, which was constructed more for the constituency at home than for either the Solomon Islanders or the missionaries in the field, my emphasis is on the mission's self-fashioning in public propaganda – popular magazines, other publications, postcards and a film entitled *The Transformed Isle* – rather than the perceptions on the ground that can be discerned, for instance, from private papers.

While, from the perspective of today's self-consciously secular Western societies, missionaries no doubt seem quaint, absurdly pious and intolerant, it is important to recall that they had not just a considerable impact on some colonized societies, but also a tremendous influence on perceptions at home of places such as the Pacific islands. Even if missionary visions and ideas were often not accepted, they were certainly widely circulated through cheap periodicals, books and photographic media. One of the central features of this propaganda was the narrative of conversion, which contrasted former savagery with a subsequently elevated and purified Christian state. This is not just a matter of religious change, but of wider social transformation. The characterization of indigenous society as 'barbaric' depended partly on practices directly associated with heathen religion, but also on general social markers such as the low status of women and their treatment as beasts of burden.

All the filthy and degrading customs associated with idol-worship obtained. Sorcery and witchcraft flourished . . . None died a natural death; all sickness was attributed to witchcraft; and the most revolting and horrible cruelty was practised to extort confessions from the unfortunate women charged with the offence.[46]

Narratives concerning particular mission 'fields' tended to dramatize one or two key practices with which the state of savagery or heathenism was identified: cannibalism, widow-strangling (in Fiji) or *sati* (in India). In the western Solomons, headhunting was rendered emblematic, as it was in some official literature and in traveller's accounts, but the manner in which this form of violence related to the characterization of a savage 'race' was crucially different to, say, the fascination with Fijian cannibalism apparent from Andrew's photograph and similar images; such practices are generally set at a temporal distance in missionary collections. The viewer is not supposed to be titillated by the actuality of these horrific practices, but is instead interested in the work that is being done or has been done to abolish them. The missionary representation thus entails temporal marking and tends to convey a narrative of barbarism as past, rather than as immediate and persisting condition.

This is often signalled by the presence of indigenous weapons in photographs of persons who are obviously converted inhabitants of a Christian order. Clubs, hatchets and shields were intricately made and thus open to being aestheticized, rendered as 'curios' or specimens of native craft. But their inclusion is obviously not a matter of simple ornamentation. What stands out is that the things are no longer used; their context of use has been abolished. Such articles are now instead the picturesque products of ingenuity, and more significantly, they are the tokens of a former order;[47] their inclusion in a picture condenses into a synchronic image a larger story of rebirth that is conveyed more fully in the film, *The Transformed Isle*: the long opening sequence representing a headhunting raid explicitly offers a fictional reconstruction of horrific events supposedly typical of the time before the missionary arrived.

In a contribution to a centennial review of Methodist work in the Pacific, John Francis Goldie, the head of the Solomons mission, drew predictably on the before–after story mentioned above: he alluded to the horrors of the past, and contrasted them with 'brighter, happier days', rhetorically asking 'Was it worth while?'[48] However, he distinguished the former state of the Solomons from that of certain other Pacific natives.

> One navigator, who visited the group many years ago, avers that the natives of New Georgia 'were the most treacherous and blood-thirsty race in the Western Pacific,' and that 'human flesh formed their chief article of diet.' This may have been true fifty years ago, but I much doubt the latter part of the statement. The people of the New Georgia group were cannibals, but not in the same sense as the Fijians, who loved human flesh as an article of diet. Those who have taken part in these cannibal feasts tell me that in connexion with human sacrifices and great religious festivals human flesh was partaken of, but few liked it; to many it was so obnoxious it made them ill. The New Georgians were crafty and cruel; but they were also remarkably clever and intelligent.[49]

The last qualification makes it clear that the point of the passage is not ethnological discrimination but the separation of the subjects of conversion from the most extreme expression of barbarism. If savages are quintessentially and irreducibly savage, the project of converting them to Christianity and introducing civilization is both hopeless and worthless. The prospect of failure would be matched by the undeserving character of the barbarians. This is why mission discourse must simultaneously emphasize savagery and signal the essential humanity, and more positive features, of the islanders to be evangelized. For writers such as Goldie, it was important to be able to differentiate one's own people from some other 'real savages' at a convenient geographic remove, and suggest ambiguity by qualifying the image of barbarism with depictions of other dimensions of indigenous life (and before the Fijians were converted the missionaries there had analogous ways of qualifying and rendering ambiguous the savagery of heathenism).

More positively, the film displayed the creativity and humanity of the Solomons people by showing the production of various types of artefacts: some extremely intricate tortoiseshell breast and forehead ornaments are upheld as 'marvels of patience and design.' The people are also seen engaged in ordinary work, playing, travelling in canoes and fishing. This is the other side of the mode of constructing savagery on the basis of *particular* forms of barbaric practice: missionaries did not suggest that it was in some sense part of the racial constitution of 'the' Vella Lavellan or 'the' Fijian that 'he' was essentially savage, at heart a cannibal. The naturalization of a certain national character, with its 'natural turn of mind', that was apparent in Buffon, Forster and other eighteenth-century writers, to be inherited by nineteenth-century racial essentialism – and, in a sociological adaptation, by British colonial government in Fiji – is quite alien to this discourse. The humanity of Solomon Islanders did not add up to any species-like entity, but was a thing of parts, some of which were condemned to the past, while others were to be drawn into the creation of a new Christian islander.

Because the depiction of artefact-working is part of a project to convey a rounded, though obviously selective, image of native life, objects are often represented in association with people, rather than being set out as stable and symmetrical arrays in the manner of ethnologists or official publications. The point is not to display the 'weapons and implements' of some bounded tribe or ethnic group, making a social geography visible for the state, but to prompt reactions of sympathy and empathy to coexist with those of horror and revulsion.

Native humanity is most directly expressed in a few photographs which include both white and black children. The remarkable 'Study in Black and White', published as a postcard, differentiates the white girl from her two native friends by showing her fully dressed, with a hat, while they are only wearing loincloths. All three however appear to be barefoot, and the fact of holding hands, and the basic conjunction in itself, seems to convey that children are all on the same level, and in some sense have the same potential. The impression is strengthened by the fact that there are only three children of more or less the same age and size in the picture. A similar message emerges from some larger, differentiated groups, but because these contain hierarchical differences based on age, the suggestions of friendship, voluntary association and equality are submerged. It is, of course, difficult to see the picture in the way that a purchaser of the postcard in 1910 would have, but, to put the proposition negatively, there is nothing in the image which implies that the boys are in any way unsuitable playmates for the girl, or that there is anything disturbing in the conjunction. The conclusion that the

Plate 8 *'A Study in Black and White'. Methodist Mission postcard*, c. 1908

work of the photograph is essentially to equate, in human worth, the three children represented, seems inescapable.

Children carry a specific burden in the before–after narrative which dominates the understanding of change in a particular mission field. Another sympathetic photograph of a small boy appeared in the magazine (on a 'children's page') with the following text.

> This picture is a photograph of a little boy born in a heathen land – the Solomon Islands. Until ten years ago, no missionary had been to the part where this boy's home is, and the people there were dark and cruel and wicked. But to-day, hundreds of them know all about Jesus, and many of them love Him. This little boy is now in one of our Mission Schools, and he, with scores of other children, is being taught the way of truth and purity. But there are thousands upon thousands of children in the islands of the Pacific still in the heathen darkness. Their homes are full of evil, their lot is very sad, for they are surrounded by wicked people. We want *you* to help to make known to them the joys of the Christian faith.[50]

There are tensions and contradictions between these stronger statements concerning the 'before' and the more positive side of native life shown, for instance, at length in the film. This passage attempts to negotiate the disjunction between the imagining of native humanity and the evil nature of the past by focusing upon children, who seem to be naturally innocent: under heathenism they might live among the wicked, in 'homes full of evil' but it is not suggested that they are wicked themselves, or even degraded. Rather 'their lot is very sad' because of surrounding circumstances. The projected child reader is invited to identify with these thousands of children who happen to inhabit the heathen darkness. The category of 'children' is stretched beyond any particular culture, and the plight of those who (as it were contingently) live with 'wicked people' is stressed. If the social circumstances change, these children can grow up being no less Christian than any others.

In an important sense the before–after story is thus generationally staged. This theme expresses itself with considerable redundancy. It is emphasized at many points that every school student is 'the son of a head-hunter';[51] the image even provides the title for

Nicholson's biography of Daniel Bula, a prominent native teacher, *The Son of a Savage*.[52] Older people (and particularly young adults) are frequently assimilated into the category of children growing out of heathenism since all are referred to as 'mission boys' or 'girls' irrespective of age; a Roviana preacher, Boaz Suga, who was probably in his twenties, is described as 'a Solomon Island boy . . . once a heathen . . . now he is a happy Christian lad.'[53] The odd conjuncture of the temporal structure and the negative imagery of savagery is encapsulated in lines quoted by Goldie in order to stress the need for a broad civilizing project: 'We are not dealing with people of the older civilizations of India and China, but "Your new-caught sullen peoples / Half devil and half child."'[54]

This infantilization of the indigenous people also, of course, contained a statement about the missionaries' relationship with them. This was clearly manifested in various photographs including missionaries or their wives which convey the hierarchy and order of a family group. This is the context in which the sharp contrast between this discourse and those which understand racial difference as analogous to species or sexual difference is most

Plate 9   *'Rev. J. F. Goldie with some of the first Converts, Rubiana, Solomon Islands',
1908*

apparent. For much secular colonial discourse, the difference between the civilized man and the savage is as clear and irreducible as that between man and woman (and the transposition of the polysemic words in eighteenth-century usage was discussed above), both kinds of physical difference being seen to be grounded in nature. If one kind takes on the attributes or environment of the other, if a process of conversion is initiated, the result can only be repugnant or dangerous, as in the parody of the native who is a 'bad imitation' of a European, manifestly threatening the British segregationist project described above. The notion that types are essentially stable in their differences, and that any admixture, hybridization or conversion can lead to no good is manifested in many specific ways: for instance in the notion that ill-health and depopulation arise partly from the natives' inability to make sensible or correct use of European clothes. In *The Essential Kafir*, Dudley Kidd noted:

> An educated native will try to make himself white; but we should be able to prevent that calamity. After all, the feat is impossible. No man in his senses would suggest that we should give our daughters to black men; no one would wish to have them sitting at our tables as a regular thing; no one would care to take a native into partnership. It is a thousand pities that we cannot banish all European clothing from native territories, and allow the Kafirs to evolve naturally, and form a society of their own, just as the Malays have been doing in Cape Town. Such a plan would be better for both black and white.[55]

The discourse of racial types very frequently operated through gender imagery: Asiatics, and particularly 'Hindoos', were effete or effeminate, as were Polynesians; Melanesians, on the other hand, were cannibal warriors with clubs and axes, men of the kind displayed by Andrew. Their race and sex were both biologically fixed; the evangelical project of incorporation, on the other hand, was powerfully captured in the familial metaphor. The mission postulated neither masculinity nor femininity but infancy, a protosocial condition from which Christian manhood and womanhood are imagined to emerge.

The tropes of missionary propaganda may thus be contrasted sharply with the essentialist understanding of racial types that, in the domain of policy, was epitomized by the British codification of 'native custom'. It follows that the missionary project is less distinct from the stereotypic French assimilationist approach, which Michael Crowder suggests combined 'a fundamental acceptance of [the Africans'] potential human equality [and] a total dismissal of African culture as of any value'.[56] While the content of what Africans lacked, and hence what the civilizing mission supplied, was quite different in official assimilationist and missionary imaginations, the form of difference and presumptions about the history that followed from it are similar. The indigenous condition is postulated not in positive markers thought to be characteristic of a particular stage of social development, but above all in absences, in the lack of enlightenment, and in this sense it echoes the vacant and generalized premodern characterization of paganism. In practice, of course, both missionary and official colonial interventions had to take existing institutions and relations into account, and incorporative policies were often placed in the background by more specific ethnological discourses about the natures of particular societies and peoples. While missionary propaganda is a distinct genre, produced and circulated through visual media and publications that made a series of assumptions about their constituency, individual missionaries, especially from the mid-nineteenth century on, often wrote for geographical and anthropological audiences as well, and were thus partible authors whose practical reactions and actions in the field reflected a range of assumptions and influences.[57]

This brings into focus a necessary qualification and elaboration of the argument that has been developed thus far. I have argued that infantilization is a crucial feature of missionary culture, but it is apparent that constructions of indigenous peoples as children, or as immature, have great generality. To refer merely to approximate contemporaries of the missionaries discussed here, Dudley Kidd observed that 'one would no more think of giving the native a vote on European matters than one would think of giving fourth-form boys at school a vote in the management of lessons.'[58] Neatly encompassing a series of unsocialized others, the administrator M. V. Portman said that he 'often likened [the Andamanese] to English country schoolboys of the labouring classes.'[59] Somewhat earlier, Stanley posed not only as an adult in relation to the black child, but also appropriated the canonical Christian trope: in his titles, Africa was not only 'dark' but 'dark-

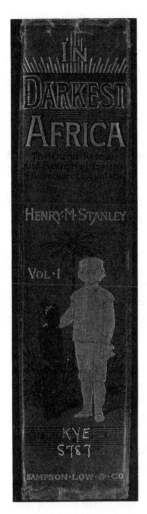

Plate 10   *Decorated book spine. From Henry M. Stanley,*
In Darkest Africa, *1890*

est', and the text at the bottom of the spine here illustrated (plate 10) reads 'Let there be light.'[60] And in evoking the half-infancy of the savage, Goldie was after all quoting not a theorist of missions, but Kipling's famous poem, 'The white man's burden'.

The distinctiveness of evangelical colonialism arises not from the terms or metaphors of its propaganda, if these are taken in isolation, but from narratives in which these tropes have specific meanings, and from practices which were inflected, if not wholly shaped, by the terms of missionary rhetoric. In one sense it is apparent that evangelical missions in both Africa and the Pacific had entirely different objectives to, say, Stanley's expedition or the Fijian administration, but it is also true more specifically that missionary work employed and enacted the notions of infantilization and quasi-familial hierarchy in a far more thorough way than any other colonial project: the construction of difference in terms of a familial relation was not a static condition, but articulated with an attempt to implement social change on the colonial periphery in a particular way. In several sequences of *The Transformed Isle* and in the literature in general, there is a great emphasis upon schooling, and more generally upon the novel creation of a social order. While the British in Fiji saw themselves as dealing with a polity that possessed an existing hierarchy and mature, if flawed, institutions, for the missionaries it was as if children were being brought up and socialized for the first time.

It is affirmed that the mission is much more than 'a house in the bush'; a whole structure of institutions was created which reorganized work and social life. To some extent the point is simply that order has been created: hence a postcard showing 'Road through mission plantation, Rubiana' constructs the image symmetrically, while group photographs convey order of various domestic and institutional kinds. There is also a particular emphasis upon work: postcards depict the hard labour of clearing a new plantation, and another shows islanders 'Discharging timber for mission house at Vella Lavella'. These images are linked with the doctrine of the 'industrial mission' which seems to have become the dominant view among the Australasian Methodists in the early twentieth century of how missions should be run. (This approach had antecedents in Moravian missions and earlier in the non-conformist societies of the nineteenth century, including the Wesleyan Methodist Mission from which the Australasian Methodist Church inherited the Pacific circuits. Moffat and Livingstone, among others, had closely identified the civilizing process and the promotion of commerce).[61] Goldie argued in a 1916 article that in other, unnamed, missions natives were allegedly Christians in name but lazy and dishonest in behaviour; a broad approach to morality, work and commerce was therefore called for.

> Is the Christianity we ask ['these savage islanders'] to accept merely a creed, and the nominal membership of a human society called

the Church, or is it a new vision, new aspirations, and a new power to will and to do – in other words, a new life? . . . all Missionary workers will agree that the real *objective* in Mission work is certainly not the successful running of a commercial undertaking, however profitable, or merely the turning out of carpenters and boat-builders, however skilful. The chief business of the Missionary is not to make boats and plantations but to make men – Christian men. Not to build houses, but to build character.[62]

Despite the masculinist language, it should be added that this programme definitely included women, and great emphasis was placed especially on sewing and garment-making, which was directly linked to conversion because those who attended church necessarily did so attired in fabric skirts and blouses or sarongs, rather than in 'heathen' dress.[63] These activities were moreover regularized: rather than being conducted individually or with friends at home in the interstices of a working day, mats and other such articles were prepared by groups working around the mission station during regular hours. *The Transformed Isle* presents 'the industrial mission' in considerable detail. The segment is signalled by an explicit reference and the claim that 'A healthy vigorous young life is springing up because they are taught that there is no such thing as a lazy Christian';[64] we see the roads, a substantial wharf built by mission labour and copra cutting (which had developed earlier in response to the demand of traders and remains an important form of petty commodity production in the Pacific).

The statements made through the film and photographs about this process of social growth and transformation do not relate merely to the before–after story, the story of the horrors of the past and the happiness of the Christian present. They also make claims about the mission's role in the civilizing process: the mission, in fact, is identified as the sole author of positive social change in the islands, a point about which Goldie was quite explicit.

We began this work amongst a purely savage people in May 1902. No track had been blazed, and we were the pioneers. We have not laboured in vain . . . They are making model villages and improving the conditions under which they live. They are learning how to utilize their idle lands, and are making plantations of food and coco-nuts.[65]

But so far as commercially-orientated native industry is concerned, many groups in the western Solomons had extensive experience of casual trading with ships before 1850, and in the second half of the nineteenth century more systematic relationships with white resident traders developed, usually involving the production of copra, ivory nuts, barter of ordinary food for guns and various other articles and the collecting of bêche-de-mer, pearlshell and tortoiseshell. The plantations which are represented in the Methodist photographs of *c.*1910 were by no means the only ones then being operated in the region.[66] More significantly, given its prominence in mission rhetoric, the notion that the mission put an end to headhunting is totally misleading: this was in fact entirely the work of the government, and the tribes of what became the Western Province had virtually all been pacified several years before the mission entered the area.

Although the activities of the government are invisible in *The Transformed Isle*, white traders do appear, and are represented exclusively as criminal exploiters of the natives. The film creates a sub-narrative around incidents supposedly typical of recruiting for the Pacific islander labour trade (mainly to Queensland canefields), and reflects a much wider controversy between those engaged in the trade and their liberal opponents, principally the missions and bodies such as the Anti-Slavery Society (whose correspondents in the islands were nearly all missionaries). The critics used the term 'blackbirding' and insisted that recruiting usually amounted to nothing other than kidnapping. So the film shows gullible islanders being lured onto a vessel's deck by unattractive thuggish-looking traders proffering strings of trinkets and hatchets. Despite their ignorance, the natives are wary and hesitant, but are nevertheless enticed on board and below decks. After a certain number have gone below, the treacherous Europeans smartly bolt the hatch and chase the others overboard, driving the substantial canoe-borne crowd away with rifle-fire: 'The brutal kidnappers weigh anchor and make for the open sea with their human freight.'[67] This scenario is rather out of place in the western Solomons, where the number of Melanesians who were ever indentured was minuscule, but in any case ignores the point that once the trade had been going on for a few years, returned labourers were telling stories at home, and indigenous men thus almost always understood what sort of work they would be engaging in and on what terms, and had various reasons for voluntarily participating. Cases of kidnapping certainly occurred, but were not typical of a system which entailed thousands of recruits and which lasted for decades.[68]

While the larger inequalities of these relationships are quite inescapable, it is apparent that the missionary view seizes upon victimization by certain whites and ignores the active and collaborative character of indigenous engagement in exploitative relations. This is not surprising, given the construction of natives as children, but underspecifies the motivation of the image. While the characterization of white traders in exclusively negative terms is curious, given that, in practice, these missionaries got on moderately well with most other white residents, this is simply the correlate of the mission's attempt to construct itself as the only civilizing agent in the heathen land. 'Industry' derives purely from missionary endeavour in a place which was savage to start with. It is implied that there are no plantations other than those of the industrial mission, and, since it can hardly be pretended that there had been absolutely no other contact between Solomon Islanders and whites, this is made out to have been purely destructive.

Not only was the mission as an entity the key actor in a larger historical drama, but individual missionaries were presented, not merely as adult parents who cared for, and naturally supervised their native children, but also as singularly transcendent and historically empowered figures in a different way. In two intriguing pictures the head of the mission, John Francis Goldie, is seen with a group, in one case of 'mission boys' (plate 9), in the other, what is evidently a school class. All look directly into the camera – except him. Perhaps Goldie merely had a personal aversion to watching the photographer, but the results convey a kind of wider engagement with the world which is not limited to immediate circumstances, and also a wider vision.[69] This implication is particularly strong in the school-group picture, because we see a globe through the window directly behind and above the missionary.

The social process of conversion and the development of a new Christian society in the native land is thus represented as a dyadic affair: the missionaries on one side show the light and provide guidance, while on the other the natives respond to the dawn and happily learn and work within the new order. Immediate reasons for this rather extravagant distortion of the actual situation are transparent: the mission had a constituency, needed to advertise its work, needed funds, needed, to convey satisfaction to those who had already made donations and, not least, was engaged in rivalry with other denominations such as the Seventh-Day Adventists. The emphasis on the 'industrial' nature of the mission was significant in the context of inter-mission competition, since it could be claimed – perhaps accurately – that certain denominations did little more than secure nominal adherence.

But at the same time there is clearly more to the project than differentiation for the purposes of advertisement. It is quite crucial to the whole structure of this discourse that the mission was not simply a religious instrument but rather a total social fact. It created an entire social geography of stations and circuits, which in some cases reflected indigenous political divisions or trade routes but gave even these entirely new functions; it sought to impose a new temporal regime of work, leisure, celebration and worship; through education it offered a new global and local history marked by the life of Wesley, the foundation of the mission society, the opening of Pacific mission fields, major events of conversion and the commemoration of martyrs; it produced not just a population of Christians, but a people that engaged in periodic plantation work, who were notionally subject to rigorous behavioural codes and who had notionally brought their social and domestic habits into conformity with Christian norms. Within this effort, ideas of the location and transformation of familial life are projected in a number of ways that are not entirely consistent; in one context native existence may be deplorably non-familial; elsewhere indigenous families are shown to be imperfect, but in the process of change; and in other cases, and particularly in the materials I have presented here, actual indigenous families seem almost dissolved within the mission station, which takes the form of a sort of macro-familial institution. The white missionaries are the parents to native boys and girls, who are instructed and brought up, not in specifically religious or technical training, but in the whole field of practical, recreational and spiritual living. The notion that the mission thus encompassed indigenous life was clearly to some extent a fantasy, but it is true that in many instances boarding schools and orphanages were created which did in fact give missionaries an enormous amount of control over children;[70] and it is also the case that individual missionaries or missionary wives often formed close attachments with converts – and especially privileged converts such as mission teachers – which the whites understood in familial terms.[71] Needless to say, the indigenous views of these friendships are usually not accessible; most of the available recollections bearing on the question were compiled or edited by missionaries, and are thus constrained in a predictable manner.[72]

While missionaries no doubt regarded Australian Aborigines and tribals elsewhere as baser or more degraded than the heathens of Asiatic civilizations, the premiss of their efforts was an ethic of human equality in Christendom. As Todorov observed with respect to premodern Christian colonialism, this was sometimes merely abstract, and accompanied by a lack of interest in concrete human inequalities, but mission egalitarianism in the eighteenth, nineteenth and twentieth centuries sometimes did contest overtly racist colonial social relationships. When missions directed their efforts among slaves or similarly oppressed colonized peoples, the unity of humankind often received rhetorical emphasis; this was manifest for instance in a Moravian painting of 'The First Fruits', depicting an assembly of converts including a 'Persian', an 'Eskimo', a 'Hottentot' and various others, but these are individuals with their baptismal names, not exemplars of races. There are general continuities between all these endeavours at an ideological level, but more fundamental parallels are found in the configuration of relations and conflicts between colonial projects. Just as the Methodists in the Solomons were extraordinarily hostile to the white traders and labour recruiters, the Boers in South Africa saw the Moravians (in the late eighteenth century) and the London Missionary Society (in the nineteenth) as entirely subversive forces that aimed to transform the native world in a revolutionary manner that would deprive them of their labour force.

> [T]he Boers firmly believed that the LMS harbored the 'Utopian idea of laying the foundation, under their own special priestly guidance, of a model kingdom of regenerated natives.' Not Moffat

nor Philip nor Livingstone, for all the clarity with which they envisaged an Eden of the Spirit, could have better phrased the charter for their civilizing colonialism.[73]

Not that there was some intrinsic missionary hostility toward slave ownership or colonial servitude: the Moravians' attitude in the West Indies was somewhat equivocal, and in North Carolina Moravian settlers were in fact slave owners;[74] if one is seeking an elementary structure of colonial discourse, it is not to be found at the level of a specific attitude or policy, nor in any particular image or metaphor, but rather in the contradictory character of the colonial objectives of distancing, hierarchizing and incorporating. It is difficult to sustain distance while creating an exclusive hierarchy; it is also problematic to assimilate the other through the disavowal of hierarchy while implicitly sustaining the inequality which all colonialism presupposes. Hierarchizing and assimilating colonialisms are, on the surface, radically opposed, and this contradiction emerges practically in the struggles between missionaries and those whose models of colonization presuppose distance and fixed relations of dominance. But these models also each have internal contradictions, partly arising from the fact that each operation presupposes something of the other; the analysis here has not explored the full range of problems, but does suggest that the missionaries had to confront a contradiction between the desirability of postulating human equality in certain contexts, and their will to control the process of conversion and the localized theocracies that were occasionally effectively established. By imagining that others were part of a family, the mission was able to reconcile common humanity and hierarchy in a manner that was as natural and intelligible in the short term as it was insecure in the long term: after all, children grow up. That is also why this metaphor was part of the common ground of colonial discourse, yet also a resource to be valorized in a specific way in evangelical propaganda.

5

Imperial Triumph, Settler Failure

A discourse is often not a set of notions and categories that exists in and for itself, but a discourse *against* another, that has an oppositional or argumentative character. The evangelical project that I have described operated in a highly contested field in the late nineteenth and early twentieth centuries. Even though the attitudes that were in people's heads are not directly documented or accessible, the clash of opinions and the hostility of some to the views subscribed to by some churches is apparent. 'Asterisk', whose letters from the New Hebrides were edited into a bestselling travel book that remains in print, wrote of the (Anglican) Melanesian Mission in 1912 that

> they are . . . very wrongheaded, insisting on the horrible doctrine of equality of races and putting their doctrine into practice. I heard of one of them who went to stay in Auckland with a parson there, quite a decent man, and his wife. The missionary brought with him a pet native teacher. The Auckland parson's wife naturally arranged that the teacher should feed in the kitchen with the other black servants. But no. The missionary insisted on his brother sitting down at dinner with the whites. The parson's wife, however, was even with him. When they were about to retire, she remarked sweetly to the missionary, 'We're so very pressed for room, Mr. X., I'm sure you won't mind putting dear Mr. Mapuna in with you. It's a large bed.'[1]

The first sentences of John Buchan's novel *Prester John* are 'I mind as if it were yesterday my first sight of the man . . . I mind yet the cold grue of terror I got from it.' The obscure and fateful figure, who disrupts the sleep of Buchan's narrator-protagonist even at the distance of the scene of retrospective composition, is the same 'inappropriate other' (to use Trinh Minh-Ha's term) that Asterisk derides. Though the missionaries' commitment to racial equality is less obvious to a reader of their paternalistic propaganda now, and though some denominations neither advocated the principle nor put it into practice, in the late nineteenth and early twentieth centuries an egalitarian or sentimental humanism in race relations was widely attributed to the churches, and objected to; the figure upon whom much of the argument turned was the native minister, presented by one side as the exemplary convert, by the other as a sinister and duplicitous evolutionary anachronism. If Asterisk's tone is primarily comic, he nevertheless finds the doctrine 'horrible', and Buchan's novel is a sustained explication of what was uncanny and terrifying in the black parson to whom he refers. The issue is paraded near the beginning of *Prester John*, when three Scottish boys reflect on the day's service in the Free Kirk.

> A black man, the Rev. John Something-or-other, had been preaching. Tam was full of portent. 'A nigger,' he said, 'a great black chap as big as your father, Archie.' He seemed to have banged the bookboard with some effect, and had kept Tam, for once in his life, awake. He had preached about the heathen in Africa, and how a black man was as good as a white man in the sight of God, and he had forecast a day when the Negroes would have something to teach the British in the way of civilization. So at any rate ran the account of Tam Dyke, who did not share the preacher's views. 'It's all nonsense, Davie. The Bible says that the children of Ham were to be our servants. If I were the minister I wouldn't let a nigger into the pulpit. I wouldn't let him farther than the Sabbath school.'[2]

Unlike Asterisk's cursory anecdote, this passage is of central importance in *Prester John*; though preceded by a few hundred words setting the scene and idealizing the Scottish coast, it is this exchange that constitutes the book's beginning. The work of this enormously popular adventure narrative, which intertwined diamond smuggling and 'Kaffir' revolt in southern Africa, is ultimately to join the boy in rejecting and denying what the black preacher asserted, not simply with respect to racial equality, but also with respect to history. Although colonial designs that rivalled those of the Methodist mission could be examined through practices and policies, or through the political and theoretical writings of Buchan and far more significant figures such as Rhodes and Milner, the novel narrates this colonial vision in a more comprehensive and unfettered form. Through what transpires and what is projected, in the positively lyrical fantasy of constructive imperialism that concludes the book, it is affirmed that white supremacy and guidance is both the necessary and best condition for the foreseeable future. Though the fiction might be considered a good source for certain British attitudes at a critical moment in southern African history, its importance can also be situated in the breadth of its readership, and hence in its location in a metropolitan debate.

This audience was no doubt secured by the economy and pace of Buchan's prose. Almost immediately after the conversation quoted, and in this time of childhood prior to the protagonist's move to the colonial frontier, the true character of the black minister is exposed: the boys, on a night excursion to the beach, see the man engaging in some kind of strange magic beside a fire, gesturing, making marks, in an alarming and 'desperately uncanny' fashion; the narrator is convinced that this was the 'black art'. Not only the man's savagery, but also his hostility, are revealed in this first chapter, since as soon as the African realizes that he is being watched, he makes chase, brandishing a knife. The character, who we later learn is the Reverend John Laputa, is thus introduced in terms of two obscure doublings or discrepancies. First of all, he falsely appears as an upright and eloquent Christian and is taken as such by everyone other than those who happen upon his secret nocturnal ritual; secondly, and more fundamentally, he has an appearance of nobility that separates him off from other members of his race, yet is at odds with his manifest savagery.

> [T]he face stamped itself indelibly upon my mind. It was black, black as ebony, but it was different from the ordinary Negro. There were no thick lips and flat nostrils; rather, if I could trust my eyes, the nose was high-bridged, and the lines of the mouth sharp and firm. But it was distorted into an expression of such devilish fury and amazement that my heart became like water.[3]

The racial aesthetic at work here, that stigmatizes certain features, is familiar, though perhaps its function in producing an ambivalence and a problem of recognition is less immediately so. The possibility of resolving or explaining the figure's ambiguous distortion derives from a stroke of fate: the novel's narrator and protagonist, David Crawfurd, hopes to enter a profession, but his father's death cuts short his university study, and an uncle finds an opening for him as a storekeeper in South Africa, with the promise that he can better himself there more quickly than would be possible at home. It is the old story: thwarted aspirations at home pave the way for the challenge of the frontier. On the boat, he encounters the black minister again, and the impressions of a few years earlier are reinforced: 'He had none of the squat and preposterous Negro lineaments, but a hawk nose like an Arab, dark flashing eyes, and a cruel and resolute mouth. He was black as my hat, but for the rest he might have sat for a figure of a Crusader.'[4]

From the time of the young man's arrival at the trading station in an isolated tract of the northern Transvaal, matters become murky: there is a sense of unease in the place that seems connected with the illegal diamond trade. Crawfurd's friend, the schoolteacher Wardlaw, speculates that colonial policy had got the native wrong – not in the sense of underestimating his intelligence, but his threat. The premonition that some uprising may occur of course foreshadows the tale's drama, as does Wardlaw's more specific fear that rebellion might arise from 'a kind of bastard Christianity'. Laputa, it transpires, is not merely a charismatic preacher, but a prophet identifying himself with the mythical Prester John, the Christian warrior-king of an independent African nation, and his power derives from his access to a fetish handed down from one black warrior-prophet to the next. The sinister and flawed character of Laputa is thus related directly to the transposition of Christianity, which is too readily mixed up with heathenism and savagery by natives (those of Haiti and the American South are mentioned as well as the 'Kaffirs'). The underlying idea that any assimilation or miscegenation can only result in ungovernable degeneracy is illustrated by Laputa's treacherous associate, the Portuguese half-caste Henriques, whose character, unlike that of Laputa, has no redeeming features whatsoever. Not only are his physical features repulsive – 'He had a face the colour of French mustard – a sort of dirty green – and bloodshot, beady eyes with the whites all yellowed with fever' – but his manner is also 'curious and furtive'; he is later characterized as a 'double-dyed traitor to his race' and a Kaffir 'in everything but Kaffir virtues'.[5] On one side, then, the integrity of Laputa's resistance is endorsed in relation to the half-caste, who is merely pursuing his own criminal ends; on the other it is differentiated from an inauthentic 'Ethiopianism' associated with the independent churches of American blacks rather than Africans themselves; 'Laputa was none of your flabby educated Negroes from America.'[6]

Although some readers applaud the 'rare imaginative sympathy'[7] manifest in Buchan's portrait of Laputa, such a response can only neglect the narrative function of this marking of positive humanity, because Laputa serves as a kind of test case, so far as the potential of the black man to benefit from civilization is concerned. If any 'Kaffir' could guide his own people and exercise responsible leadership, Laputa could: his nobility, his masculinity, his education, his genuine power and his feeling for his people are frequently attested to, yet there is no doubt that the whole project of the uprising constitutes a historical regression that expresses the leader's essential backwardness and savagery: his education can never be more than a misleading veneer. ' "... I said he was an educated man, but he is also a Kaffir. He can see the first stage of a thing, and maybe the second, but no more. That is the native mind. If it was not like that our chances would be worse." '[8] Hence, while the speaker here, one Captain Arcott, has tremendous admiration for Laputa's genius and bravery, the fact of racial origin is absolutely fundamental and constraining: ' "If he had been white he might have been a second Napoleon ... He has the heart of a poet and a king, and it is God's curse that he has been born among the children of Ham." '[9]

In fact, then, every hyperbole that affirms Laputa's capacities and learning – his Latin, his occasional moments of generosity and humanity, his selflessness – serves really to affirm the absolute difference between black and white, and the association of the former with a barbaric past, and the latter with the future, with peace, progress and industry. Crawfurd's final struggle with the minister takes place in a cave, a sacred place for the messianic cult, and after the black leader, fatally wounded by the treacherous half-caste, has jumped to his death, the young man still has the awesome challenge of climbing a subterranean waterfall to freedom. As he regains open country, the darkness of his own violent experience in the conflict of the uprising, and the darkness of Laputa and the place, are condensed and repudiated in an extraordinary passage that displays not only the colonialist equations of black and white, rebellion and progress, past and future, but also the aesthetic and possessive identifications between the landscape here and at home.

> It was little more than dawn . . . before me was the shallow vale with its bracken and sweet grass, and farther on the shining links of the stream, and the loch still grey in the shadow of the beleaguering hills. Here was a fresh, clean land, a land for homesteads and orchards and children. All of a sudden I realized that at last I had come out of savagery. The burden of the past days slipped from my shoulders. I felt young again, and cheerful and brave. Behind me was the black night, and the horrid secrets of darkness. Before me was my own country, for that loch and that bracken might have been on a Scotch moor.[10]

With respect to nineteenth-century landscape painting, Bernard Smith has suggested that 'European control of the world required a landscape practice that could first survey and describe, then evoke in new settlers an emotional engagement with the land that they had alienated from its aboriginal inhabitants.'[11] Buchan's text effects in prose the second, affective element of this appropriative operation: the features of the landscape are translated into a Scotch idiom; the scene is pure, free not only of natives, but even of any marks or traces of their occupation, and is instead absolutely available to a youthful settler domesticity. This moment of vision marks the end of the uprising, and because Crawfurd appropriates the movement's treasure – mostly derived from diamond theft and smuggling – he can return to Scotland to realize his dream of university education. One of his associates discovers a diamond mine and uses some of the resulting fortune to establish 'a big fund for the education and amelioration of native races'. A training college was set up at Blaauwildebeestefontein, the site of Crawfurd's great conflict.

> It was no factory for making missionaries and black teachers, but an institution for giving the Kaffirs the kind of training which fits

them to be good citizens of the State. There you will find every kind of technical workshop, and the finest experimental farms, where the blacks are taught modern agriculture. They have proved themselves apt pupils, and to-day you will see in the glens of the Berg and in the plains Kaffir tillage which is as scientific as any in Africa. They have created a huge export trade in tobacco and fruit; the cotton promises well; and there is talk of a new fibre which will do wonders.[12]

This passage thus directly addresses that which was quoted first: the native condition is not to be 'ameliorated' by religion, by the false effort to make teachers of those who are not ready and not properly formed for such a station in life. However, it would have been more accurate had Buchan written that the training college fitted the Kaffir out to be subjects, not citizens, of the State, since everything in the passage suggests that work under white guidance is the appropriate and possible form of development. The blacks are not just at school, but their whole way of life is *in statu pupillari*; there is for instance 'a rule that all the Kaffir farms on the Berg sound a kind of curfew', and there is no doubt what reference point informs the recreation of the land: 'The loch on the Rooirand is stocked with Lochleven trout, and we have made a bridle path up to it'.[13] Bizarre as it may seem, a great deal of expense and effort actually was in put into acclimatizing trout; this was a topic that Buchan had discussed more extensively in his journalistic book, *The African Colony*, in the chapter entitled 'The future of South African sport.'[14]

Prester John directly reflects turn-of-the-century imperialist thinking and, specifically, administrative attitudes in the period of Buchan's own South African service between 1901 and 1903 – most conspicuously in its principal silence. What is completely elided is the fact that, from the imperialist perspective, the struggle was not between whites and natives, but between the British and the Afrikaners; the conflict carried the burden of the global issue of imperial unity. The evident threat was not the resistance of colonized populations, but colonial nationalism; and the theoreticians who advocated imperialism as a noble and vigorous idea were principally reacting to a far less ethereal problem: the erosion of imperial influence and authority in the colonies.[15] One of the most zealous writers and administrators of this persuasion was

Lord Milner, who recruited Buchan to the South African service while he was High Commissioner there. In Milner's view, 'the gospel of creative imperialism'[16] (which was more or less Rhodes's 'social imperialism') was not a continuation of British colonial policy, but a new and visionary departure.

> Imperialism . . . has all the depth and comprehensiveness of a religious faith. Its significance is moral even more than material. It is a mistake to think of it as principally concerned with extension of territory, with 'painting the map red.' There is quite enough painted red already. It is not a question of a couple of hundred thousand square miles more or less. It is a question of preserving the unity of a great race, of enabling it, by maintaining that unity, to develop freely on its own lines, and to continue to fulfil its distinctive mission in the world.[17]

Despite the extent and pomposity of Milner's writing, the only clear and significant notion in this doctrine was its emphasis on 'the importance of the racial bond', which, since it referred to the British rather than the white 'race', bore a highly problematic relation to the South African context. In a military sense, the issue had been resolved in favour of the British in 1902, but control was rapidly lost over political developments, and Afrikaner parties had gained the upper hand before their decisive electoral victory in 1907.[18] In the period of Buchan's service, however, the mood was evidently highly optimistic, and the preoccupation with rebuilding a united and loyal settler population, in which Afrikaners and British had the same rights, almost entirely eclipsed any other questions of policy or development. There was a conspicuous lack of interest in reforming or reorientating native policy; though Afrikaner mistreatment of blacks entered into British propaganda, the extent to which this was merely propaganda can be judged by Milner's statement: 'You have only to sacrifice "the nigger" absolutely, and the game is easy.'[19] It subsequently 'proved possible to discover large areas of agreement between the administration and the white population.'[20] At certain moments, the government asserted that civilization rather than colour should be the basis for determining political rights, but these tentative moves toward a more assimilationist or paternalist approach were either qualified in the face of white resistance or of such limited effect that the basic forms of institutionalized racism were unmodified. Political failure in the short term has also obscured the extent to which Milner's policies had enduring effect; they 'laid the foundations for a state which not only reflected the demands of twentieth-century British imperialism but also fulfilled them', notably through the segregationist policies that have remained notorious.[21]

In this context, it is less surprising that there is not a passage in *Prester John* that dramatizes the difference between the Dutch and the British or indeed uses it to any narrative effect; there is barely a remark reminiscent of the frequently expressed British prejudice against those who were unrefined, indolent and literally boorish, nor is there any observation upon differing attitudes towards native policy or the Dutch propensity to mistreat and abuse black labour. Buchan's lack of interest in drawing these issues into his novel may be explained partly because Buchan himself sympathized paternalistically with the farmers of the veld, though not the slick town Afrikaners; the former reminded him of the peasants of Scotland.[22] Just as women are virtually unmentioned in a book preoccupied with a conflict between black and white men,[23] the Dutch are passive elements of the context and background, not figures whose interest and perspective are at all relevant in the story's rationale.

In a sense, then, Buchan's focus on the Kaffir–white conflict could be seen primarily as a way of evading what had been perceived in his milieu as the real struggle, and its almost unqualified failure, given that the British military victory had failed to secure British political supremacy in southern Africa.[24] But the book does manifest Buchan's service under Milner, and reflects his ideas on race relations in quite a precise and direct fashion – not surprisingly, since Milner's charisma and personal dominance over his appointees and subordinates was well known. In Buchan's case, adherence to the general conception of imperialism is conspicuous even in an autobiography written nearly forty years later.[25] Milner's position (like that of Cecil Rhodes) was grounded in commonplace evolutionism, which performed the specific function of permitting him to reject conventional Boer racism, while enabling the perception of contrasting stages of advancement that ultimately specified an equally essential and radical gap.

> The white man must rule, because he is elevated by many, many
> steps above the black man; steps which it will take the latter centu-
> ries to climb, and which it is quite possible that the vast bulk of the
> black population may never be able to climb at all . . . But if you are
> going to defend white supremacy on this ground, and if at the
> same time you recognize, as I believe you do, the duty and wisdom
> of doing everything you can to raise the black man as far as he can
> be raised, what is the consequence? Is it not a consequence of
> taking your ground on the firm and inexpugnable ground of
> civilization as against the rotten and indefensible ground of colour,
> that if a black man, one in a thousand – perhaps it would be more
> correct to say one in a hundred thousand – raises himself to a white
> level of civilization . . . should not his treatment be that of a white
> man . . . ?[26]

Milner thus sought to place himself on the high moral ground,
by repudiating racism in principle, yet understood the black capacity for civilization in such negative and pessimistic terms that
the practical implications were negligible, while political equality
was often explicitly excluded.[27] It is notable, also, that in suggesting that colonized peoples were too far behind the British to
govern themselves, Milner saw others such as the Egyptians in the
same terms as the South African blacks.[28] This position was taken
for granted by all of the characters in Buchan's *Lodge in the Wilderness*, a tedious fictional debate about the nature of imperialism in
which issues such as colonial nationalism and dominion status,
but not race relations, are discussed extensively and vacuously: a
character based on Cecil Rhodes however expresses the consensus
at one point: 'You cannot annihilate ten strenuous centuries by
assuming that they have not existed, and inviting the native to
crowd the work of them into a year or two.'[29]

The narrative of evolution was central, and its crucial implication echoed the analogy between the life cycle and social-develop-
mental time that Forster had noted so much earlier. In this
imagination, the native was not ready for rapid advancement; the
wrong sort of training could only produce walking anachronisms
such as Laputa: 'do not aim at higher education, for that means
black parsons and black school-masters . . . Above all things teach
them trades and handicrafts . . . Don't try and make out of them
theologians or schoolmasters or bagmen or electioneering hum-
bugs. Leave the scum of civilisation for civilisation to deal with.'[30]

It is ironic that the main argument here was with 'Exeter Hall', that is, with missionary and philanthropic opinion at home, since in many cases the training conducted by missionary societies was in fact of a technical and agricultural character. In its emphasis on carpentry and plantation work, the Methodist 'Industrial Mission' that was fantasized but also partially realized under Goldie's direction actually had a good deal in common with the great native training institution imagined by Buchan. Though there were certainly native teachers and a few ordained ministers, the education of the vast mass of converts was entirely in the domain of 'trades and handicrafts'.

This raises the broader question of the distinctness of the colonialism projected by Buchan – and more generally the conservative 'social imperialism' of Rhodes and Milner – in relation to the projects and discourses I have discussed in the previous chapter. Though Milner might on occasion defer to the opinion of the Aborigines' Protection Society in acknowledging the desirability of sustaining the 'existing system of communal tenure and of tribal government'[31] he never took the principle seriously, and as imperialism's liberal critic, J. A. Hobson, demonstrated, there was a direct contradiction between any preservation of tribal structures and life, and the demands of the white farmers and mine owners for labour, which colonial administrations effectively represented. Hobson argued that an 'enlightened policy of civilized assistance' would follow an entirely different course.

> If we or any other nation really undertook the care and education of a 'lower race' as a trust, how should we set about the execution of the trust? By studying the religions, political and other social institutions and habits of the people, and by endeavouring to penetrate into their present mind and capacities of adaptation, by learning their language and their history, we should seek to place them in the natural history of man; by similar close attention to the country in which they live, and not to its agricultural and mining resources alone, we should get a real grip on their environment. Then, carefully approaching them so as to gain what confidence we could for friendly motives, and openly discouraging any premature private attempts of exploiting companies to work mines or secure concessions, or otherwise to impair our disinterested conduct, we should endeavour to assume the position of advisers. Even if it were

necessary to enforce some degree of authority, we should keep such force in the background as a last resort, and make it our first aim to understand and to promote the healthy free operations of all internal forces for progress which we might discover.[32]

Hobson was calling for an anthropological colonialism, and a distinctively modern kind of government founded on consent and implicit authority rather than force. Gordon's approach in Fiji approximated this ideal, though he lacked uncertainty about the appropriateness and legitimacy of colonial authority; like Lugard, he took it as axiomatic that 'the subject races' 'are not yet able to stand alone.'[33] Fiji, was, of course, an unusual case: Gordon had particular scope for taking protectionist rhetoric seriously, because the relatively small and economically unsuccessful settler population's interest could be subordinated to this higher purpose. The 'native policy' did not, in any case, seriously compromise the colonial economy, which came to be structured more by the combination of big monopoly capital in the form of the Colonial Sugar Refinery and indentured Indian labour. The labourers, needless to say, were treated in an entirely different fashion to indigenous Fijians: they had no customs or culture that might be respected, and there was no equivalent to indirect rule through prominent Indian men either on the plantations or in the communities of 'free' Indians that grew as indentures were completed.[34] Colonial policy, then, could only be liberal with respect to one population at a time: while the Indians were treated in precisely the fashion that Hobson found execrable, the insulation of the indigenous population from the space of economic imperatives made it possible to deal with them paternalistically. The benevolent protectionism was linked with Gordon's construction of himself and the work of the colonial state in terms that were supremely confident, omniscient, rational and unselfish. While Milner insisted that government could not 'deal with the native question regardless of colonial settlement'[35] – meaning that settler racism had to be pandered to – Gordon pretended wilfully to ignore the interests of planters and paraded his claim to a disinterested spirit that indeed drew upon the kind of ethnological understanding of the Fijian's place 'in the natural history of man' that Hobson recommended. The specification of physical and mental characteristics, and of socially peculiar manners and customs, which had been essentially an intellectual project for men such as Forster, had discovered its application in an elaborated form in the work of colonial government. Rather than there being a savage to be conquered, there was a variety of native to be documented, enumerated, disciplined and uplifted.

While this approach, and later notions of indirect rule, were informed by an abstract sense of imperial duty, 'social imperialism' conceived the purpose and role of the colony quite differently. Milner maintained: 'Imperialism, properly conceived, is just such a draft of oxygen as is needed to revitalise the used-up atmosphere of British politics.'[36] There was a more general notion that the 'congested' character of society at home and the low living standard of a substantial proportion of the population could be remedied by migration to 'vast undeveloped areas under our own flag simply clamouring for more and ever more inhabitants.'[37] In *A Lodge in the Wilderness*, 'State-organised emigration' is explicitly advocated: 'You will give our empty lands population and reduce the congestion of our English slums.'[38] As E. J. Hobsbawm noted, the idea that 'a safety valve for overpopulated countries' might be created in this fashion 'was little more than a demagogic fantasy.'[39] However, it clearly enters into Buchan's narrative: Crawfurd, though not a member of the underclass, is cramped and destined for some lowly clerical occupation if he remains at home, whereas the opportunities in the colonies are virtually unlimited. The scope for accomplishment on the frontier is projected into the atmosphere and the landscape, which is paradoxically both reminiscent of Britain, in its pastoral beauty, yet also enlarged, vigorous, and fresh: 'The winds blow as clean as in mid-ocean, soil and vegetation are as wholesome as an English down. I have entered the place from different sides . . . on each occasion I seemed to be crossing the borders of a *temenos*, a place enchanted and consecrate.'[40]

Setting aside the specific congruence of this response with the imperial wish to maintain the dominion status of the settler colony – which is a new endeavour but one firmly subordinate to 'home' not only politically and economically but also aesthetically – there is a point of similarity between this discourse and that of the evangelical missionaries, in the sense that both seek to recreate in the colony a better form of society in the centre. There is no question that what already exists on the periphery has validity or

merit in its own terms; what is positive relates only to identifications that can be made between the centre and the margin, and
the scope that these mark out for the fashioning of something
new, for the rebirth of people and place in terms defined by the
colonists. The difference, however, is that the pioneering discourse, expressed by Buchan in a peculiarly comprehensive and
fantastic form, privileges the landscape as the raw material for a
divinely ordained work, in which there is a kind of opportunity for
growth and progress that seems lacking in the old world. The
pioneer is inspired by majestic and clean spaces, and the fanciful
associations between these newly revealed tracts and the appearance of his own country. This sentimental conflation legitimizing
the appropriation of native land is also conspicuous in Australian
history and in the representation of pioneering in films and other
works dealing with the settler experience.[41] The missionaries, of
course, aimed to create a purer Christian community, under their
own tutelage, than was possible in the corrupted and secularizing
societies of the centre. While both of these projects denied indigenous autonomy, the settler interest in developing the terrain
could potentially dispense with natives altogether, and in many
instances the direct conflict of interest over rights to land gave it
a genocidal orientation. In contrast, the missionary project did
not aim to dispossess (though valuable land was often acquired by
missions) and was more contradictory in its projected and actual
development. Even when evangelists such as Goldie set out with
the manifest desire of directing social advancement and creating
a localized theocracy, the structure of their endeavour, which
provided for the training and authorization of mission teachers,
embodied its own redundancy: most Protestant churches were
'indigenized' within one or two generations, and a degree of
autonomy thus regained (as is manifest in the case of the Solomon
Islands Christians, discussed at the end of chapter 2).

A more radical underlying difference was between the essentialist assumptions of official colonialism and the evangelical preoccupation with mutability. While the ambiguity of native character
and the scope for its conversions was fundamental to the missionary effort, both Gordon and Buchan saw the native being as fixed
and coherent, and both positioned it in evolutionary terms, but in
different ways, that echo two possible assessments that had been

available to evolutionary thought since the eighteenth century. Buchan's understanding, like John Barrow's response to the Hottentot, placed the black at 'the beginning', in a remote and primordial moment of human emergence; in the early twentieth century this was a way of scientizing and sanitizing a racist attitude by avoiding simple colour hierarchy while establishing a radical difference between the stage of development of one race and the other that represented the extremes on a continuum. Though the need for European government might theoretically be diminished at some point in the future, the development of the native race was understood as such a long-term and gradual process that white supremacy was in effect a permanent necessity. Certainly the elite visitors at the 'lodge in the wilderness' felt no compulsion to discuss decolonization, and it is telling that there was little talk of India. Gordon, on the other hand, saw the Fijian order as resembling that of Scotland a few centuries earlier; it was therefore backward, but feudal rather than primordial, and – like the condition of the Tahitians which Enlightenment writers understood in classical terms – was not absolutely distanced from civilized society. Hence progress towards self-government was not necessarily remote, and could be encouraged by administrators as it was in the Pacific; the crucial precondition of this paternalism was of course that a colony was not a settler colony, a space reserved for a white future and white accomplishments.

More negatively, evolutionary discriminations provided for a systematically uneven approach to indirect rule, such that less centralized or aristocratic populations were not accorded the modicum of cultural respect or autonomy bestowed upon more 'advanced communities' – to use Lugard's terms.[42] While a contrast can be made between Gordon on one side and Buchan and Milner on the other, Gordon's attitude to Fiji can also be contrasted with his attitude to the Solomons, and, for reasons of economic exigency rather than evolutionary categorization, with the administration's subsequent approach to indentured Indians. Both Gordon and Milner thought through a language of racial essentialism; Milner employed it to legitimize social relations in what was basically a conquest state,[43] while Gordon's project engendered hegemony and compliance rather than sheer dominance. The mere fact of racial stability was crucial to the first position; anthropological itemization of the nature of the distinctive race was fetishized by the second. While Buchan could fantasize a triumph of assimilation, in which indigenous society was absorbed into a generalized training institution, it is ironic that this project was realized approximately by the targets of his polemic. Evangelical missionaries, unless dabblers in ethnology under another hat, lacked an interest in the distinctive customary regimes of the races they sought to convert; as had been the case before 'national character' and natural history, the other was lacking and was a lack – but once transformed into a Christian adult was also a worker, adept with his copra knife or her needle. If that fantasy was partially realized in the Solomons, that fact must be attributed to the peculiarities of that highly marginal colony, in which missions were less constrained and less resisted than they were elsewhere; but it could have been the same in many other places, were there not a crucial difference between a project and a mere projection.

Critics of colonial discourse often write, unavoidably, from within the terrain that they wish to interrogate: as critics of and in the Western literary and theoretical canon, or as historians trained in one Western historiographic tradition or another. The claim and aspiration to speak in some sense from a native or colonized perspective has been intensively debated.[44] If one speaks on behalf of 'others', there is a risk of creating false identifications and assimilating 'their' perspectives to one's own; if one makes one's own interest explicit, and is content only to speak about 'them' and 'their' self-representations, one may be accused of recapitulating what is seen as the paradigmatic exclusion of Orientalist discourse, namely constituting the presence of an author and an authority on the basis of the other's absence.

I do not wish to pursue these questions here, because their politics cannot be adequately registered through global terms such as 'others' and 'authors'. It makes a difference whether an author is a historian, a cultural theorist, a film critic or an ethnographer. It makes a great deal of difference, in particular, whether this author has produced his or her representations on the basis of sustained involvement with the people involved, and whether they therefore have particular expectations arising from that encounter. It also makes a difference who 'they' are; Tolai, Inuit,

Chicanos and Tamils are not discursively interchangeable 'others' but peoples with very different locations, different access to state resources and education and different concerns. In one case they may regard it as highly inappropriate for anyone other than a member of the immediate community to narrate or represent their histories and identities; in other cases they may welcome the assistance of someone who is an outsider or partial outsider such as a diaspora-trained scholar.

In these debates it sometimes seems to be assumed that colonial studies is primarily about 'others' – about representing 'them' in some way that is more acceptable politically, epistemologically and ethically. A number of writers have now pointed out that this fetishization of alterity easily recapitulates an us/them disjunction which has in fact long been fissured and cut across by migration and transactions in both directions.[45] There is also a risk that it neglects the extent to which colonial studies cannot take the identities of colonists as an unproblematic reference point.

In this context a further problem arises for work that deals with colonial literature, or that works within particular discourses such as the visual and textual propaganda of the Methodists' Solomons mission. A text such as Buchan's novel, or a colonial governor's report, or a missionary film, certainly provides appropriate source material for an analysis of the way in which particular colonizing agents imagined and represented their projects, but these texts may be misleading and false if taken to represent the workings of these colonial projects. Colonial literature occludes not only the voices of the colonized, but those of many colonizers as well – because they are disreputable, because they are women or simply because they are ordinary and working-class. Published missionary texts may also disguise and censor the sense of failure or uncertainty often made explicit in private missionary writing; the colonial governor is certainly unlikely to pass on his subordinates' frustrated sense that Fijians are in the end ungovernable; if Buchan's fantasy is more obviously remote from the actualities of colonial experience, it provides us with no ground from which to seek out or understand what might be a plethora of common colonizers' representations and narratives.

The risk here is not simply that a dimension of colonialism might be neglected, but that its coherence can be radically overstated. Even a text such as Conrad's *Heart of Darkness*, famous as an expression of the collapse of colonial reason into murky tropical insanity, nevertheless preserves a point from which this degradation can be narrated and accounted for. What that novel may leave us unprepared for is the extent to which failures of colonialism could also be failures of articulation. John Buchan's coherent fiction of triumph may represent a text at one end of a continuum: at the other are barely written, badly written letters, that register a truth of failure.

Vernon Lee Walker wrote to his mother from Australia, Fiji, New Caledonia (or Kanaky) and the New Hebrides (now Vanuatu). The last of his letters overlaps with Stanley's expeditions into the Congo, although Walker was dead before the triumph of those journeys was established, before the publication of *In Darkest Africa* in 1890. It is difficult to avoid the view, however, that that book, a model of aggressive pioneering masculinity, would not have helped Walker much. While Stanley epitomized the success of imperialism at its most confident moment, Walker's world was inhabited by failed businesses, bad debts and recalcitrant and aggressive natives; in a series of brief and frustratingly uninformative letters, this obscure and inconsequential racist seems to anticipate the 'turn of the tide', the moment at which Marlowe told his story of Kurtz.

The mood of Walker's first letters is positive; they describe a trip to Fiji, his clerical work in Melbourne and then in Sydney and the apparent prosperity of his older brother Howard, who drives around in a trap, sets up a pleasant Sydney house and is about to be married. For reasons which are not clear, the marriage falls through and Howard's business collapses; Lee moves from office work to Noumea, where he is first handling stores and subsequently engaging in petty trading and labour recruiting between there and the New Hebrides. He evidently finds the settler town difficult, miserably lonely and stifling, but seems to enjoy the rough life on the boat and the confrontations with unpacified islanders. But this pleasure – if it is pleasure – cannot be reconciled with any sense of value that privileges Walker's location on the frontier, rather than a 'home' for which he has become unsuitable. This shift from the sub-imperial capitals of Australia to the extreme periphery, from a white man's town to a boat crewed by 'niggers', from prospects to wreckage, can be witnessed in the following extracts.

The natives . . . are a fine strong clan of men, but most fearfully lazy, and as they live on nothing but fish and fruit, it is as much as you can do to get them to work at all: We had some good fun with them, throwing money into the water, and letting them dive for it. If you throw a threepenny bit as far as ever you can, they will run to the place where it dropped in the water, and then dive down, and are sure to get it before it, gets to the bottom. The women and men wear no clothing but a piece of rag round their middle (sometimes not even that much) and the children nothing at all . . . It was a little queer at first having a whole crowd of niggers round you, but after a little time you don't notice them at all, and get quite used to them . . . At 'Rewa' we saw the greatest sight that was to be seen, namely a meeting of all the native chiefs and their tribes (this meeting only takes place either only once a year, or every ten years, I forget which).

> (19 January 1878, from Melbourne, describing a visit to Fiji)

I am such an awful bad correspondent, and there is no news of any interest to those at home.

> (18 December 1883, from Sydney)

Things here, have changed greatly, since I last wrote to you . . . I am very, very sorry to hear of Louie's return home . . . I am afraid that she will not have a good opinion of me, & I daresay that there are lots of little things, which I might have done, to make her stay more pleasant, but having been out of decent society for so many years, I am afraid that I must have appeared a rather uncouth brute . . . I have been for a trip round the coast, and although it was very rough work, I enjoyed myself thoroughly & only wish that I was going to start the same trip over again tomorrow, for I am miserable in Nouméa, as I have no friends & I see very little of Howard I have just a bedroom, & take my meals out, & hardly speak a word to anyone from the time I get up until I go to bed. I come home after dinner (as to-night) and write letters, or if I do not write letters, go to bed, as the offices open here, at seven o'clock in the morning, so one has to get up early . . . I have an idea that I owe Nellie a letter, however I will try to write to them next mail, but letter writing is an awful job for me, for I am an awful bad hand at it.

> (29 July 1884, from Noumea)

I ought to be ashamed of myself for not writing oftener to you, and have no excuse to offer, except that I am an awfully bad hand at letter writing . . . Our schooner is in the 'labour trade', that is, she goes down to the islands, gets canaques, they have to come of their own free will (the government have their agent on board to see that everything is done lawfully) & you have to pay their friends for them either in muskets, money, powder &ct). When the ship is full, she returns to Nouméa & their you sell them to whoever likes to buy them for domestiques &ct Some of them are engaged for 3, 4 & 5 years. The longer they are engaged for, the more money you can get for them. Some of them we got as much as £30/-/- a head for them. The buyer has to give them wages at the rate of, from 9 to 12 francs per month, but does not pay them until their engagement is finished . . . There is any amount of danger for the ship in going amongst the Islands, as every time a ship comes back we hear of ships being fired at & white men killed by the canaques, & often eaten . . . 'Willie' is in Australia now, but I am afraid that I will not be able to see him . . . Luck seems to be against me.

(3 February 1885, from Noumea)

I have just returned from a trading trip to the New Hebrides as super-cargo on board our schooner. Our last super-cargo was killed by the natives & when the schooner returned we could not find a man to fill his place, as it is a rather difficult position to fill. I told Howard that I was sure I could do it better than anyone else, & that I would go for him. He seemed to think that I was not capable, but at the last moment when he could get no-one else to go, he told me to go. I rather surprised him when I returned two weeks earlier than he thought I could do the trip in. I made a better trip than anyone who had gone down before me. I can get along with the natives better than most people & have no fear of them. You would hardly know me now, I am more than brown almost black from the sun. Clothes do not trouble one much in the Islands. Pajama trousers & singlet are full dress, always bare-footed, as I am in the water nearly all day jumping from the boat ashore. In fine weather it is not so very bad, & there is a kind of fascination in the kind of risks you run.

(3 January 1886, from Noumea)

I have been waiting, waiting, waiting to see if the time would not come, when I could write good news, but I am afraid that it will be a long time before I shall be able to do that . . . For the last eighteen months I have been living on board this small schooner, all the time in the New Hebrides coming from one Island to the other, selling trade, collecting copra &ct, & when the ship is full taking it to Nouméa & then bringing fresh trade down again. It is a very rough life but I do not dislike it, certainly you have not got much comfort on board, for instance sometimes when short of water we cannot even get a wash for perhaps a week. Dress does not trouble one much, a pair of trousers & singlet, nothing else. My arms, feet, and face, are nearly as dark as a natives, from sunburn. There is a fascination about the life. You never know one minute but you might get knocked on the head by a tomahawk, or shot at with rifle by the natives, as they are all armed. The man whose place I took in the vessel was speared by the natives and killed; I had been with him the trip before. However all the time that I have been in the Islands I have never had any trouble with the natives and have always got on well with them. Howard wants me to go home, but what is the use of my going home, after being down here for so long, I would be fit for nothing at home.

> (25 December 1886, at sea near Erromango,
> southern New Hebrides).[46]

Even Walker's early visit to Fiji is marked by a failure, though not one of the usual kind, that entails some recognizable injury, loss or collapse of personal efficacy. What is conspicuously absent from the first long letter quoted, written to an Englishwoman who has no personal familiarity with the Pacific, is any evocation or even description of scenery. Walker's lack of interest in landscape, perhaps even his sense that his mother would not be interested, marks an incompleteness in his effort to represent his experience of the Pacific, given the extent to which the appreciation of place was never simply an innocent or neutral aesthetic response, which was evoked by landforms that were somehow objectively interesting or beautiful, but part of a larger project of imaginative appropriation. As was especially clear in *Prester John*, possessive identifications could be effected at the same time as a place was found to be almost divine in its freshness and suitability as a site for new endeavours and new families. In many familiar and banal ways, the idea that the Pacific islands are delightful, lush, benign and welcoming has been reiterated through travel and tourist literature since before Walker wrote and ever since. What is striking is that, in quite a long letter describing a voyage past many islands and a trip up a river, he never takes scenery as a detached thing to be produced and accentuated.

Walker's letter can be contrasted with another account of the same trip, by a journalist he mentions in passing, which appeared over five parts in the Melbourne *Age* newspaper: 'The result of a recent trip to Fiji has been to impress me most favourably in regard to the industrial capabilities of the country, and its future commercial prosperity.' Recommending that Victorians might invest there, the writer proceeded to more optimistic claims – that Fiji could be for Australia what the West Indies had been to Europe – and came back to such questions at many points in his report. But the islands were attractive to the tourist as well as the investor or settler.

> During the greater part of the voyage you sail over placid, summer seas, sighting innumerable islands, which raise their brown and purple peaks above the sunlit waves. You see some features of nature peculiarly characteristic of that quarter of the world, and to be met with nowhere else, as, for instance, the coral reefs which form beautiful but dangerous circles round each of the islands, and the cocoa-nut palm trees which supply the natives with food and drink and almost all they need. You see the way in which the natives live, blending in their character a good deal of the barbarism out of which they are just emerging, and a little of the Christian civilization which has been placed within their reach. You see new aspects of nature, and new phases of life.[47]

Walker's letter refers rather to the hazards and displeasure of the trip – a drunken captain, reefs and storms – but what is striking about the newspaper account is not its trite fabrication of a sanitized, pleasant tour, but the article's larger coherence. It is a typically dull piece of colonial journalism, hard to distinguish from many other accounts of Fiji of the period, which were extremely repetitive on the subject of the islands' resources and prospects, but the text possesses a certain completeness and composure, which Walker's franker and fragmentary narrative lacks. The journalist positions Fiji on the periphery of an expanding frontier; people are about to know the place better, to visit in greater numbers, to expand settlement and increase production. The islands present themselves both as novel prospects and novel sights; just as the eye is excited and inspired by the scenery and the natives, energy is stimulated by the scope for investment and development. This vision is informed both by precise geographical knowledge (the total area is 'nearly equal to that of Wales') and ethnological understanding: land tenure and traditional government through chieftainship can be described. Fijians are at once objects of anthropological speculation (could their cannibal natures really be altered by Christianity?) and bizarre characters who provide amusement and spectacle.

> They were . . . not repulsive. They were rather an appropriate adjunct of the scene. How could we have believed that we were in Fiji at all, unless we had seen just such grotesque fellows as those we saw clustering on the deck, or squatting on the bows of their canoes, or swimming about in the water.[48]

Fiji, then, is not somewhere that one can simply be; one needs to be persuaded that one is in such an exotic place; and belief can be confirmed by a kind of measurement: the natives are as grotesque as one expects. Walker appears uninterested in this larger narrative that the *Age* writer imagines. Of course, he comes out with some of the standard observations: the Fijians are utterly idle, though their fastidiousness in preparing for their dances attests to their jealousy and vanity; and he, like so many others, was at least mildly titillated by the prospect of owning a cannibal's club. But just as Walker is not interested in the specific natures of Fijians – they and the Solomon Islander indentured labourers alike are simply 'niggers' – neither is he concerned with the future of Fiji, which is such a weighty issue for the ponderous report. Walker refrains from representing the island and the journey in terms of an aesthetic and inquisitive possessiveness that would accompany economic appropriation; his 'ethnological' observations are marked by a carelessness that is almost refreshing after the false and tedious precision that so characterizes much colonial anthropological and travel writing: the feast witnessed at Rewa took place 'either only once a year, or every ten years, I forget which'.

If a colonial imagining was to be rounded and coherent, it had to draw together an affective and aesthetic response to a place with a scientific delineation of its resources and some reduction of its natives to barbaric, picturesque or vanishing types. These elements envisaged particular forms of development on the part of settlers identified with a landscape, which they could legitimately appropriate because its natives were either imagined away (as in Buchan's account), or construed as incapable of asserting serious claim to the land. In fact, in Fiji this imperialist understanding far outran the capacities of settlers to profit from the little land that had been alienated, and as we have seen the administration was governed by an entirely different colonial vision. But the comprehensiveness of the journalist's account does mirror a wider breadth and power in imperial writing, and from this point of view Walker's oft-repeated statement that he is 'an awful bad hand' at letter-writing acquires greater significance. The settler letter can be understood as a text through which an imperial vision was constructed for oneself and one's addressees, just as Buchan constructed it for a national and imperial readership. If this statement appears to inflate the significance of personal correspondence, it should be recalled that at this time, when visits 'home' took place infrequently or perhaps never, the letter was the only means by which a migrant to the colonies could sustain a personal connection with society at home, and for some who saw newspapers and other texts infrequently it was one of very few links even at an impersonal level. The letter was a crucial context through which a colonist accounted for himself or herself and projected that construction of self back to those at home. It is therefore of considerable significance that even in his early letters Walker fails to position himself in a prospectively settled landscape, fails to situate himself with respect to the resources and prospects of the colony and thus fails to write himself into an expansionist future.

Not only is Walker unable to represent himself in any positive way as a colonial actor, transforming other lands or peoples, he comes to doubt his identity as a white person and a member of his own society. He has become not brown but nearly black, such that he doubts his mother would recognize him; and he is not only coarse in his manners but 'fit for nothing at home'. This self-deprecation recapitulates the environmentalist arguments of the eighteenth century, which sought to refute racial essentialism on the grounds that blacks in temperate climates would eventually acquire fair skin, as whites in the tropics would become dark and succumb to tropical lethargy. Though these issues were generally explored by natural-history writers hardly vulnerable to such transformations themselves, early twentieth-century fiction suggests that Walker's self-perception registered a broader concern.

> [T]here are men – one finds them on almost every beach in the wide South Sea – who in other days and other climes have held their heads high with the highest, but who now, because of some queer kink in their mental make-up ... have shed their white men's ways and drifted by easy stages into the dingy inertia that places them level with the beasts. They live native fashion; in many cases they have native wives. They are not black men, but neither are they white.[49]

It is impossible to speculate on the basis of Walker's letters about whether guilt over sexual relations with native women (or native men) lies between the lines. In a larger sense, however, the risk that the colonizer would not remake a colonized space but be remade himself as a native was epitomized by cross-racial sex, which expressed a contradiction in the identity of the masculine pioneer, between the sexual ramifications of conquest and the interest in preserving an untarnished and distinct white subject. This was, of course, not only a problem at a semiotic level (the liminal being impure) but a political issue, and the same one that made the 'black parson' problematic for imperialists such as Buchan; white settlers could not be imagined as a united population unless distinguished from, and ranked above, blacks or natives.

The case of Vernon Lee Walker establishes that colonialism could fail not only because its impositions were resisted by the colonized, or because one colonial project undermined another, but also because colonizers were often simply unable to imagine themselves, their situations and their prospects in the enabling, expansionist, supremacist fashion that colonial ideologies projected. The non-correspondence between idealized portrayals of colonists and their self-accounts could be attested to in a variety of ways; for example, through diaries that make it clear that individual missionaries sometimes came to see themselves as unhelpful intruders who in fact had little to offer the heathen, or through similarly disillusioned administrators' accounts. This qualifies the significance of readings such as those I have provided of the official representations from Fiji and the Methodist propaganda from the Solomons. Certainly, these texts reflect colonial imaginings and are real discourses within European experience. But they cannot be imagined in any simple way as expressions of whole colonial projects: the texts mostly obscure the messy circumstances and confusions of the encounters they related to. Still less can they be understood as expressions of what was imposed upon the colonized: often these constructions of relationships and futures are best understood as discourses that Europeans imposed upon themselves – or that missionary societies imposed upon their subscribers and patrons. Though usually indirectly related to real (and often disruptive and violent) impositions upon colonized peoples, these representations must be seen largely within the contexts of their circulation and reception, which were often within metropolitan societies rather than the colonized terrains that form their notional subject-matter. The supreme confidence often present in colonial discourse may indeed manifest epistemic megalomania, but also perhaps expresses the geographical and social distances between scenes of writing and the realities of colonial success and failure. Texts grounded more directly in the liminality of colonial confrontations frequently exhibit not authority but literary confusion and the awkward sense that the writer is marked more than superficially by a tropical climate and constituted not so much by a metropolitan origin, as by his or her diasporic location, and perhaps also by social and sexual transactions with indigenous people.[50]

While some colonial discourse certainly appears impervious to the faulty and limited realization of its projections in practice, Walker's letters stand at the other extreme on the continuum; not only did he see his own career as a failure, he was simply unable to imagine it within a larger narrative of empire. His vulnerability was not merely textual or cultural. The most poignant aspect of this unimportant racist's correspondence was his precise anticipation of his own death. He referred on several occasions to the 'fascination' that aroses from the 'risks you run'; at any time 'you might get knocked on the head by a tomahawk.' His brother wrote on Christmas Day 1887

> He left here on the 16th for the Island of Pentecost where I have a large property, after visiting this place, he went up the coast to purchase yams, & landing at Steep Cliff Bay, (or rather he did not

land at all) as soon as the boat touched the shore about 100 natives fired on him, he had a couple of shots with his Winchester & was then shot in the arm, & tomahawked at the back of the head, the whole affair did not take two minutes & I think he died without pain. The little vessel could render no assistance as they had only the one boat, but they fired about 100 shots. They were about a mile away the next day when they fell in with a Fiji vessel & went ashore in two boats, the natives had all cleared, but they recovered Lee's body, it had not a stitch of clothing on & was simply hacked to pieces . . . As you may imagine this has been a great shock to me, I have been in bad health for a long time, & it has been a great strain on my weak nerves, & I have been in bed the last two days . . . I have about 20 people here to dinner today many being asked long ago by Lee, & who of course did not know of his death, I am afraid it will not be a very merry affair, but I must do my best.[51]

6

The Primitivist and the Postcolonial

Of the forms that colonialism takes in the present, the development projects and military interventions on the part of First World states are perhaps the most conspicuous. Though development takes many forms, some of which are no doubt as constructive as others are pernicious, and though arguments about the Gulf war or Panama might be rather different to those around Vietnam, both military interventions and 'economic assistance' are manifestly linked with investments and spheres of informal political control. If global power has certainly undergone numerous displacements and destabilizations over the second half of the twentieth century, its dynamics and asymmetries remain recognizably imperialist; if this colonialism seeks to convert 'newly industrialized' or 'less developed' economies, rather than pagan souls, it nevertheless retains the intrusive character that missionary interventions always possessed, even when local people had their own reasons for adopting whatever introduced practices or discourses were at issue.

This chapter explores neither economic neo-colonialism nor the New World Order that cost so many Iraqi lives.[1] I pass over these topics partly because they have been extensively discussed by many others, but mostly because I wish to focus on forms of contemporary cultural colonialism which left-liberal culture in the West is not dissociated from, but deeply implicated in. It is easy to denounce government policies and bodies such as the IMF, but perhaps more difficult to explore constructions of the exotic and the primitive that are superficially sympathetic or progressive but in many ways resonant of traditional evocations of others. Though these, in their time, may similarly have appeared enlightened, they often now look restrictive and exploitative. One of the tasks of cultural critique can be an exposure of the tension between the apparent strategic value of these rhetorical forms and their underlying or longer-term limitations.

I have argued that colonialism's culture should not be seen as a singular enduring discourse, but rather as a series of projects that incorporate representations, narratives and practical efforts. Although competing colonizing visions at particular times often shared a good deal, as the racist discourses of one epoch superficially resembled those of others, these projects are best understood as strategic reformulations and revaluations of prior discourses, determined by their historical, political and cultural contexts, rather than by allegedly eternal properties of self–other relations, or by any other generalized discursive logic. Accordingly, contemporary primitivisms possess a good deal in common with earlier reifications and fetishizations of notionally simple ways of life, but have a distinctive character that derives from the politics of identity in the present.

The primitivist discourses I describe here cannot be straightforwardly located in particular, institutionally circumscribed colonizing projects such as that of the Australasian Methodist mission or the British administration in Fiji; rather, like the capital-I Imperialism which Rhodes, Buchan and Milner championed, contemporary primitivism is diffused through consumer culture and a variety of class and interest groups. However, the variants that I am concerned to explore are located in societies of a distinct type, that is, settler colonies. While eighteenth-century primitivism is associated mainly with French and British Enlightenment writers who were reflecting on accounts from remote America or the South Pacific, whites in Australia, New Zealand, Canada and elsewhere are now idealizing indigenous peoples in similar terms, but with reference to Australian Aborigines, Maori and native Americans.[2] The key question is whether affirmations of native spirituality and harmony with the environment (of the sort exemplified by the furniture mentioned in chapter 1) actually entail a consequential revaluation of indigenous culture (or in what contexts, and for whom?), or whether they instead merely recapitulate appropriations familiar from the history of settler colonies, in which Australians and others have defined themselves as 'natives' by using boomerang motifs and Aboriginal designs and by claiming similar attachments to land.

These issues are rendered more complicated by the range of indigenous statements in the debate. 'Primitivist' idealizations are advanced not only by whites but also by some Aborigines and some Maori, and their evident strategic value in advancing the recognition of indigenous cultures clearly precludes any categorical rejection of the whole discourse. What is at issue is not whether current representations match some check-list of what is or is not politically correct, but the play between essentialist and hybridized identities in a field of affirmations and contests.

My main reason for concluding *Colonialism's Culture* with these themes is that they loom large in public debate around the scene of its composition. However, a book about the directions and techniques of colonial cultural studies might have another reason for privileging the construction of indigenous identities in this way: because it redresses the marginalization of these issues – and these people – in the contemporary discourses of critical multiculturalism and postcolonial theory, especially as they are fashioned in the United States, which (despite all the talk of 'decentering') remains the key arena for the legitimization and the marketing of scholarship and theory. It is understandable, but regrettable, that debates about race, minority identities, representations of ethnicity and cognate questions are almost always about Afro-Americans, Hispanics and other immigrant people of colour within the United States or about histories of colonialism in other regions. In US journals that address race,[3] more reference is made to racism and colonial conflicts elsewhere – in South Africa or Britain – than to native American struggles, and there is no widely read theoretical text that speaks from the indigenous perspective in the way that the work of Gates, bell hooks, Cornel West and many others speak from Afro-American experience, or as Said's *Orientalism* and Spivak's work presents the positions of diasporic intellectuals from the Middle East and south Asia respectively.

If this is readily explicable on the grounds of the limited presence of native Americans in the academy, it is in other ways puzzling: native Americans and narratives of conquest are prominent in major popular genres such as Hollywood Westerns, but scarcely enter into the literature on colonial discourse and the 'representation of the other'. While the blindness may have been partially ameliorated by the debates around native American issues in the Quincentenary year, it remains to be seen whether contemporary issues and localized protests receive as much enduring attention as work on the conquest itself by prominent theorists such as Stephen Greenblatt. It is notable that *Marvelous Possessions* relates the violence and wonder of cross-cultural contact gesturally to Zionism, and in more detail to the paradigmatically exotic Bali, but not to the encounter that continues between the indigenous peoples and the dominant society within North America.[4] It is no doubt desirable for the fifteenth- and sixteenth-century histories to be reinterpreted, but it is a pity if an emphasis on that period paradoxically reinforces the marginalization of contemporary native Americans.[5] There thus seems scope for the marginal societies of Australia, New Zealand and Canada, in which indigenous assertions and identities are far more powerfully present, to write something back into the debates in the United States. This is simply that American societies are settler societies too, and that indigenous perspectives and histories cannot be equivalized with those of other 'others'.

Although the 'primitive' and the 'exotic' are sometimes conflated, exoticism has more to do with difference and strangeness than an antithetical relation to modernity. The Middle East, India and China were often constructed as 'feudal' or otherwise premodern, but their significance in Western representation tended to derive from emblematic customs such as the harem, caste, footbinding and so on, rather than from their archaism as such. The importance of difference – as opposed to sheer inversion – is manifest for instance in the interest in Indian architecture shown in Salt's engraving, reproduced in chapter 2 (plate 3). The potential disconnection of exoticism from evolutionary time is marked also by the fact that Japan, Korea, Singapore and Hong Kong remain exotic for Europeans and Americans, even though their modernity can hardly be in doubt. The primitive, on the other hand, is not generally significant because of some specific attributes that say Australian Aborigines possess and 'Hottentots' do not, but above all because of an originary, socially simple and natural character.

Even in eighteenth-century expressions, this simplicity can be understood in terms of a lack of the material possessions by which Europeans are corrupted or dulled, rather than enhanced.

[N]ature in her more simple modes is unable to furnish a rich European with a due portion of pleasurable sensations. He is obliged to have recourse to masses of inert matter, which he causes to be converted into a million of forms, far the greatest part solely to feed that incurable craving known by the name of vanity. All the arts are employed to amuse him, and expel the *tedium vita,* acquired by the stimulus of pleasure being used till it will stimulate no more; and all the arts are insufficient. Of this disease, which you are here so terribly afflicted, the native Americans know nothing. When war and hunting no longer require their exertions, they can rest in peace. After satisfying the more immediate wants of nature, they dance, they play; – weary of this, they bask in the sun, and sing. If enjoyment of existence be happiness, they seem to possess it; not indeed so high raised as yours sometimes, but more continued and more uninterrupted.[6]

'Primitivism', typified by this sort of contrast, is something more specific than an interest in the primitive: it attributes an exemplary status to simple or archaic ways of life, and thus frequently shares the progressivist understanding of tribal society as an original and antecedent form, but revalues its rudimentary character as something to be upheld. At this level of generality, it is the conformity of contemporary primitivism with the longer tradition that seems striking.

In *Voices of the First Day: Awakening in the Aboriginal Dreaming* (1991), Robert Lawlor argues that Aboriginal culture is everything that the West is not. In particular, he emphasizes that Aboriginal dreaming constructs the world as a unified field of psychic energy, and that in many fundamental respects this worldview has been conducive to higher forms of happiness and sociality than those 'we' are able to experience. Western civilization, associated with the 'puritanical oppression' of Christianity, colonialism, 'capitalism and its socialistic variations', scientific thinking and so on amounts to a massive detour from healthy human development; it is fortunately one that we appear now to be in a position to rectify. Although Lawlor had earlier pursued his interests in ancient civilization in south India, living among 'Dravidian people whose language and way of life had remained virtually unchanged for the last four thousand years', he was drawn away from that 'land blanketed with layers of history and burdened with overpopulation' toward 'the most ancient of all cultures'.[7]

Not content with the standard archaeological view that Aborigines have been in Australia for 40,000 or 50,000 years, or even the more speculative claim that occupation may extend back to around 150,000 years before the present, Lawlor finds mounting evidence for an Australian origin for humanity; the facts have been neglected by archaeologists predisposed to look to Africa. Aborigines are seen to have developed a kind of pre-Stone Age wood-based culture, which has persisted to the present day without evolving perhaps 'because their revelations, or Dreamtime laws, prevented them from doing so.' In many respects, for Lawlor, 'The Australian Aborigines seem to be a predecessor or prototype in that they exhibit, throughout their populations, distinctive characteristics of all the other four major races.'[8] Some points of Lawlor's argument lend themselves more readily to quotation than paraphrase.

> It is as if the Aborigines are the quintessence of the primary four-fold division of the races [White, Yellow, Black, and Red, or Caucasian, Mongoloid, Negroid, and Capoid] . . . It may seem to be a coincidence that modern astronomers have designated the four major phases in the life cycles of stars as black holes, red giants, white dwarfs, and yellow suns. However, their respective qualities are related to and consistent with other symbologies of the four colors.[9]

Aboriginal culture is thus original in a radical and absolute sense. Lawlor asserts again and again that what can be witnessed of Aboriginal life in the present expresses and recapitulates a truth that humanity has otherwise lost: a typical caption to an 1890s photograph reproduced by Lawlor reads 'The ceremonies of the Aborigines call us back to the primal origins of creation.' Many particular aspects of Aboriginal sociality thus compare favourably with Western practices because the former preserve a sense of the interconnectedness of all things. Even the domain of gender relations, generally thought to entail domination and a variety of social and ritual asymmetries across most of the continent, illustrates for Lawlor the superiority of 'early societies' that escaped 'the crackdown on fertility rites by state religions'. He finds that 'The bestowal of women in Aboriginal society supports a stable social order based on nonpossessive attitudes. It also fulfills a more positive function than the repressive pornographic forms found in our own society.'[10]

While the idea that 'our society' possesses any unitary form of sexuality is untenable (where would this place the voguing of Jenny Livingstone's film *Paris is Burning?*) the idea that non-European sexualities might be preferable to the objectifications of pornography and advertising is entirely reasonable, as is the thesis that non-industrial forms of production make the obscenity of pollution and overproduction visible. This is commonplace, of course, but may be justified if juxtaposition with other societies somehow adds rhetorical force to the denunciation of modernity; we need not only to see that Los Angeles would be nicer if there were fewer cars, but also that Aborigines got on very well without cars at all.

If this was only silly it would hardly warrant discussion. What is problematic is the extent to which this New Age primitivism reiterates the negative as well as the potentially positive features of the archaism attributed to Aborigines. Constructing them as culturally stable since the beginning of humanity does imply an ahistorical existence, an inability to change and an incapacity to survive modernity; this essentialism also entails stipulations about what is and what is not appropriately and truly Aboriginal, which marginalizes not only urban Aboriginal cultures, but any forms not closely associated with traditional bush gathering. The book's interest in contemporary Aboriginality may be judged from the fact that nearly all the photographs of people are from the Baldwin Spencer collection of outback images from the turn of the century, that are said to provide 'an authentic glimpse into the oldest known human society.'[11] The other images include exploration-period engravings and numerous drawings based on colonial images, and a range of colour photographs of dot and x-ray animal paintings (it nowhere being made explicit that these are distinctively modern styles). Other recent photographs feature the landscape, the desert, kangaroos and other wildlife; only one is of an Aboriginal person, a head-and-torso portrait of a girl, dots painted across her forehead, apparently not wearing any European clothing, and naturalized by a bird standing on her hand.

The caption reads 'Wild birds bring messages from unknown realms.'

The anthropologist Spencer's images are thus decontextualized from the history of contact between the people depicted and Europeans; despite the fact that some were clearly posed on Spencer's request, what we see reflects not a particular population, but a generic Aboriginal culture which has existed since the beginning of time. Lawlor is, of course, ignoring the archaeological evidence for various shifts in technology, art and production systems – evidence which is often frustratingly inconclusive, but which presumably reflects wider social and cultural changes and a larger dynamism. But it is hardly surprising to find this undiscussed: were the historical vigour of Aboriginal societies acknowledged, their prelapsarian status would of course be prejudiced.

Being radically anti-modern, it is not surprising that Aborigines are profoundly threatened by modernity. The worn and misleading 'fatal impact' thesis is aired again in passing allusions such as those to the destructive effects of alcohol and to an old man who is 'the last member of his tribe' still able to make stone tools. More problematically, it is asserted that the Tasmanian Aborigines (especially attractive to Lawlor because of their ecologically sound nudity and alleged inability to light fires) were in fact eliminated: 'by 1850, the extermination of this primeval people had swept from the earth the last rituals of human innocence.'[12] This kind of statement is of course offensive to modern indigenous Tasmanians (though no doubt from Lawlor's point of view they are half-castes and hence not 'real' Aborigines).

Aboriginality can thus be cherished only in so far as it is a stable form that can be made to correspond with New Age metaphysics; Aboriginal history contributes to the picture only by showing that the relation of white Western culture to Aboriginal life was purely destructive. In so far as histories might establish that Aborigines resisted colonization, or accommodated themselves to it, or appropriated Christianity, Western art styles and other objects, discourses and institutions to serve Aboriginal needs and ends, they are irrelevant, and are occluded. This celebration of Aboriginality is thus limited to the traditional, and presents contemporary Aboriginal life through works of art that can be construed as traditional by a primarily American readership unfamiliar with the postwar history of Aboriginal painting. Though alluding to the oppressed and damaged character of Aboriginal society, the book has no space for Aboriginal political movements, not even for the Land Rights struggle which in fact establishes the enduring importance of attachments to country. Is it possible to avoid concluding that this evocation is little more than a rip-off, that the 'Aboriginal Dreamtime' here is like the woman in the glossy pornographic photograph, construed 'appreciatively' in terms specified by the image-maker?

Kevin Costner's *Dances with Wolves* was more than just another movie. It was widely applauded; its sympathetic treatment of American Indians was regarded as unprecedented;[13] it took a lion's share of the 1991 Oscars; and despite being long and very predictable, it was rereleased in a director's cut with an additional 40 minutes of footage in late 1991.[14] In production, the film was in fact progressive to the extent that native American actors, rather than white stars, took the Indian parts. Beyond this, and the realist device of presenting subtitled speech in the native languages, the film is strikingly unoriginal in its reiteration of primitivist tropes and the stereotypic understanding of colonial histories that I evoked in chapter 1.

As several commentators have pointed out, *Dances*, like a number of earlier 'liberal' Westerns, merely inverts the Manichean oppositions associated with the more conventional triumph of 'how the West was won'.[15] The frontier whites are degenerate and evil; the Indians are noble and courageous, and live in harmony with the land and with one another. What is remarkable is not the reappearance of these terms in a Hollywood film, or the New Age re-emphasis on indigenous spirituality, but the way in which the master-caption of Costner's voice-over reduces the complexities and ambiguities of characters to categorical truths. In fact, there is some tension within the Lakota Sioux community which the alienated Lieutenant Dunbar joins, between Indians favouring hostile and more accommodating responses to whites, and though this energizes much of the film's implicit emotional dynamism, the voice-over resists the implication that the native community is divided by any inequity or conflict: 'It seems every day ends with a miracle here . . . I've never known a people so eager to laugh, so devoted to family, and so dedicated to each other, and the only word that came to mind was harmony.'

This reinforces the sense noted earlier in which primitivism, unlike exoticism, is concerned less with difference than sheer inversion and juxtaposition: the specificity of Indian cultures (marked by the canonical teepees and feather headdresses) serves no narrative function, but merely authenticates a portrait of a type of society opposed to our own, which possesses virtues that are plainly absent from a rapacious and expanding white modernity. This primitivism is therefore distinct from the anthropological tradition dedicated to the itemization of cultural difference, which informed a colonial governmentality that operated in Fiji and elsewhere upon the various native societies or cultures that it defined. While neutralizing those differences through idealization, primitivism however shares with that anthropological project a legislation of authenticity: others are acceptable in so far as they conform to their proper natures, but are degenerate and improper in 'acculturated' or hybridized forms. *Dances* refrains from presenting the inauthentic Indian, but accords with familiar primitivist logic in displacing the negative attributes of savagery onto another tribal population, in this case the Pawnee, whose characterization as lawless barbarians has been overlooked by those who celebrate the film. Hence, as with the Cook voyage responses to Pacific islanders, discussed in chapter 3, it is not the case that a romantic noble savage discourse has been opposed to another set of representations that denigrated ignoble savages; rather a unitary discourse could deploy both figures in different contexts or for different narrative purposes. The ambiguity that Marianna Torgovnick noted in very different Western reflections on the primitive is again manifest: while overtly aiming to displace ideas of savagery and white superiority, liberal texts air and deploy the very notions that they notionally question, and in the end perhaps do more to reaffirm than subvert them.[16]

Dances naturalizes the Sioux by revealing them within a remarkable, brilliantly photographed landscape. The 'big screen' is as crucial here as it is in David Lean's *Lawrence of Arabia*, creating an image of heroic proportions, a cinematic equivalent to the history painting that, despite the film's unoriginality, is not remotely to

be seen as a succession of generic allusions or postmodern ironies, but a fatal-impact narrative saturated with human meaning,
morality and tragedy.

The lamentation of the fatal impact is perhaps the film's
profoundest subterfuge. The idealization of the Sioux entails
their incompatability with colonial society and makes their elimination inevitable. Dunbar explains near the beginning that he
wants 'to see the frontier . . . before it's gone', and though the
viewer is spared any horrific massacre, the closing text frames,
over the smouldering fires of an abandoned camp, record that
'Thirteen years later, their homes destroyed, their buffalo gone,
the last band of free Sioux submitted to white authority at Port
Robinson, Nebraska. The great horse culture of the Plains was
gone and the American frontier was soon to pass into history.'
This conclusion thus affirms what Dunbar's initial statement an-
ticipates, and privileges the indigenized Dunbar as a resourceful
backwoodsman, striding off into the snow with his wife and child,
in a principled action aimed to draw the military's attention away
from the tribe that has hosted him. The evocation of the natives
Americans has a conditional quality: not 'here they are', but 'here
is their passing'. As in E. S. Curtis's classic images of noble Indians
vanishing into the mists, the landscape or their own melancholy,
so also in Lindt's studio portrait, Raffles's print of the Papuan
slave staring toward his homeland and many settler-colonial representations of 'The last of the . . .', this fading to absence is
determined by the presence of another figure, a white protagonist
who is in some cases a settler, in others a writer able to record the
truth of an extinguished culture.[17]

While *Dances* denigrates actual settlers and is not centrally preoccupied with ethnographic authority, it does ennoble the figure
that Lieutenant Dunbar exemplifies. In its allegory of accomplishment and identity, the film may possess a singularity which its
conformity with a long and diversified primitivist lineage would
leave us unprepared for. In other words, and in terms of the
argument I have advanced earlier in this book, the film is not
merely another specimen of an enduring colonialist discourse,
but a distinctive project that resonates with wider peculiarities of
the present.

One of the more powerful sections of the film is the opening
display of the sheer insanity of the Civil War, which is followed by

the corruption and cowardice of frontier officers Dunbar encounters on his way into Sioux country. Just as the Vietnam experience
has been revealed cinematically as a debased madness from which
nationalist truths of emancipation and military honour had been
evacuated, both the Union's war and the civilizing mission in the
West are exposed as struggles devoid of principled motive and
expression, as corruptions from which Dunbar can only be alienated. Though initially deeply disorientated and confused, he is
therefore not so much an agent of conquest, as a traveller; unlike
Crawfurd in *Prester John*, he goes not to bring a people within the
ambit of colonial order and power, but to prejudice his own
customary truths, to transgress and experiment. With help from
firearms appropriated from the military outpost he has abandoned, Dunbar aids his community in fighting off Pawnee raiders;
as the chaos of the conflict subsides around him, Dunbar's voice-
over tells us:

> It was hard to know how to feel. I'd never been in a fight like this
> one . . . there was no dark political objective . . . It had been fought
> to preserve the foodstores that would see us through the
> winter . . . I gradually began to look at it in a new way. I felt a pride
> I'd never felt before. I'd never really known who John Dunbar was.
> Perhaps the name itself had no meaning. As I heard my Sioux
> name being called over and over, I knew for the first time who I
> really was.

Dunbar's nominal indigenization is also a moment of conquest
in two senses. Not only does he help defeat the Pawnee, but he
establishes himself as a champion among the Sioux, who recognize the power of the weapons he has introduced and make him
the hero of the moment, calling his name over and over. This
interpellation does not identify Dunbar as a Sioux, and this is not
what his self-discovery consists in. Instead, his prior self-recogni-
tion as a soldier in battles possessing 'dark' political significance is
transmuted into his recognition by the Sioux as a heroic warrior;
he never becomes a common member of their community, but
retains the privilege of the colonizer to act forcefully and with
historical effect, yet his individual heroism is stripped of its associations with conquest and authenticated by the Sioux. This is, in
fact, the only narrative work that the Indians can accomplish;
everything else in the story is done to them or for them.

The simultaneity of Dunbar's self-assertion and partial in-digenization is allegorized by his 'dancing with wolves', his mystical association with an intractably wild creature that he paradoxically succeeds in partially domesticating and feeding, that becomes a kind of mascot and guardian spirit, occasionally visible and audible even after it is callously shot by the soldiers attempting to police Dunbar's dereliction of duty and reabsorb him to their side of the frontier. Costner/Dunbar, dissociated from the flaws of modernity and white society, as an indigenized white man, is a profoundly different figure to the acculturated Indian; while the latter can only acquire the corruption of white society and the half-caste morality typified by Henriques in *Prester John*, the white traveller retains the authority of presence that the passing Indian perforce lacks, while substituting integrity and an identification with the land for the discredited expansionist narratives of conquest and environmental destruction. What *Dances with Wolves* re-dresses is not history but a dominant masculine identity, and it does this not by narrating the other side of the story, but through the appropriation of Indian garb that lacks the stains of discarded uniforms.

At any time a plethora of narratives of national identity are no doubt circulating in a conflicted field. It would be unwise to claim any emblematic status for *Dances with Wolves*, but the film may typify a liberal response to the declining appeal of modernization, patriotism and civic conservatism. With the rise and institutionalization of multiculturalism, 'identity' is associated increasingly with cultural difference and minority status, which is unavailable to the dominant culture, or at least to men. Liberal men, who cannot take the option of overtly denigrating minority identities and reaffirming the value of imperialism, environmentally destructive modernization and so on, are therefore prompted to reconstruct their own identities on the model of a minority. This curious, recursive reformulation, or moment of 'symbolic obviation' in Roy Wagner's terms, seems to lie behind such projects as the New Age redefinition of male sexuality, the 'Men's Movement' presided over by primitivist intellectuals like Robert Bly and the refashioned American individual of *Dances with Wolves*. Kevin Costner, dissociated from the Vietnam-Civil War, having discovered the Sioux in himself, and sanctimoniously lamented their departure from a land that now constitutes a vacant space for his own achievements, can re-emerge as a crusader for honesty and freedom in Oliver Stone's *JFK.*

This marks another sense in which 'the primitive' is profoundly different from 'the exotic'. The force of the primitive in Costner's appropriation, and in similar operations in Canadian, Australian and New Zealand culture, derives precisely from the fact that the native is not foreign but indigenous: self-fashioning via the Sioux or the Aborigines does not exoticize oneself, but makes one more American or more Australian. (This is precisely what Paul Hogan, the folkloricized Australian hero, does in *Crocodile Dundee*, as is manifested particularly by his participation in a corroboree.) In this mode, primitivism has something in common with the long tradition of white settler appropriations of indigenous names and motifs – the use of the boomerang as an Australian emblem, for example – but augments these by defining ethos and being, rather than merely the icons of identity, through indigenous models. If the legitimacy of traditional narratives of nationhood is destabilized to the point that the epoch can be characterized as 'posthistorical', primitivism can now serve not only the general-ized New Age interest in spirituality and new masculinity, but also a specifically national truth.

It is difficult to tell this tale without recapitulating the vanishing trick that *Dances with Wolves* itself performs upon native Ameri-cans. The cultural dynamic seems to establish the permanence of colonial asymmetry, the fact that dominant white cultures seem to abandon one form of exploitation only to proceed to another: having stolen Aboriginal land, Australians are now stealing the Dreamtime. Depressingly plausible as it is, this pessimism might leave us unprepared for the distinct dynamics of these transac-tions, and the potentially empowering aspect of even their 'New Age' manifestations. The example of Aotearoa New Zealand rein-forces the argument that there is a new appropriative dynamic of nationalized indigenous identity, but would undermine the view that this is no more that a further tactic of white dominance.

New Zealand, like Australia, is a 'postcolonial' society in the sense that it is no longer formally a British colony. It is also conspicuous that Maori culture now possesses a degree of prestige and legitimacy unprecedented in the period of colonization: even over a period of right-wing backlash and National (conservative)

Party government, the notion that New Zealand should be a 'bicultural' society is gaining acceptance. But in what form is Maori culture recognized and celebrated?

One telling expression is the projection of Maori identity in major exhibitions of *taonga* (valuables or treasures); the success of the *Te Maori* exhibition in New York in 1984 was regarded as a major boost for the Maori 'cultural renaissance' of the last decade, and a subsequent, related exhibition, *Taonga Maori*, more recently toured Australia and formed a long-term display in the National Museum in Wellington. What is striking about this collection of fine carvings, weaving, featherwork and nephrite is a radical aesthetic decontextualization that excludes non-traditional contexts of production, colonial processes and European influences of all kinds. Despite the fact that most of the material was nineteenth century, and was therefore made and collected during a period of intensive contact and rapid change, it was unambiguously associated through display captions and in the catalogue with a stable, authentic and radically different social universe that is characterized particularly by its holism, archaism and spirituality.

> Being a Maori, therefore, is knowing who we are and where we come from. It is about our past, present and future. Our kinship ties and descent expressed through our *whakapapa* (genealogy) are what binds us to our past and to our ancestors, and where our *mana* (power), *ihi* (prestige), *wehi* (fear) and *tapu* (sacredness) come from. This is our identity; without it we have no foundation, no refuge. It is expressed in the following words:
> *He mana Maori motuhake*
> *He mana tuku iho ki a tatou.*
> (Maori spirituality set apart
> A spirituality that has been handed down to us).
> The answer to the question 'Who are the Maori people?' is about the separation of . . . the two primal parents of the Maori . . . It is about the many tribal traditions, myths, and stories which provide a solid foundation for our lives . . . it is about love and respect for our culture, our fellow man, and our environment.[18]

On the face of it, this evocation has a good deal in common with the discourse of *Voices of the First Day*. A number of objections to its content might be rehearsed, but it is important then to consider what the effect of *Taonga Maori* has been in its context.

Certainly, the catalogue's larger description of Maori culture cannot be seen as an unproblematic self-presentation on the part of Maori: the section on kinship, for example, is highly reminiscent of anthropological systematizations, such as those of Sir Raymond Firth, that happen to be consistent with the projection of a cohesive kin-structured world because they emphasize the nesting together of descent lines, clans, and tribes. Similarly, though it should not be denied that categories such as *mana* and *tapu* were important notions in precolonial Maori culture, the descriptions in the catalogue do owe something to the traditional colonialist and anthropological representations, and on the whole they lean toward a construction of Maoriness as mystical and spiritual: 'The Maori psyche revolves around tribal roots, origins, and identity.'[19] George French Angas, in *New Zealanders Illustrated* (1847), in his captions to depictions of a variety of artefacts, carvings, weapons and the like often alluded to the 'sacred' character of particular objects but associated this with irrational and constrained superstition: some *tiki* represented 'the supposed *taniwa* or river god'; 'so strict is the law of *tapu* that no one dare touch these valuable relics.'[20] The *Taonga Maori* catalogue reproduces this emphasis on the mystical associations of the objects, supplanting a rationalist progressivism with white society's craving for non-industrial authenticity.

The critique that might be put forward is not that this projection of identity is merely a derivative discourse, but that it partakes of a cultural essentialism that construes Maoriness primarily in terms of its difference from pakeha (white New Zealander) identity, and thus reduces it to terms that complement white society's absences: against the alienations of modernity are 'intimate connections' that constitute 'roots, origins, and identity'. In the discussion of the *marae*, the meeting ground that was and is the site of various formal celebrations, that is generally central to tribal affairs, it is stated that the *marae* 'is intimately connected with the ceremonial experiences in life crises such as birth, death, and marriage. To return to the *marae* from the brashness of urban life is to return to a simpler time, to a place of enduring human values.'[21] What is oddly elided here is one of the most significant developments of the Maori renaissance, namely the great expansion of urban *marae* to serve the interests of Maori now remote from rural tribal homelands.

The Maoriness evoked here, like some representations of Aboriginality, is available to white settlers seeking to establish national identities that are not merely impoverished versions of Britishness or limited to the pioneer experience to which relatively few can directly relate.[22] The *Taonga Maori* show was part of a surge of interest that received particular impetus in the mid-1980s from the earlier *Te Maori* exhibition and the success of Keri Hulme's Booker-Prizewinning novel, *The Bone People*. The exhibitions might be criticized through similar arguments to those I adduced against Lawlor's *Voices of the First Day*: the construction of authentic spirituality marginalizes most Maori who, though not part of a homogeneous pakeha society, must negotiate identities in urban contexts, with non-traditional social relations, institutions, jobs and so on. In relation to folkloricized identities such as that paraded in the *Taonga Maori* exhibition, they stand as poor copies of a correct ethnic authenticity that is at once inaccessible to many urban Maori and inappropriate in so far as it is associated strongly with the past, rather than with the contemporary circumstances within which they, like everyone else, have to operate. In the specific domain of art, this excludes or marginalizes innovations, non-traditional media and any forms of modernist style: the few contemporary pieces that figured in the *Taonga Maori* exhibition were either modern examples of wholly traditional forms, such as weavings and carvings, or other works that manifested the persistence of traditional patterns and designs.[23] The extensive body of modernist and postmodernist Maori art was excluded.

In the Maori case, however, this kind of critique would neglect the extent to which characterizations of Maori tradition, spirituality and mythology have played a crucial empowering role in a wider struggle that has not been limited to the legitimization of traditional culture. This struggle has involved many campaigns against the desecration of tribal lands, against development or for compensation, and for better services and funding for Maori development and education programmes, such as Kohanga Reo, which aims to reverse the long-term decline in Maori language use through teaching programmes directed especially at primary school children.[24] These efforts have ranged from occupations of land and direct action against anti-Maori racists to lobbying and bureaucratic reforms. In many cases the issues and objectives are not directly linked with tribes or with Maori culture and language, but nevertheless draw inspiration and legitimacy from the same range of symbols and traditions that seem to be reprimitivized in exhibitions such as *Taonga Maori*. In Alan Duff's remarkable novel *Once were Warriors*, an urban Maori population devastated by alcohol and violence is shown to redeem itself through the organization of pragmatic local projects that are not themselves essentially or peculiarly indigenous, but that derive their coherence from a sense of continuity with Maori ways, and are inspired by the dignity and power of the elders' oratory.[25]

The issue here resonates with one raised earlier, in chapter 1. I referred to James Clifford's criticisms of Edward Said, whose rejection of the Orientalist postulate of radical difference between East and West was seen to rest sometimes upon the evocation of a 'real' Orient and common humanity. Clifford suggests that Said's work 'frequently relapses into the essentializing modes it attacks' and proposes that Said's hybridized position as an Arab-American intellectual typifies the question that needs now to be explored: 'What processes rather than essences are involved in present experiences of cultural identity?'[26] For his part, Said has more recently attacked nativism on much the same grounds that I have criticized primitivism: it reinforces the imperialist notion that there is a clear-cut and absolute difference between ruler and ruled by merely 'revaluating the weaker or subservient partner'. He claims that such manifestations of nativism as Leopold Senghor's negritude, Wole Soyinka's explorations of the African past and Rastafarianism lead to 'compelling but often demagogic assertions about a native past, history, or actuality that seems to stand free not only of the colonizer but of worldly time itself'. He accuses this 'abandonment of history' of degenerating into millenarianism, craziness and 'an unthinking acceptance of stereotypes'.[27]

What both these critiques pass over is the extent to which humanism and essentialism have different meanings and effects in different contexts. Clifford writes as though the problem were merely intellectual: difference and hybridity are more appropriate analytically to the contemporary scene of global cultural transposition than claims about human sameness or bounded types. I would agree, but this does not bear upon the uses that essentialist discourses may have for people whose projects involve mobilization rather than analysis. Said might be able to argue that nativism as a political programme or government ideology has been largely pernicious, but nativist consciousness cannot be deemed undesirable merely because it is ahistorical and uncritically reproduces colonialist stereotypes. The main problem is not that this imposes academic (and arguably ethnocentric) standards on non-academic and non-Western representations, but that it paradoxically essentializes nativism by taking its politics to be historically uniform. On the contrary, I suggest that representations of identity such as the *Taonga Maori* exhibition, which certainly inverts colonialist stereotypes and reproduces the idea of essential difference, have different meanings at different times, and for different audiences. My initial response to the show arose from an aesthetic similar to Clifford's: I was disturbed by its fetishization of an unacculturated authenticity. However, the exhibition, and more particularly the broader reputation of its predecessor *Te Maori*, was clearly enabling and empowering for many Maori. Just as Aboriginal art and the Dreamtime mythology helped promote the legitimacy of Aboriginal culture at a time when it was not widely respected by the dominant population, this essentialism played a progressive role by capitalizing on white society's primitivism and creating a degree of prestige and power for Maori that did not exist before the 1980s.

Discourses of this kind must thus be understood as ambiguous and historically mutable instruments, as projects that possess one value at one time and another subsequently. In the 1970s and 1980s the gains produced by nativism were probably more significant than the drawbacks arising from the recapitulation of a restrictive primitivism; complemented by other political movements and discourses concerned more directly with contemporary indigenous lives and needs, essentialist constructions of native identity are likely to continue to play a part in gaining ground for indigenous causes among conservative populations, whose ideas of authenticity are generally still defined by the 'anthropological' tradition traced in chapter 3: particular peoples are the bearers of distinct characters or cultures, and hybridized natives (unless models of perfect assimilation) are seen as degenerate and untrue to their natures. Nativism may remain even more important for native Americans in the United States, who remain considerably more marginal than Australian Aborigines, Maori and native Americans within Canada. Nativist-primitivist idealizations can only be politically productive, however, if they are complemented by here-and-now concerns, and articulated with histories that do not merely recapitulate the 'imperialist nostalgia' of the fatal-impact narrative. Thus, for all its elisions, *Taonga Maori* can be empowering, while the positive effects of *Dances with Wolves* seem limited to the point of being negligible.

Like James Clifford, Paul Gilroy is attracted to a pluralist view of identity – specifically in the context of black diasporic cultural creativity – but points out that both essentialist and pluralist identities have limitations. The latter, which emphasizes divisions internal to ethnicities based on 'class, sexuality, gender, age and political consciousness', tends towards an 'uneasy but exhilarating' libertarianism. The emphasis on the constructed and shifting character of race 'has been insufficiently alive', Gilroy suggests, 'to the lingering power of specifically 'racial' forms of power and subordination.'[28] While this is a comment specifically on the British scene, it perhaps has the broader correlate that a preoccupation with divisions and hybridity may often be more compatible with individual artistic creativity than the forms of collective representation and mobilization that remain crucial in many political domains.

These difficulties however seem less significant in the present than those arising from the opposed position. An 'over-integrated sense of cultural and ethnic particularity' has led in Gilroy's view to 'a volkish political outlook', particularly among artists and middle-class blacks claiming to speak for communities while mystifying the differences within them.[29] Again, the specific observations resonate with problems which arise elsewhere: like most other codifications, such as the colonial administration's representation of Fijian sociality, constructions of indigenous identities almost inevitably privilege particular fractions of the indigenous population who correspond best with whatever is idealized: the chiefly elites of certain regions, bush Aborigines rather than those living in cities, even those who appear to live on ancestral lands as opposed to groups who migrated during or before the colonial period. Such asymmetries are transposed in various ways from colonial discourses to nativist assertions, frequently through being opportunistically refashioned by the privileged codifiers of nativist identity. These constructions notably often rigidify gender and age relationships that were formerly more fluid; in Aotearoa New Zealand, for example, despite the evidence concerning nine-teenth-century practice, it has become traditionalist dogma that women were not permitted to speak at *marae*. This 'fact' of Maori culture has been significant not only for contemporary practice on those meeting grounds but has been drawn into other do-mains: conservative Maori clerics, for instance, have used it to oppose the ordination of women. Similarly, while elders gain prestige from the nativist representation of Maori culture, others find the association with archaism problematic and constricting: 'Being Maori doesn't come from my heart. I think that in Maoritanga everything is going backwards instead of going for-wards. I just want to go forward.'[30]

I have suggested that modern colonial discourses have repre-sented native peoples in a number of ways: as heathens but poten-tial Christians, as savages to be wished away, as primitives defined through the negation of modernity and as distinct 'races' or 'cultures' possessing particular natures. While the evangelists pur-veying the first of these constructions were often racist or at least paternalistic and ethnocentric in their attitudes, it is significant that the basic model was anti-essentialist: the mutability of people, not a fixity in their character, was pivotal to its narrative of conver-sion and improvement. It is, of course, this anti-essentialism which makes it possible for Christianity to be appropriated by anti-racist movements, such as the struggle against apartheid. Both primitiv-ism and anthropological typification, in contrast, are deeply es-sentialist, and the projects that Gilroy refers to, that affirm identities in non-nativist, pluralistic terms, are at the same time struggles against the fixed types projected by colonial cultures.

Just as colonial culture needs to be understood, not as an essence, but as a plurality of projects including, most recently, the primitivist renovation of white identity via indigenous culture, anti- and postcolonial culture cannot be taken as a unitary set of meanings or a stable position. The ways of subverting limiting constructions of Maoriness and Aboriginality are thus as diverse as the practices, media and genres through which such subversions are effected. While colonialist preoccupations with fixed bounda-

ries and authentic types were once undone by millennial movements which appropriated European symbols, books, banknotes
and rituals, hybridized performances that assert above all the
positions and presence of indigenous actors can be expressed
through graffiti, tattoos and reggae music, or novels, theatre,
photography and painting.

One such performance is *Bran Nue Dae*, a remarkable, very
funny and very sexy musical written by Jimmy Chi of the Aboriginal community of Broome, in the far northwest of Western Australia, and performed mostly by actors from that community.[31] In
a range of parodic and amusing but sometimes also haunting
songs, the story works through mission station experiences, presided over by terrifyingly orderly German Lutherans, and presents
a series of people coming back together in their country. Tadpole
has been in and out of gaol – 'I bin drovin' I bin drinkin' I bin
christian I bin everything and now it's time I gotta go home see
old people'; young Willie has been brought up on the mission and
knows little of bush life. They meet up with an urban dropout,
Marijuana Annie, and her German hippy boyfriend Slippery, both
of whom discover that they are in fact part-Aborigines who had
been fostered into white society during the notorious period of
assimilation in the 1950s and 1960s. Slippery, it turns out, is son of
the German missionary: 'Ich bin Ine Aborigine!!' he proclaims,
mimicking to ambiguous effect Kennedy's famous assertion in
Berlin. The Broome community is an unusually hybrid one, reflecting various phases of Asian immigration associated with
fishing and pearling, as well as white settlement, but *Bran Nue Dae*
presents histories and predicaments that have counterparts across
Australia. In particular it defines Aboriginality through the experience of assimilation and its rejection, as something that can be
recovered through self-identification, rather than a quantity that
'authentic' Aborigines possess more of than others. The musical
evoked not stable cultural differences but experiential predicaments, some of which (to do with drugs and drink) are rendered
through the character of Marijuana Annie to belong to urban
youth rather than one 'race' or the other. Through its north
Australian kriol (Aboriginal English), the performance had an
unmistakable cultural location, but appealed to commonalities
and shared aspirations rather than differences. As Tadpole says,
'He's a Christian, I'm a Christian, she's a Christian, We all bloody

Christian'; and as the chorus concludes 'On the way to a Bran Nue Dae, everybody, everybody say.' The sheer zest of *Bran Nue Dae* is difficult to convey in a text of this kind (suffice it to say that rather than merely advocating safe sex in one song, the chorus facilitated it by distributing condoms to the audience). Against the humourlessness of colonialist and nativist codifications of identity alike, Chi's work conveys truths of biography and identity that stabilized cultures cannot.

I return briefly to the three terms of my subtitle. Travel appears a less ambiguous instrument than Said's evocation of the highest form of academic freedom might lead us to expect; it is too often the appropriative project effected by Dunbar, that re-empowers a dominant subject even if it destabilizes his customary truths. Despite Said's reference to 'a realistic sense of the terrain', the image evokes movement that is inspired by curiosity rather than constrained by structures of power. Said's own writing suggests instead that travel needs to be written about more than it should be performed, and that writing within and against colonial texts can only proceeds more anxiously and reactively than images of transgression and discovery suggest.

I have suggested that what might loosely be called an 'anthropological' perspective on colonialism and colonial representation is more adequate than theories that approach these as global, unhistorical terms. All this really means is that colonialism is examined through localized, practically mediated expressions, through projects constituted through discursive agency rather than by either individual historical actors or dehistoricized discourses. This need not be called an 'anthropological' approach; what is appealing about doing so is the paradox that is generated, since anthropology – like travel, collecting, ethnography and curiosity – is more conspicuously part of the problem than part of a solution. An 'anthropology of colonialism' cannot situate 'the colonial' as an external object of study; this lack of comfortable distance from the power structures and the discourses being analysed seems appropriate, given the continuing energy of various colonial forms, such as those of settler primitivism exhibited in *Dances with Wolves*. Government, manifest in cultural domains through the operations of anthropological typification, seems likely to long outlast more literal kinds of colonial rule, but has

Plate 11   *Tracey Moffatt, 'Some Lads II', 1986*

always been irrelevant or ineffective for some, such as Vernon Lee Walker, and does not now proceed uncontested.

Tracey Moffatt's sequence *Some Lads* could be seen as a response, not only to the studio portraits that she alludes to, and that my frontispiece to this book exemplifies, but also to much of the other colonial representation discussed here. Andrew's image of Fijian cannibalism, the British appreciations of Indian architecture and Buchan's legislation of the authentic savage are of course not literally studio products, but they are all constructions in which others are reified in surroundings that specify their attributes and our appropriate responses to them. If a studio can be defined theoretically as a frame for representation that permits a photographer or narrator to surround decontextualized bodies with meanings of his choice, the studio portrait is, in this loose and extended sense, the paradigmatic form of colonial representation. What I have argued, for post-Enlightenment discourses, is that essentialized typifications acquired increasing salience, even though the nature of essentialism – national, racial or cultural – and the attendant content of typifications, shifted over time. Anthropological evocations of other cultures have partaken of this studio logic by constructing cultures that were abstracted from the dynamics of interactions between colonizers and colonized, which were thus rendered singular and authentic, and which were construed in terms of Western absences and the viewers' interests; picturesque Bali may amount to an unusually clear expression of this tendency, but in form it is not unique or even particularly atypical. It would, of course, be illogical to expect a Western photographer or narrator to construct another culture in terms that had no relation to some sort of Western agenda; if meanings enter into circulation in a particular cultural domain, they must have some salience within that domain that can hardly be true to their origins or to a radically autonomous set of values. Postcoloniality cannot privilege a chimera of some radical alterity that can be represented by 'Westerners' or by others in 'Western' contexts, but that magically eludes some 'Western' inflection.

Postcoloniality, however, is not an inaccessible condition, but rather one that can be worked through by replacing identities in the experiences constitutive of contemporary indigenous life; put more theoretically, this fractures authenticities and reconstitutes events and encounters and biographies through an anti-essentialist, anti-teleological history that Prakash has called postfoundationalist.[32] *Bran nue dae's* narration of Aboriginality and mockery of assimilationism lyricizes pluralized identities that emerge through historical dislocations rather than from a stable ethnicity. Critique can also become postcolonial by turning its attention to the logic of representation, to the business of establishing studios: typifications can only be undone if their historical contingency and mutability are exposed. The 'Arab' or the 'Javan' is not naturally this or that; such types are not natural entities, but constructions that travellers, governors and anthropologists have struggled to articulate and specify, particularly over the last 300 years. This is not to say that Middle Eastern or southeast Asian peoples do not have their own ethnic representations that are no more or less real than those of colonizers' imaginings. Indeed, the Maori exhibition and similar presentations of other native peoples suggest that indigenous groups sometimes put themselves in studios, in a fashion which may – or may not – subvert the colonialist discourse that is imitated.

I have rejected the idea that we can complacently situate ourselves in a postcolonial epoch. To do that, we would need to have transcended the cultural forms and procedures associated with colonial dominance, and this is something that liberal films like *Dances with Wolves*, that exhibitions such as *Taonga Maori*, have not done. But this is not to say that contemporary cultures and cultural projects are locked within an impervious discourse, that lacks internal contradiction or redundancy. Colonial cultural studies can draw attention to these fissures and failures most effectively by evading total objects such as 'colonial discourse' that obscure the multiplicity of colonizing projects and the plurality of potential subversions of them. If the time and consciousness of whole societies cannot be characterized as postcolonial, then particular critiques, images and narratives can be. Moffatt's *Some Lads* mocks and transforms the studio portrait; in this book I have tried to undo the naturalized characterization that such portraits exemplified. These efforts are postcolonial because they disfigure the workings of colonialism's culture; but postcoloniality necessarily follows, and is highly engaged with colonialism. If we had transcended colonial images and narratives more comprehensively, perhaps we would not need to discuss them at all – but there is no emptiness at present in which such a confident silence can be heard.

Notes

INTRODUCTION

1 Ian Watt, *The Rise of the Novel* (London: Chatto & Windus, 1957), p. 65.

2 Edward W. Said, 'Identity, authority, and freedom: the potentate and the traveler', *Transition* 54 (1991), p. 18.

3 Johannes Fabian, *Time and the Work of Anthropology* (Chur: Harwood Academic Publishers, 1991).

CHAPTER 1

1 Ann Laura Stoler, 'Rethinking colonial categories: European communities and the boundaries of rule', *Comparative Studies in Society and History* 31 (1989), 135–6.

2 Cf. Michael Taussig, *Shamanism, Colonialism, and the Wild Man: a Study in Terror and Healing* (Chicago: University of Chicago Press, 1987), esp. pp. 128–35.

3 Stoler, 'Rethinking colonial categories', p. 137.

4 Some writers, such as Todorov, see racism as 'a type of behaviour which consists in the display of contempt or aggressiveness toward other people on account of physical differences' ('"Race", writing, and culture', in *'Race', Writing, and Difference*, ed. Henry Louis Gates, Jr. (Chicago: University of Chicago Press, 1985) p. 370). I find this far too general and advocate in chapter 3 an understanding that privileges the conceptual dimension of racism – that is, the notion that 'races' constitute definite, natural entities which can be associated with temperamental propensities as well as physical attributes. The superiority of one 'race' over another is obviously a key element

of the discriminatory ideology, but is not what makes it historically and culturally distinctive. Todorov's definition – which approximates woolly liberal notions of 'prejudice' – is also criticized by Henry Louis Gates Jr. on the grounds that 'Afro-American history is full of examples of "racist" benevolence, paternalism, and sexual attraction which are not always, or only, dependent upon contempt or aggression' ('Talkin' that talk', in *'Race', Writing, and Difference*, p. 403).

5 Johannes Fabian, 'Religious and secular colonization: common ground', *History and Anthropology* 4 (1990), p. 339; reprinted in Fabian, *Time and the Work of Anthropology: Critical Essays 1971–1991* (Chur: Harwood Academic Publishers, 1991).

6 See Renato Rosaldo, 'Imperialist nostalgia' *Representations* 26 (1989), 107–22.

7 This is a theme of my book *Entangled Objects: Exchange, Material Culture, and Colonialism in the Pacific* (Cambridge, Mass.: Harvard University Press, 1991). On indigenous adoptions of Christianity in particular, see Geoffrey M. White, *Identity through History: Living Stories in a Solomon Islands Society* (Cambridge: Cambridge University Press, 1991), and Jean and John Comaroff, *Of Revelation and Revolution: Christianity, Colonialism and Consciousness in South Africa* (Chicago: University of Chicago Press, 1991).

8 See N. Thomas, 'Alejandro Mayta in Fiji: narratives of millenarianism, colonialism, postcolonial politics, and custom', in *Clio in Oceania: Toward a Historical Anthropology*, ed. Aletta Biersack (Washington: Smithsonian Institution Press, 1991), pp. 297–328; and Homi K. Bhabha, 'Of mimicry and man: the ambivalence of colonial discourse', *October* 28 (1984), pp. 125–33.

9 See particularly Sara Suleri, *The Rhetoric of English India* (Chicago: University of Chicago Press, 1992); this sentence draws upon her point of view but does not precisely reflect it.

10 This literature is very considerable indeed, but it may help some readers if useful works dealing with various aspects of the field are mentioned here. For representations of others and blacks in antiquity see François Hartog's superb *The Mirror of Herodotus: the Representation of the Other in the Writing of History* (Berkeley: University of California Press, 1988) and Frank Snowden, *Blacks in Antiquity* (Cambridge, Mass.: Harvard University Press, 1983); for Renaissance images of the New World, Bernadette Bucher, *Icon and Conquest: a Structural Analysis of the Illustrations of de Bry's* Great Voyages (Chicago: University of Chicago Press, 1981) and Anthony Pagden, *The Fall of Natural Man: the American Indian and the Origins of Comparative Ethnology*, 2nd edn (Cambridge: Cambridge University

Press, 1986). Tzvetan Todorov, *The Conquest of America* (New York: Harper, 1985), is highly readable but has been criticized for over-reliance on W. H. Prescott's classic *History of the Conquest of Mexico* (numerous editions). For a poststructuralist analysis, see Peter Mason, *Deconstructing America: Representations of the Other* (London: Routledge, 1990). Stephen Greenblatt has edited an important special issue of *Representations* (31, 1991) on 'The New World'; see also his own books *Learning to Curse: Essays in Early Modern Culture* (New York: Routledge, 1990) and *Marvelous Possessions: the Wonder of the New World* (Chicago: University of Chicago Press, 1991). I discuss Todorov, Pagden, and Greenblatt further in chapter 3. Benjamin Keen's *Image of the Aztec in Western Thought* (New Brunswick: Rutgers University Press, 1971) is extensive but not especially penetrating. For the modern period, V. G. Kiernan's *The Lords of Humankind: European Attitudes to the Outside World in the Imperial Age* (Harmondsworth: Penguin, 1972; 1st edn 1969) remains a readable introduction.

On India, important texts include Eric Stokes, *The English Utilitarians and India* (Delhi: Oxford University Press, 1959); Partha Mitter, *Much Maligned Monsters: History of European Reactions to Indian Art* (Oxford: Clarendon Press, 1977); and Ronald Inden, *Imagining India* (Oxford: Basil Blackwell, 1990). The Subaltern Studies group has also, to some extent, been concerned with colonial representation; see n. 13 below.

On Africa, Philip D. Curtin, *The Image of Africa: British Ideas and Action, 1780–1850* (Madison: University of Wisconsin Press, 1964) is thorough and informative but deals only with West Africa; both this and *Africa and the Victorians*, by Ronald Robinson with John Gallagher and Alice Denny (London: Macmillan, 1981) (which is more wide-ranging) belong definitely to the conventional 'images of' kind of scholarship rather than the genre informed by Foucault and Said. For southern Africa, Jean and John Comaroff's important *Of Revelation and Revolution* (Chicago: University of Chicago Press, 1991) deals partly with evangelical constructions, and is particularly useful in its emphasis on connections between mission projects at home and abroad. An article also emphasizing missionary representations is Annie E. S. Coombes, ' "For God and for England": contributions to an image of Africa in the first decade of the twentieth century', *Art History* 8 (1985), 452–66. Sander Gilman among others has written on the 'Hottentot Venus' ('Black bodies, white bodies: toward an iconography of female sexuality in late nineteenth century art, medicine, and literature', in *'Race', Writing and Difference,* ed. Henry Louis Gates, Jr., Chicago: University of Chicago Press, 1985, pp. 223–61). There have been a number of studies focused on colonial culture in particular domains such as education, language and medical policy; see, for example, Megan Vaughan's *Curing their Ills: Colonial Power and African Illness* (Cambridge: Polity Press, 1991) and Johannes Fabian, *Language and Colonial Power: the Appropriation of Swahili in the Former Belgian Congo* (Cambridge: Cambridge University Press, 1986). John MacKenzie's *The Empire of Nature: Hunting, Conservation, and British Imperialism* (Manchester: Manchester University Press, 1988) provides a fascinating account dealing mainly with Africa and India. This book is part of a series, Studies in Imperialism, which includes collections on education, juvenile literature, sexuality and a number of other topics, which are of uneven value, although David Arnold's *Imperial Medicine and Indigenous Societies* (Manchester: Manchester University Press, 1988) is extremely useful. Much more provocative theoretically is John Noyes's *Colonial Space: Spatiality in the Discourse of German South West Africa, 1884–1915* (Chur: Harwood Academic Publishers, 1991), which deals particularly with fiction.

For Australia, *Seeing the First Australians*, ed. Ian Donaldson and Tamsin Donaldson (Sydney: Allen & Unwin, 1985), is a good set of essays; Paul Carter's *The Road to Botany Bay* (London: Faber and Faber, 1987) is an innovative though controversial discussion of constructions of space and topography; Alison Broinowski's *The Yellow Lady: Australian Impressions of Asia* (Melbourne: Oxford University Press, 1992) is useful especially for literary texts. For the Pacific, see especially Bernard Smith's *European Vision and the South Pacific*, 2nd edn (New Haven: Yale University Press, 1985), which I discuss further in chapter 3; Smith's arguments are extended in *Imagining the Pacific* (New Haven: Yale University Press, 1992). His work covers both graphic material and ideas up to 1860, but is particularly strong on the Cook voyage period, also explored by Harriet Guest, 'Curiously marked: tattooing and masculinity in eighteenth-century British perceptions of the south Pacific', in *Painting and the Politics of Culture*, ed. John Barrell (Oxford: Oxford University Press, 1992). A range of voyage, official colonial, missionary and pioneer interests up to the 1920s are discussed in my book *Entangled Objects: Exchange, Material Culture, and Colonialism in the Pacific* (Cambridge, Mass.: Harvard University Press, 1991), ch. 4. A useful review dealing with later constructions and their relations with postcolonial self-constructions in indigenous Pacific societies is Roger M. Keesing's 'Colonial discourse and codes of discrimination in the Pacific', forthcoming in a UNESCO volume ed. M. O'Callaghan; for an analysis of gender and missionary material, see Margaret Jolly, '"To save the girls for brighter and better lives": Presbyterian missionaries and women in the south of Vanuatu', *Journal of Pacific History* 26 (1991), 27–48.

There are other works dealing with representations of particular regions or populations include Colin Mackerass, *Western Images of China* (Hong Kong: Oxford University Press, 1989) and Adrian Vickers, *Bali: a Paradise Created* (Ringwood: Penguin Australia, 1989).

There are numerous compendia presenting visual material, of which the series under the general editorship of Ladislas Bugner, *The Image of the Black in Western Art* (Cambridge, Mass.: Harvard University Press/Menil Foundation, 1976–) stands out. Others of value for the material presented or for commentary include: *Terra Australis: the Furthest Shore*, ed. William Eisler and Bernard Smith (Sydney: Art Gallery of New South Wales, 1988); *Europa und der Orient, 800–1900*, ed. Gereon Sievernich and Hendrik Budde (Bertelsmann: Gütersloh/München, 1989); *The Raj: India and the British, 1600–1947*, ed. C. A. Bayly (London: National Portrait Gallery, 1990), includes important essays as well as a fascinating range of reproductions. Briony Llewellyn, *The Orient Observed: Images of the Middle East from the Searight Collection* (London: Victoria and Albert Museum, 1989) contains a selection of images but superficial commentary; Guy C. McElroy, *Facing History: the Black Image in American Art, 1710–1940* (San Francisco: Bedford Arts, 1990) includes essays by Henry Louis Gates, Jr. among others. Studies specifically on photography include: Christopher Pinney, 'Classification and fantasy in the photographic construction of caste and tribe', *Visual Anthropology* 3 (1990), 259–88; David Prochaska, 'The archive of *Algérie imaginaire*', *History and Anthropology* 4 (1990), 373–420; and Elizabeth Edwards (ed.) *Anthropology and Photography* (New Haven: Yale University Press, 1992).

The material cited here ranges widely in theoretical orientation: some of the works mentioned are conventional studies in the history of ideas, or are useful primarily for documenting or presenting material; others exemplify recent critical, feminist and post-structural theoretical perspectives. Gates's collection, *'Race', Writing, and Difference*, provides a good introduction to the range of current discussion (which has various manifestations in journals including *Comparative Studies in Society and History, Critical Inquiry, Critique of Anthropology, Gender and History, History and Anthropology, New Formations* and *Representations*); other works specifically associated with 'colonial discourse theory' (which is in fact not a unified or homogeneous approach) are discussed in chapter 2. I stress that this listing is very selective indeed, and is intended mainly to convey a sense of the range of writing available.

11 See Greenblatt, 'Learning to curse: aspects of linguistic colonialism in the sixteenth century', in *Learning to Curse*, pp. 16–39 (partly on *The Tempest*); Gayatri Chakravorty Spivak, 'Three women's texts and the critique of imperialism', in *'Race', Writing and Difference*, ed. Henry Louis Gates, Jr., pp. 262–80 (on *Jane Eyre, Frankenstein* and *Wide Sargasso Sea*); and Edward W. Said, 'Narrative, geography, and interpretation', *New Left Review* 180 (1990), 81–97 (on Camus).

12 See particularly the special issue of *American Ethnologist*, on *Tensions of Empire*, ed. Frederick Cooper and Ann L. Stoler (vol. 16, no. 4, 1989) and Nicholas B. Dirks (ed.) *Colonialism and Culture* (Ann Arbor: University of Michigan Press, 1992).

13 See especially the work of the Subaltern Studies group: Ranajit Guha's *Elementary Aspects of Peasant Insurgency* (Delhi: Oxford University Press, 1983); *Subaltern Studies I–VI*, ed. R. Guha (Delhi: Oxford University Press, 1983–9); and, among other recent extensions and commentaries upon the project, Dipesh Chakrabarty, 'Postcoloniality and the artifice of history: who speaks for "Indian" pasts?', *Representations* 37 (1992), 1–26. The best critical commentary is probably Rosalind O'Hanlon's 'Recovering the subject: *Subaltern Studies* and histories of resistance in colonial south Asia', *Modern Asian Studies* 22 (1988), 189–224.

14 The key collection for the earlier wave of critique was *Anthropology and the Colonial Encounter*, ed. Talal Asad (London: Ithaca, 1974). For American and French debates see Kathleen Gough, 'New proposals for anthropologists', *Current Anthropology* 9 (1968), 403–7, and G. Leclerc, *Anthropologie et colonialisme* (Paris: Fayard, 1972). The radical impulse in anthropology then shifted to more substantive economic studies of imperialism, and further reflection on the intellectual dimensions of anthropological colonialism was not substantially advanced until the publication of Johannes Fabian's *Time and the Other: How Anthropology Makes its Object* (New York: Columbia University Press, 1983; see also the same author's *Time and the Work of Anthropology: Critical Essays 1971–1991*, Chur: Harwood Academic Publishers, 1991). *Writing Culture: the Poetics and Politics of Ethnography*, ed. George E. Marcus and James Clifford (Berkeley: University of California Press, 1986) is often cited as the central collection of 'postmodern' anthropology, but has often also been criticized for its reiteration of anthropological authority and particularly its marginalization of feminism: see Frances E. Masica-Lees, Patricia Sharpe and Colleen Ballerino Cohen, 'The postmodernist turn in

anthropology: cautions from a feminist perspective', *Signs* 15 (1989), 7–33; bell hooks, *Yearning: Race, Gender and Cultural Politics* (Boston: South End, 1990), pp. 123–33. Trinh Minh-Ha's work has aroused a great deal of interest in this context, though her critique of anthropology is flawed by a highly restricted and stereotyped view of the subject (see her *Woman, Native, Other: Writing, Postcoloniality and Feminism* (Bloomington: Indiana University Press, 1989), pp. 47–76, which makes easy game of Malinowski and his diary). For useful commentaries see Henrietta Moore, 'Anthropology and others', *Visual Anthropology Review* 6 (2) (1990), 66–72, and Christopher Pinney, 'Other explanations of itself', *Third Text* 16/17 (1991), 145–56, which draws attention to divergences between Trinh's films and texts.

15 Gyan Prakash, 'Writing post-Orientalist histories of the third world: perspectives from Indian historiography', *Comparative Studies in Society and History* 32 (1990), 383–408.

16 bell hooks, *Yearning*, pp. 12–13.

17 Here I am thinking particularly of texts such as *Discipline and Punish* (New York: Viking, 1979) and the first volume of the *History of Sexuality* (New York: Pantheon, 1978). The earlier work, in particular, does not accord with the same model.

18 Cf. Edward W. Said, 'Reflections on American "left" literary criticism', in *The World, the Text, and the Critic* (London: Faber & Faber, 1984), esp. pp. 141–2.

19 Chicago Cultural Studies Group, 'Critical multiculturalism', *Critical Inquiry* 18 (1992), 531.

20 By pluralizing 'locations' I intend here to underline the differences among critics, rather than evoke a community of 'us readers and writers'. Here and elsewhere I use 'critics' to refer to those engaged in cultural debate, including historians and anthropologists and some writers outside the academy as well as literary critics.

21 Michel de Certeau, *The Practice of Everyday Life* (Berkeley: University of California Press, 1984), p. 50.

22 Pierre Ryckmans (aka Simon Leys), 'Orientalism and Sinology', *Asian Studies Association of Australia Review* 7 (3), 20. These comments are typical of a number of statements which appeared in a review symposium running over several issues of that periodical.

23 Homi Bhabha, 'The other question: difference, discrimination, and the discourse of colonialism', in *Literature, Politics and Theory*, ed. Francis Barker, Peter Hulme, Margaret Iversen and Diana Loxley (London: Methuen, 1986), p. 149.

24 Thomas Bacon, *First Impressions and Studies from Nature in Hindostan*

(London: W. H. Allen, 1837), i, 233.

25 Edward W. Said, *Orientalism* (New York: Viking, 1978), p. 94.

26 In the Palestinian case, this has of course been literally true, since the political and diplomatic struggles have long been about the right of the Palestine Liberation Organization to be recognized and represented as a national entity and a party to negotiation.

27 E.g. Michael Richardson, 'Enough Said', *Anthropology Today* 6 (4) (1990), 17–18. For a searching and intriguing discussion of the passage from *The Eighteenth Brumaire of Louis Bonaparte*, see Gayatri Chakravorty Spivak, 'Can the subaltern speak?' in *Marxism and the Interpretation of Culture*, ed. Cary Nelson and Lawrence Grossberg (Urbana: University of Illinois Press, 1988), pp. 276–8.

28 *Orientalism*, pp. 325–6.

29 James Clifford, 'On *Orientalism*', in *The Predicament of Culture* (Cambridge, Mass.: Harvard University Press, 1988), pp. 263, 273.

30 Edward W. Said, *The Question of Palestine* (New York: Times Books, 1979); *Covering Islam: How the Media and the Experts Determine How we See the Rest of the World* (London: Routledge, 1981); and *Blaming the Victims: Spurious Scholarship and the Palestinian Question*, ed. Edward W. Said and Christopher Hitchins (London: Verso, 1988). While these books are primarily critiques of the Western media, Said has also discussed Palestinian perspectives in *After the Last Sky* (New York: Pantheon, 1986), a photo-essay with Jean Mohr.

31 *Orientalism*, p. 301.

32 Like any similarly broad statement this requires qualification; more generous or tolerant attitudes towards Australians on the part of various Europeans could be cited; see, for example, Rhys Jones, 'Images of natural man', in *Baudin in Australian Waters*, ed. Jacqueline Bonnemains, Elliot Forsyth and Bernard Smith (Melbourne: Oxford University Press, 1988).

33 See Julian Thomas, *Showman: the Photography of Frank Hurley* (Canberra: National Library of Australia, 1990).

34 Edward Alexander, 'Professor of terror', *Commentary*, August 1989, pp. 49–50.

35 I am thinking here of Robert Flaherty's famous film *Nanook of the North* (1922). The heroic confrontations and the interest in universals of human survival (the struggle for food and shelter) offer a useful counter-example to the dominant idea in colonial cultural studies that the literature and art of travel is preoccupied with difference and otherness. See, however, Richard Barsam's *The Vision of Robert Flaherty: the Artist and Myth and Filmmaker* (Bloomington: Indiana University Press, 1988).

36 For further discussion of primitivism, see Marianna Torgovnick, *Gone Primitive: Savage Intellects, Modern Lives* (Chicago: University of Chicago Press, 1990); James Clifford, *The Predicament of Culture* (Cambridge, Mass.: Harvard University Press, 1988); and Hal Foster, 'The primitive unconscious of modern art, or white skin black masks' in *Recodings: Art, Spectacle, Cultural Politics* (Seattle: Bay Press, 1985). The very considerable earlier literature includes the series 'Contributions to the History of Primitivism' published in the 1930s by Johns Hopkins Press.

37 'Out of Africa', *The Good Weekend*, supplement to *The Sydney Morning Herald*, 1 September 1990, p. 85.

38 Jeremy Beckett, 'The past in the present; the present in the past: constructing a national Aboriginality', in *Past and Present: the Construction of Aboriginality*, ed. Jeremy Beckett (Canberra: Aboriginal Studies Press, 1988), p. 194.

39 For example, *The Resolution Journal of Johann Reinhold Forster*, ed. Michael E. Hoare (London: Hakluyt Society, 1982), p. 396.

40 Robert Bage, *Hermsprong, or Man as He is Not* (London: William Lane, 1796), iii, p. 23.

CHAPTER 2

1 For a brief discussion of Andrew, with reproductions of some of his Samoan photographs, see City Group, 'Thomas Andrew', *Photofile* 6 (3), 30–3. The photo discussed here was part of a sequence; in some versions these have handwritten captions, this being 'The Vanquished', another with bodies spread on an earth oven being 'The Banquet' and so on.

2 I have no information about the circumstances of Andrew's work in Fiji, and do not know who specifically he was photographing, but, even if it might be hypothetically argued that his Fijian models would have preferred to obtain money some other way, it is most unlikely that any kind of coercion was involved.

3 Rana Kabbani, *Europe's Myths of Orient: Devise and Rule* (London: Macmillan, 1986), p. 4.

4 Abdul R. JanMohamed, 'The economy of Manichean allegory: the function of racial difference in colonialist literature', in *'Race', Writing and Difference*, ed. Henry Louis Gates, Jr. (Chicago: University of Chicago Press, 1985), pp. 86–7.

5 I am not supposing that 'colonial discourse theory' constitutes a unitary approach. I focus here on the work of Homi Bhabha partly

because it is widely read and partly because it represents a strong form of the global theory impulse I want to criticize. The name of Gayatri Spivak is often also associated with colonial discourse theory; I refer to her work only in passing, because it is in fact far less concerned with constructing a general set of arguments around colonial representation; while, as I indicate below, I tend to agree with the criticisms that Gates and Parry have made of her work, much of my critique of Bhabha and JanMohamed does not apply to her.

6 Though the earlier model of biased perceptions or images is still frequently expressed: 'It is unfortunate that the bulk of European travel narrative about the East was so strongly coloured by bias and supposition' (Kabbani, *Europe's Myths of Orient*, p. 139). The weakness of this kind of formulation is its implication that the subtraction of prejudice leaves a clear picture, whereas what requires attention is the wider range of textual devices that present others in particular terms; difference is produced, not simply distorted.

7 Peter Hulme, *Colonial Encounters: Europe and the Native Caribbean, 1492–1797* (London: Methuen, 1986), p. 2.

8 Edward Said, 'Yeats and decolonization', in *Remaking History*, ed. Barbara Kruger (Seattle: Bay Press, 1989), p. 6.

9 Cohn, 'The census, social structure, and objectification in South Asia', in *An Anthropologist among the Historians and Other Essays* (Delhi: Oxford University Press, 1987), p. 243.

10 Cohn, 'The command of language and the language of command', in *Subaltern Studies IV*, ed. R. Guha (Delhi: Oxford University Press, 1985), pp. 276, 283–4.

11 Ibid., pp. 312–13.

12 'Difference, discrimination, and the discourses of colonialism' in *Literature, Politics, Theory*, ed. Francis Barker, Peter Hulme, Margaret Iverson and Diana Loxley (London: Methuen, 1986), p. 154; see also 'Signs taken for wonders: questions of ambivalence and authority under a tree outside Delhi, May 1817', in *'Race', Writing and Difference*, pp. 172–3.

13 'Of mimicry and man: the ambivalence of colonial discourse', in *October: the First Decade*, ed. Annette Michelson, Rosalind Krauss, Douglas Crimp and Joan Copjec (Cambridge, Mass.: MIT Press, 1987), pp. 318, 322, 320 (this article originally appeared in *October* 28 (1984), 125–33). This argument overlaps with that developed in the essays cited in the previous note. If I seem to attach excessive importance to these essays, it is worth pointing out that they have been widely reprinted and cited.

14 Benita Parry, 'Problems in current theories of colonial discourse',

Oxford Literary Review 9 (1987), p. 40. This article offers an extremely useful review and critique of some of the more influential essays published in the field up until the mid-1980s.

15 For reasons related both to the limits of my own competence and to the overall direction of this book's arguments, I have not pursued Bhabha's uses of Fanon and Lacan here; these are addressed by Parry (see previous note) and Henry Louis Gates, Jr., 'Critical Fanonism', *Critical Inquiry* 17 (1991), 457–70. Gates finds that Fanon has been narcissistically decontextualized by numerous critics into a precursor of their own positions and an icon of Third World resistance.

16 Michel Foucault, *Discipline and Punish* (New York: Viking, 1979), p. 194. See also, in particular, the article 'On governmentality', *Ideology and Consciousness* 6 (1979), 5–21 (reprinted in *The Foucault Effect: Studies in Governmentality*, ed. Graham Burchell, Colin Gordon and Peter Miller (Chicago: University of Chicago Press, 1991)).

17 *Discipline and Punish*, p. 143.

18 E.g. Nicos Poulantzas, *Political Power and Social Classes* (London: Verso, 1975; 1st edn, 1968), pp. 44–50 and *passim*. For a useful review of the debates see Anthony Giddens, *A Contemporary Critique of Historical Materialism* (London: Macmillan, 1981), pp. 202–29.

19 'On governmentality', pp. 17, 20.

20 While this would in, say, the case of Conrad or *The Tempest* seem too obvious to require reiteration, I would take the point that it is important to show the imperialist implication and logic of some canonical works that have not generally been seen in this way; such a contextualization of earlier nineteenth-century fiction is argued for by Suvendrini Perera in *Reaches of Empire: the English Novel from Edgeworth to Dickens* (New York: Columbia University Press, 1991).

21 Such functional idioms also come up in writers who otherwise differ from Bhabha theoretically: according to Hulme, colonial discourses are 'unified by their common deployment in the management of colonial relationships' (*Colonial Encounters*, p. 2); while JanMohamed suggests that what should be of interest is the 'ideological function [of colonial discourse] in relation to actual imperialist practices' ('The economy of Manichean allegory', p. 80).

22 JanMohamed, 'The economy of Manichean allegory', pp. 84, 86.

23 Tony Tanner, 'Frames and sentences', in *Scenes of Nature, Signs of Men* (Cambridge: Cambridge University Press, 1987), p. 239. The Derrida passage immediately precedes this and is quoted from the essay 'Living on: Border lines'.

24 Peter Miller and Nikolas Rose, 'Governing economic life', *Economy and Society* 19 (1990), 7.

25 'Difference, discrimination, and the discourses of colonialism', p. 158.

26 In a brief discussion near the end of the book, he suggests censoriously that American-style consumerism is rampant in the region, leading to a 'vast standardization of taste' and to 'the paradox of an Arab regarding himself as an 'Arab' of the sort put out by Hollywood' (*Orientalism*, pp. 324–5). This merges the problem of colonial dominance with a widely established denigration of mass consumption (criticized effectively by Daniel Miller in *Material Culture and Mass Consumption* (Oxford: Blackwell, 1987)) and exaggerates the penetration of Western ideas and products while neglecting the autonomous or resistant interests that may accompany their appropriation. For a much more satisfying discussion of one set of responses to Orientalism and the West, see Timothy Mitchell, *Colonising Egypt* (Cambridge: Cambridge University Press, 1988).

27 'Of mimicry and man', p. 321.

28 Bhabha, 'Postcolonial authority and postmodern guilt', in *Cultural Studies*, ed. Lawrence Grossberg, Cary Nelson and Paula Treichler (New York: Routledge, 1992), p. 63.

29 Ranajit Guha, 'On some aspects of the historiography of colonial India', in *Subaltern Studies I*, ed. R. Guha (Delhi: Oxford University Press, 1982); Partha Chatterjee, 'Gandhi and the critique of civil society', *Subaltern Studies III*, ed. R. Guha (Delhi: Oxford University Press, 1984), pp. 155–6; see also Chatterjee, *Nationalist Thought and the Colonial World: a Derivative Discourse?* (London: Zed Press, 1986).

30 'Of mimicry and man', p. 322.

31 *Fiji Times*, 27, 28 March, 10 April 1918; this material is discussed further in N. Thomas, 'Alejandro Mayta in Fiji: narratives about colonialism, millenarianism, postcolonial politics, and custom' in *Clio in Oceania: Toward a Historical Anthropology*, ed. Aletta Biersack (Washington: Smithsonian Institution Press, 1991), pp. 297–328.

32 Quoted in Saul Dubow, 'Race, civilisation and culture: the elaboration of segregationist discourse in the inter-war years', in *The Politics of Race, Class and Nationalism in South Africa*, ed. Shula Marks and Stanley Trapido (London: Longman, 1987), pp. 71–94.

33 Robert Young, *White Mythologies: Writing History and the West* (London: Routledge, 1990), p. 151. The sentence which follows this reads: 'If the latter is the case, what is their relation to the general text of colonialism?' It might also be asked what a concept such as 'the general text of colonialism' is doing in a text concerned to deconstruct and decolonize the totalizations of 'History'.

34 Parry, 'Problems in current theories of colonial discourse', p. 29.

35 Cf. Gates, 'Critical Fanonism', p. 466.
36 Peter de Bolla, *The Discourse of the Sublime: History, Aesthetics, and the Subject* (Oxford: Basil Blackwell, 1989), p. 7.
37 'Signs taken for wonders', p. 171.
38 'The economy of Manichean allegory', pp. 83–4.
39 For a convergent critique of these fetishizations of alterity, see Sara Suleri, *The Rhetoric of English India* (Chicago: University of Chicago Press, 1992); see also 'Woman skin deep: feminism and the postcolonial condition', *Critical Inquiry* 18 (1992), 756–9.
40 The history of encounters and representations in west Africa is well synthesized by Philip Curtin, *The Image of Africa: British Ideas and Action, 1780–1850* (Madison: University of Wisconsin Press, 1964).
41 Tzvetan Todorov, *The Conquest of America: the Question of the Other* (New York: Harper and Row, 1984), pp. 42–3, 49–50. Cf. Peter Mason, *Deconstructing America: Representations of the Other* (London: Routledge, 1990), p. 101.
42 As Michael Ryan noted, in the fifteenth and sixteenth centuries 'the manners and customs of exotic peoples excited few. Explorers themselves seemed to take this new humanity in stride, when they took it at all' ('Assimilating new worlds in the sixteenth and seventeenth centuries', *Comparative Studies in Society and History* 23 (1981), 519). For further discussion see J. H. Elliot, 'Renaissance Europe and America: a blunted impact?' in *First Images of America*, ed. F. Chiapelli (Berkeley: University of California Press, 1976).
43 Ronald Inden, 'Orientalist constructions of India', *Modern Asian Studies* 20 (1986), 401–46; *Imagining India* (Oxford: Basil Blackwell, 1990).
44 See Jeremy Beckett, 'Children of conquest: miscegenation in some colonies of settlement', unpublished paper.
45 John Sweetman, *The Oriental Obsession: Islamic Inspiration in British Art and Architecture* (Cambridge: Cambridge University Press, 1988), pp. 86–102.
46 William Hodges, *Select Views in India* (London: privately printed, 1785–8); Thomas and William Daniell, *Oriental Scenery* (London: Richard Bowyer, 1797–1810); Henry Salt, *Twenty-four Views* (London: William Miller, 1809); James Baillie Fraser, *Views in the Himala Mountains* (London: Rodwell, 1820). For scholarly republications, see Mildred Archer, *Early Views of India: the Picturesque Journeys of Thomas and William Daniell, 1786–1794* (London: Thames & Hudson, 1980) and Mildred Archer and Toby Falk, *India Revealed: the Art and Adventures of James and William Fraser, 1801–35* (London: Cassell, 1989).
47 Of course it could be suggested that European views and buildings would be represented in the same way, but so far as the Daniells are

concerned this would seem incorrect. Taking the work of Thomas's nephew William – who co-operated with Samuel in various Orientalist publications, and who also produced a volume of *Sketches Representing Native Tribes, Animals, and Scenery of Southern Africa* (London, 1820) – it is apparent that his plates for Richard Ayton's *Voyage round Great Britain . . . with a Series of Views Illustrative of the Character and Prominent Features of the Coast* (London: Longman, 1814–20) approach their subjects in a manner that has little in common with *Oriental Scenery*. In particular, work and activity are frequently depicted as fishing vessels are entering or leaving harbours, while labour was almost totally elided in the Indian views; out of 150, only one showed people engaged in agriculture, which must be seen as something of an accomplishment, given the extent to which India was and is a farming country. More generally, and without going into an extensive discussion, it might be suggested that the facts of social life are far less thoroughly displaced into the picturesque in the British views. On the major point that ways of imaging Asia might often have counterparts in depictions of Europe, the conclusion, so far as, say, British painters in Italy are concerned, might not be that the Indian images are therefore not distinctively colonial, but rather that those from Italy partook of a similar interest in past glories and larger qualities of light and topography that marginalized the contemporary population or construed it as faded and degenerate. This is crude, but various aesthetic and classicist elisions broadly comparable to the treatment of India are conspicuous in Mediterranean travel books from Addison to Henry Miller and more recent examples. The colonialist dimension of tourism of course persists and is sufficiently familiar to require no further comment here.

48 'Problems in current theories of colonial discourse', p. 43.

49 Gayatri Chakravorty Spivak, 'Can the subaltern speak?' in *Marxism and the Interpretation of Culture*, ed. Cary Nelson and Lawrence Grossberg (Urbana: University of Illinois Press, 1988), p. 307. Spivak's argument is sustained in this case by the powerful example of *sati*; but while this is certainly emblematic of British and evangelical interventions in indigenous gender relations, 'saving brown women from brown men', it does not follow that immolated widows should be rendered as canonical subalterns or even as canonical subaltern women. To make this step is to define the 'sexed subaltern subject' on the basis of her inability to speak, and to neglect a variety of enunciations that might be heard or recorded. Spivak rejects such publications as Gail Omvedt's *We will Smash this Prison! Indian Women in Struggle* (London: Zed Press, 1980) on the grounds that the assumption that dialogue between a radical white woman

and her particular urban interlocutors is representative of Indian women, 'or touches the question of "female consciousness in India"' (ibid., p. 311), is harmful in its context of First World publication. However legitimate this objection may be to the particular text or the way it tends to be interpreted, it is obviously a problem that could be raised about any and all quotations or expressions of subaltern perspectives, and seems ultimately to be a tactic for evading engagement with material, which is simply presumed to be politically tainted by its context of elicitation or contaminated by nativism. The problematic issue of speaking of or for 'the other' has been extensively debated, often in terms inspired by, or in reaction to, Spivak's article (see, for example, Julie Stephens, 'Feminist fictions: a critique of the category "non-western woman" in feminist writings on India', in *Subaltern studies VI*, ed. R. Guha (Delhi: Oxford University Press, 1989), pp. 92–5, and Susie Tharu, 'Reply to Stephens', ibid., pp. 126–31). Similar problems have been debated in the Pacific context by Margaret Jolly: 'The politics of difference: feminism, colonialism, and decolonization', in *Intersexions*, ed. G. Bottomley, M. de Lepervanche and J. Martin (Sydney: Allen & Unwin, 1991), pp. 52–74.

50   Even if counter-colonial practice is, by definition, frequently reactive, the notion that indigenous discourse is wholly contained or structured by a form of 'nativism' that requires no specification or pluralization reinstates an essentialism of subalternity and resistance – and perforce its own categories of privileged subjects. Although, in another essay ('The inversion of tradition', *American Ethnologist* 19 (1992), 213–32), I have argued for a perception of colonial and postcolonial representations of identity in the Pacific as a succession of reactive transformations, in opposition to the anthropological tendency to ignore or marginalize the ramifications of colonialism for Pacific islands 'cultures', my intention was not to suggest that colonizing endeavours ever entirely enframed or encompassed indigenous responses, and in the context of the debates about colonial discourse, it seems necessary to reverse the emphasis and point to the *partial* effect of colonization.

51   Guha, 'On some aspects of the historiography of colonial India', p. 4.

52   For a survey of such material, see John M. MacKenzie, *Propaganda and Empire: the Manipulation of British Public Opinion, 1880–1960* (Manchester: Manchester University Press, 1984).

53   The source of my image is of course Werner Herzog's classic, *Aguirre, the Wrath of God*, but accounts of the expedition on which the film was based suggest that Herzog hardly overstated Aguirre's

madness (*The Expedition of Pedro de Ursua and Lope de Aguirre* (London: Hakluyt Society, 1861)).

54 Pierre Bourdieu, *Outline of a Theory of Practice* (Cambridge: Cambridge University Press, 1977), p. 10.

55 Bourdieu, *Distinction: a Social critique of the Judgement of Taste* (London: Routledge, 1984), pp. 100–1.

56 For an example from the colonial historiography of Fiji, see N. Thomas, 'Taking sides: Fijian dissent and conservative history-writing', *Australian Historical Studies* 95 (1990), pp. 239–51.

57 Geoffrey M. White, *Identity through History: Living Stories in a Solomon Islands Society* (Cambridge: Cambridge University Press, 1991), p. 36.

58 Ibid., p. 8.

59 *Identity through History*, pp. 113–14 and *passim*; for Fijian parallels, see Martha Kaplan, 'Christianity, chiefs, and people of the land,' in *The Rthnography of Christianity in the Pacific*, ed. John Barker (Lanham, Maryland: University Press of America, 1991); for the case of the Tolai in Papua New Guinea, see Klaus Neumann, *Not the Way It Really Was: constructing the Tolai past* (Honolulu: University of Hawaii Press, 1992).

60 White points out that an Anglican missionary in the late 1930s, Richard Fallowes, organized a network of church chiefs and catechists who gathered together in an indigenous 'parliament' which the administration found sufficiently threatening to warrant the missionary's deportation; on Isabel these gatherings were later regarded as forerunners of the postwar Maasina Rule, a politico-religious movement which was probably the most substantial threat to colonial domination in the history of the Solomons.

61 See Hudson Lagusu, 'Smoke and ashes for the Knabu gods', in *Pacific Rituals: Living and Dying* (Suva, Fiji: Institute of Pacific Studies).

62 This theme is developed more extensively in my book *Entangled Objects: Exchange, Colonialism, and Material Culture in the Pacific* (Cambridge, Mass.: Harvard University Press, 1991).

CHAPTER 3

1 Peter Mason, 'Seduction from afar: Europe's inner Indians', *Anthropos* 82 (1987), 588–93; E. P. Thompson, *Whigs and Hunters: the Origin of the Black Act* (Harmondsworth: Penguin, 1977), p. 151.

2 For the most effective of a number of analyses of such parallels, see Jean and John Comaroff, *Of Revelation and Revolution: Christianity,*

Colonialism and Consciousness in South Africa (Chicago: University of Chicago Press, 1991).

3   Bernard McGrane, *Beyond Anthropology: Society and the Other* (New York: Columbia University Press, 1989), p. 51.

4   Ibid., pp. 77–8.

5   Tzvetan Todorov, *The Conquest of America: the Question of the Other* (New York: Harper and Row, 1984), p. 5; Stephen Greenblatt, 'Learning to curse: aspects of linguistic colonialism in the sixteenth century', in *Learning to Curse: Essays on Early Modern Culture* (New York: Routledge, 1990); *Marvelous Possessions: the Wonder of the New World* (Chicago: University of Chicago Press, 1991); Anthony Pagden, *The Fall of Natural Man: the American Indian and the Origins of Comparative Ethnology*, rev. edn. (Cambridge: Cambridge University Press, 1986).

6   Cf. on India, Gyan Prakash's passing comment in 'Writing post-Orientalist histories of the third world: perspectives from Indian historiography', *Comparative Studies in Society and History* 32 (1990), 386.

7   Johannes Fabian, *Time and the Other: How Anthropology Makes its Object* (New York: Columbia University Press, 1983), p. 26.

8   J. H. Elliott, *The Old World and the New* (Cambridge: Cambridge University Press, 1970), pp. 41–4; Pagden, *The Fall of Natural Man*, pp. 15–16.

9   François Hartog, *The Mirror of Herodotus: the Representation of the Other in the Writing of History* (Berkeley: University of California Press, 1988), p. 174. This is specifically in relation to the Scythian pantheon.

10 Ibid., p. 186.

11 Reinhart Koselleck, 'The historical-political semantics of asymmetric counterconcepts', in *Futures Past: on the Semantics of Historical Time*, tr. Keith Tribe (Cambridge, Mass.: MIT Press, 1985), pp. 165–73.

12 In the sixteenth century, 'barbarous' was occasionally used in the sense of 'non-Christian' (*OED*).

13 Pagden, *The Fall of Natural Man*, p. 69. Cf. Koselleck, 'The historical-political semantics', p. 165 and *passim.*

14 H. L.-V. de la Popelinière, quoted by John Howland Rowe, 'Ethnography and ethnology in the sixteenth century', *Kroeber Anthropological Society Papers* 30 (1964), 5.

15 Todorov, *The Conquest of America*, p. 34. The condition of nakedness is presented categorically even though it is clear that certain girdles or loin-cloths were worn. Peter Mason has discussed the voyeuristic aspect of observations of this kind in *Deconstructing America* (London: Routledge, 1990), pp. 171–2.

16 Pagden, *The Fall of Natural Man*, p. 19.

17 *The Journal of Christopher Columbus*, tr. Cecil Jane (New York: Bonanza Books, 1989), p. 24; cf. pp. 33, 196. The original journal is not extant, and what survives appears to be from a copy transcribed by Bartolomeo de las Casas, which evidently contains emendations.

18 Ibid., p. 50.

19 For example William Hodges, *Travels in India, During the Years 1780 . . . 1783* (London: the author, 1793); see Harriet Guest's discussion: 'The great distinction: figures of the exotic in the work of William Hodges', *Oxford Art Journal* 12 (2) (1989), 36–58.

20 Walter Ralegh, *The Discoverie of the Large, Rich and Bewtiful Empyre of Guiana* (London: Robert Robinson, 1596), p. 96. There is, in effect, a contrast made with Peru; earlier in the book the Spanish emperor is said to have had that country's maidenhead.

21 Ibid., p. 92. Compare Lawrence Keymis, *A Relation of the Second Voyage to Guiana* (London: Thomas Dawson, 1596), which is similarly economical in its references to the inhabitants.

22 See for example Greg Dening, *Islands and Beaches: Discourse on a Silent Land* (Melbourne: Melbourne University Press, 1980), pp. 9–11.

23 Gerald H. Anderson, 'The Philippines: reluctant beneficiary of the missionary impulse in Europe' in *First Images of America*, ed. Fredi Chiappelli (Berkeley: University of California Press, 1976), p. 393.

24 Cf. Urs Bitterli, *Cultures in Conflict* (Cambridge: Polity Press, 1989), p. 55; Koselleck, 'The historical-political semantics', pp. 182–3.

25 Nathan Wachtel, *The Vision of the Vanquished* (Brighton: Harvester, 1977), p. 39.

26 William H. Prescott, *History of the Conquest of Peru* (London: Routledge, 1882), i, 369–78.

27 Joseph de Acosta, *The natural & moral history of the Indies*, tr. Edward Grimston, ed. C. R. Markham (London: Hakluyt Society, 1880, orig. 1604), pp. 354–5. For an extremely valuable discussion of Acosta's work in its context, see Pagden, *The Fall of Natural Man*, ch. 7.

28 Of course, a more adequate account of this period would have to deal with the specific inflections and arguments of particular texts; it is notable, however, that this statement holds generally true of quite different representations of the period, such as the Protestant Jean de Léry's *History of a Voyage to the Land of Brazil*, tr. Janet Whatley (Berkeley: University of California Press, 1990; 1st edn 1578); the tropes of absence and falsity emerge in the account of religion, pp. 134–51.

29 Todorov, *The Conquest of America*, pp. 106–7.

30 See, for example, Peter Fryer, *Black People in the British Empire: an Introduction* (London: Pluto Press, 1988), pp. 66–72.

31 See, for example, Bernard Smith, *European Vision and the South Pacific*, 2nd edn (New Haven: Yale University Press, 1985); Philip D. Curtin, *The Image of Africa* (Madison: University of Wisconsin Press, 1964).

32 Frank M. Snowden, *Before Color Prejudice: the Ancient View of the Blacks* (Cambridge, Mass.: Harvard University Press, 1983), p. 63. See also Snowden, *Blacks in Antiquity* (Cambridge, Mass.: Harvard University Press, 1970).

33 Nancy Stepan, *The Idea of Race in Science: Great Britain 1800–1960* (London: Macmillan, 1982), p. xii.

34 The case of the Portuguese is of some interest for the forms of premodern racism, especially because the alleged racial tolerance characteristic of Portuguese colonialism was long upheld in national ideology, but also, rather puzzlingly, by scholars who should have known better, such as Urs Bitterli (*Cultures in Conflict*, p. 68). See C. R. Boxer, *Race Relations in the Portuguese Colonial Empire, 1415–1825* (Oxford: Oxford University Press, 1963), Marvin Harris, *Patterns of Race in the Americas* (Westport: Greenwood, 1980, 1st edn 1964), and, for a useful review of the debate, M. N. Pearson, *The Portuguese in India* (Cambridge: Cambridge University Press, 1987), pp. 102–5.

35 Henry M. Stanley, *In Darkest Africa, or the Quest Rescue and Retreat of Emin Governor of Equatoria* (London: Sampson Low, 1890), ii, 355–6.

36 Cf. Christopher Pinney, 'Classification and fantasy in the construction of caste and tribe', *Visual Anthropology* 3 (1990), 259–88.

37 Among the key texts are those of Blumenbach: see *The Anthropological Treatises of Johann Friedrich Blumenbach*, ed. Thomas Benyshe (London: Longman, 1865). Recent critical studies of early physical anthropology include Londa Schiebinger's 'The anatomy of difference: race and sex in eighteenth-century science', *Eighteenth Century Studies* 23 (1990), 387–405, and Stepan, *The Idea of Race in Science*, but most work places greater emphasis on early nineteenth-century sources.

38 George Louis le Clerc, Count of Buffon, *A Natural History, General and Particular*, tr. William Smellie (London: Thomas Kelly, 1866), i, 355. Forster himself read the French original, but the translation quoted was published first in the 1770s and thus reflects the text received by the British readership.

39 Ibid., i, 531.

40 Ibid., i, 406.

41 Samuel Pufendorf, *An Introduction to the History of the Principal Kingdoms and States of Europe*, 7th edn (London: Dan Midwinter, 1711), e.g. pp. 142, 211, 584. It could be argued that such typifications had

a much longer history, but it is notable that earlier examples tend to be comic or explicitly political, while from Pufendorf onward they are invested with a good deal of authority.

42 M. Adanson, *A Voyage to Senegal, and the Isle of Goree, and the River Gambia* (London: J. Nourse, 1759). Though the translator suggests that Adanson made 'diligent inquiry into the various curiosities, natural and artificial, of Negroland' (p. iii), it is quite clear at several points that the author himself did not see the description of customs as an element of his endeavour: 'I was even present once at their ceremony of marriage: but this would make me digress too far from my subject; I shall only observe that they are very humane and hospitable' (p. 214). The last statement is exemplifies such cursory 'ethnographic' comment as is found in the book.

43 Johann Reinhold Forster, *Observations Made During a Voyage round the World* (London: G. Robinson, 1778), p. 227.

44 Ibid., p. 235.

45 Ibid., pp. 250–1.

46 *The Journal of Christopher Columbus*, p. 194.

47 Mungo Park, *Travels in the Interior Districts of Africa . . . in the Years 1795, 1796, and 1797* (London: W. Bulmer, 1799), pp. 16–21.

48 Franz Boas, 'The aims of anthropological research' (1932), in *Race, Language and Culture* (Chicago: University of Chicago Press, 1982), p. 255. The best critical discussions of Boas are those of George Stocking, for example his introduction to *A Franz Boas Reader*, ed. G. Stocking (Chicago: University of Chicago Press, 1974).

49 Tim Ingold, *Evolution and Social Life* (Cambridge: Cambridge University Press, 1986), pp. 54–6.

50 Diane J. Austin, 'Symbols and culture: some philosophical assumptions in the work of Clifford Geertz', with comments by Steven Kemper, J. A. Barnes, W. W. Sharrock, Roy Wagner and Don Handelman, *Social Analysis* 3 (1979), 45–86.

51 This borrowing is discussed more extensively in my essay, 'Partial texts: representation, colonialism, and agency in Pacific history', *Journal of Pacific History* 25 (1990), 148–9.

52 George E. Marcus and Michael J. J. Fisher, *Anthropology as Cultural Critique: an Experimental Moment in the Human Sciences* (Chicago: University of Chicago Press, 1986).

53 Clifford Geertz, *Islam Observed: Religious Developments in Morocco and Indonesia* (New Haven: Yale University Press, 1968), pp. 9–11.

54 Ibid., pp. 25–35.

55 Ibid., p. 19.

56 Though I discuss Geertz's writing on the Balinese state, similar criticisms have been made of his well-known discussion of Balinese

time. This is a non-durational notion, a steady state, through which Balinese life 'takes place in a motionless present'. This exoticist argument has been effectively criticized by Maurice Bloch (among others). He notes that Geertz acknowledged that durational ideas of time like our own were not entirely absent from Balinese life, in reference to national politics for instance, but were 'unstressed and of distinctly secondary importance'. Bloch points out that not only is it 'difficult to see how the political parties and Sukarno could have been of so little importance for the Balinese' either at the time of fieldwork or in earlier colonial periods, but that there is also evidence for linear constructions of time in 'traditional' domains such as village politics. 'It seems therefore misleading to say that the Balinese have a non-durational notion of time. *Sometimes* and in *some* contexts they do, sometimes and in other contexts they do not . . .' (Maurice Bloch, 'The past and the present in the present', in *Ritual, History and Power* (London: Athlone, 1989), p. 10. This makes the Balinese sound dull and unexotic, which is presumably one of the reasons why anthropologists devote little space to analysing beliefs and dispositions of particular peoples that do not differ particularly from our own (cf. Roger M. Keesing, 'Exotic readings of cultural texts', *Current Anthropology* 30 (1989), 460). It is not that universalism with respect to people's ideas of space and time would be attractive or plausible, but rather that the anthropological fix on cultural difference denies both certain psychological generalities and, perhaps more importantly, a variety of other differences that split and fracture cultures or nations.

57 Louis Dumont, *Homo hierarchicus* (Chicago: University of Chicago Press, 1980, 1st edn 1966); among many critiques see Arjun Appadurai, 'Is homo hierarchicus?', *American Ethnologist* 13 (1986), 745–61, Ronald Inden, 'Orientalist constructions of India', *Modern Asian Studies* 20 (1986), 401–46; and Gloria Godwin Raheja, 'India: caste, kingship, and dominance reconsidered', *Annual Review of Anthropology* 17 (1988), 497–522.

58 Clifford Geertz, *Negara: the Theater State in Nineteenth-Century Bali* (Princeton: Princeton University Press, 1980), p. 13.

59 Ibid., pp. 15, 121.

60 Ibid., p. 136.

61 Marianna Torgovnick, *Gone Primitive: Savage Intellects, Modern Lives* (Chicago: University of Chicago Press, 1990), pp. 85–95.

62 We are reminded at several points that its key features seem to have been the same for ever: 'The expressive nature of the Balinese state was apparent through the whole of its known history, for it was always pointed not toward tyranny . . . but toward spectacle . . .';

'they struggled with this paradox of cultural megalomania and organizational pluralism to the very end . . . Had not the modern world at length caught up with them, they would no doubt be struggling with it still' (ibid., pp. 13, 19).

63 David Pryce-Jones, *The Closed Circle: an Interpretation of the Arabs* (London: Weidenfeld & Nicolson, 1989), p. 25.
64 Ibid., p. 41.
65 Ibid., pp. 21, 35.
66 Ibid., p. 406.
67 Ibid., p. 405.
68 G. E. R. Lloyd, *Demystifying Mentalities* (Cambridge: Cambridge University Press, 1990).
69 Pryce-Jones, *The Closed Circle*, p. 405.
70 *European Vision*, p. 123.
71 Ibid., p. 339.
72 My discussion here draws upon Margaret Jolly's paper, "Ill-natured comparisons": racism and relativism in European perceptions of ni-Vanuatu from Cook's second voyage', in *Colonialism and Culture*, ed. N. Thomas (special issue, *History and Anthropology* 5 (1992), 331–64). Jolly emphasizes that while most of the observers did denigrate the people of Vanuatu, George Forster's assessments were distinctly relativistic and uncertain.
73 These developments are surveyed in N. Thomas, 'The force of ethnology: origins and significance of the Melanesia/Polynesia division', *Current Anthropology* 30 (1989) 27–41; 211–13.
74 Forster, *Observations*, pp. 418, 421–2. This is discussed more extensively in editorial comment by Harriet Guest and Nicholas Thomas, in a forthcoming republication by the University of Hawaii Press of Forster's book.
75 Cf. N. Thomas, *Entangled Objects*, p. 132.
76 George Forster, as quoted in the title of Jolly's paper.
77 Jocelyn Linnekin, 'Ignoble savages and other European visions: the La Pérouse affair in Samoan history', *Journal of Pacific History* 26 (1991), 26.

CHAPTER 4

1 This section draws upon N. Thomas, 'Sanitation and seeing: the creation of state power in early colonial Fiji', *Comparative Studies in Society and History* 32 (1990), 149–70, which may be consulted for more extensive documentation and discussion.
2 Peter France, *The Charter of the Land: Custom and Colonization in Fiji*

(Melbourne: Oxford University Press, 1969).

3   Colo East Provincial Council, 12–13 October 1892, National Archives of Fiji, Suva (hereafter NAF).

4   Cf. Ronald Inden, *Imagining India* (Oxford: Basil Blackwell, 1990).

5   Judith A. Bennett, *Wealth of the Solomons: a History of a Pacific Archipelago, 1800–1978* (Honolulu: University of Hawaii Press, 1987), pp. 127–9.

6   *Arrow of God*, 2nd edn (London: Heinemann, 1974) pp. 54–9.

7   Sir Arthur Hamilton Gordon (Lord Stanmore), *Fiji: Records of Private and of Public Life, 1875–1880* (Edinburgh: privately printed, 1897–1912), i, 212.

8   Ibid, p. 210.

9   Cf. P. Corrigan and D. Sayer, *The Great Arch: English State Formation as Cultural Revolution* (Oxford: Basil Blackwell, 1985).

10   Timothy Mitchell, *Colonising Egypt* (Cambridge: Cambridge University Press, 1988), p. 32.

11   Cf. Paul Rabinow, *French Modern: Norms and Forms of the Social Environment* (Cambridge, Mass.: MIT Press, 1989).

12   John F. Goldie, 'The Solomon Islands', in *A Century in the Pacific*, ed. James Colwell (Sydney: Methodist Book Room, 1915), p. 564.

13   *Report of the Committee Appointed to Inquire into the Decrease of the Native Population* (Suva: Government Printer, 1896), pp. 6–7. I have asserted at several points that particular stereotypes or observations tend to have a good deal of generality across epochs and among colonial actors with quite different projects; here the notion of the heedlessness of mothers echoes a missionary remark – Charles Abel's view that Papuan women looked after their children about as well as ducks – but it will be seen from the discussion of the Methodist mission in the next section that such similarities in the vocabulary or surface imagery of colonial representation are substantially less important than more fundamental questions of the approach to difference and the postulated historical relation between colonizer and colonized.

14   *Report*, pp. 23–9.

15   Norma McArthur, *Island Populations of the Pacific* (Canberra: Australian National University Press, 1967), pp. 66–7.

16   *Report*, 73–4.

17   Cf. Megan Vaughan, *Curing their Ills: Colonial Power and African Illness* (Cambridge: Polity Press, 1991), pp. 66–70.

18   (Governor) Donald Cameron, 1925, quoted in John Iliffe, *A Modern History of Tanganyika* (Cambridge: Cambridge University Press, 1979), p. 321. For an important elaboration of these views slightly later, see J. C. Smuts, *Africa and Some World Problems* (Oxford: Oxford

University Press, 1930). This is discussed by Saul Dubow, 'Race, civilisation and culture: the elaboration of segregationist discourse in the inter-war years', in *The Politics of Race, Class and Nationalism in South Africa*, ed. Shula Marks and Stanley Trapido (London: Longman, 1987), pp. 71–94.

19 On Thurston's 'horror of miscegenation' and related attitudes, see John Young, 'Review of *The Majesty of Colour* (vol. 1) by Deryck Scarr', *Journal of Pacific History* 9 (1974), 214. The matter is obscure in the biography itself.

20 See also Martha Kaplan, 'Luveniwai as the British saw it', *Ethnohistory* 36 (1989), 349–71.

21 For comparative studies of sanitation, medicine, and colonialism, see those collected in *Imperial Medicine and Indigenous Societies*, ed. David Arnold (Manchester: Manchester University Press, 1988) and in *Disease, Medicine and Empire*, ed. Roy MacLeod and Milton Lewis (London: Routledge, 1988).

22 See e.g. A. J. C. Mayne, *Fever, Squalor and Vice: Sanitation and Social Policy in Victorian Sydney* (St. Lucia: University of Queensland Press, 1982), especially pp. 89–140. On the role of photography in documenting slum conditions, see John Tagg, 'God's sanitary law', in *The Burden of Representation: Essays on Photographies and Histories* (London: Macmillan, 1988); the photographic documentation of native types was crucial in administrative efforts in various colonies, but not particularly in Fiji. See Christopher Pinney, 'Representations of India: normalisation and the "other"', *Pacific Viewpoint* 29 (1988), pp. 144–62.

23 On Fiji's Indians generally, see K. L. Gillion, *Fiji's Indian Migrants* (Melbourne: Oxford University Press, 1962) and *The Fiji Indians: Challenge to European Dominance 1920–1940* (Canberra: Australian National University Press, 1977). For more recent and critical perspectives, see the work of Brij Lal, e.g. 'Veil of dishonour: sexual jealousy and suicide on Fiji plantations', *Journal of Pacific History* 20 (1985), 135–55, and of John D. Kelly, e.g. 'Discourse about sexuality and Fiji Indian history', *History and Anthropology* 5 (1990), 19–61. My statements here relate only to the question of sanitation and plantation management; in later periods the free Indian population would have been subject to Public Health legislation.

24 *Annual Report on Indian Immigration for 1900* (Fiji Legislative Council Paper 28 of 1901), p. 23. It is consistent with this that mortality statistics are not generally analysed. While assessments of figures for Fijians would always have featured speculation about the causes for fluctuations, the Indian rate is typically 'fairly satisfactory' (e.g. *Annual Report . . . for 1899*, Legislative Council Paper 24 of 1900, p.

19). There are a small number of other passing references to sanitation, infant care, etc. but these mainly blame the filth upon those obliged to inhabit it – sickness among children derived from the 'apathy and ignorance of mothers' – sounding a note familiar both in accounts of Fijians and of the metropolitan poor (*Annual Report . . . 1898*, Legislative Council Paper 25 of 1899, p. 16; *cf.* Mayne, *Fever, Squalor and Vice*, pp. 98–9). Even such statements, however, were marginal within reports overwhelmingly concerned with the management and legitimation of a labour system, a concern expressed in statements such as 'there is no doubt that prosecution is indispensable to enforce work from a considerable minority of labourers' (*Annual Report . . . for 1898*, p. 25).

25 Fiji-based missionaries expressed some of this (see e.g. John Wear Burton, *The Fiji of To-day* (London: Kelly, 1910), pp. 272–3, though there is a tendency to blame the 'coolies' themselves – p. 312). For more principled and critical accounts, see the reports of the remarkable Charles Freer Andrews: *India and the Pacific* (London: Allen & Unwin, 1937) is more accessible than others.

26 E.g. *Annual Report . . . for 1894*, CP 24 of 1895, 13–14.

27 Colo North Provincial Council, 1913 Minutes, resolution VIII, NAF.

28 F. E. Williams, *Orokaiva Society* (Oxford: Oxford University Press, 1930), p. 68.

29 Again, there are parallels both in other colonized societies (cf. Mitchell, *Colonising Egypt*) and in the Victorian social management of the urban 'lower orders' (cf. Mayne, *Fever, Squalor and vice*).

30 Ibid.

31 Colo North Provincial Council Minutes, Resolution IV, NAF. This was later judged an unreasonable restriction and abandoned in 1913 (Colo North, special Provincial Council, 19 February 1913).

32 Colo West report for January and February 1902, Colonial Secretary's Office Minute Paper (hereafter CSO) 1496/02, NAF.

33 C. S. L. Chachage, 'British rule and African civilization in Tanganyika', *Journal of Historical Sociology* 1 (1988), 211–12.

34 This further manifests the rigidifying nature of administrative inscription. The complex matter of land tenure and registration was discussed by France in *The Charter of the Land*.

35 Colo West report for March 1888, CSO 801/1888, NAF.

36 E.g. CSO 3295/1891. It was also acknowledged in the 1896 inquiry that there seemed to be no difference in statistics from sanitary and insanitary sites (*Report*, p. 82).

37 Colo North Provincial Council, 1902 minutes, NAF.

38 *Report*, p. 212. These matters were discussed under the heading of 'Decentralization' – placing village distribution in a negative state of dispersal which could logically then be rectified.

39   Colo North Provincial Council, 1904 minutes, NAF.

40   *Report*, p. 212.

41   Rabinow, *French Modern*, pp. 231–2.

42   David Prochaska, *Making Algeria French: Colonialism in Bône, 1870–1920* (Cambridge: Cambridge University Press, 1990), p. 85.

43   Both the agricultural and military connotations were often elaborated upon. The symbolic importance of the latter is especially explicit in a much earlier text, John Williams's *Missionary Enterprises in the South Sea Islands* (London: John Snow, 1838).

44   The WMMS was established in 1813, and was active in India and South Africa, among other places. Its south Pacific missions were taken over by the Australian Wesleyan Methodist Missionary Society in 1855 (Niel Gunson, *Messengers of Grace* (Melbourne: Oxford University Press, 1978), p. 17).

45   J. F. Goldie (head of the Solomons mission) to J. G. Wheen (General Secretary of the Australasian Methodist Missionary Society), 2 January, 18 July 1920, Methodist Overseas Mission collection, Mitchell Library, Sydney, box 554.

46   Goldie, 'The Solomon Islands', in *A Century in the Pacific*, ed. James Colwell (Sydney: Methodist Book Room, 1915), p. 563. It is interesting that witches in the mission accounts are always female, since other reports from the area make it clear that they could be of either sex.

47   See *Australasian Methodist Missionary Review* (sometimes known simply as *Missionary Review*, hereafter *AMMR*), 4 April 1912, for another example. The point is explicit in the caption to a later photograph in a Seventh-Day Adventist periodical of a western Solomons man 'holding in one hand the Bible, and in the other some relics of heathen worship and customs' (*Australasian Record*, 1 October 1956) and a vignette of a 'Group of rejected war weapons' at the end of a nineteenth-century memoir (William Gill, *Gems from the Coral Lands; or, Incidents of Contrast between Savage and Christian Life in the South Sea Islanders*, (London: Yates and Alexander, n.d. (*c.*1875), p. 344).

48   Goldie, 'The Solomon Islands', pp. 573, 574.

49   Ibid., p. 563.

50   *AMMR*, 4 April 1912.

51   Goldie, 'The Solomon Islands', p. 573.

52   London, 1924. The central structure of this narrative form may be further illustrated from Goldie's overview of the history of the mission. He began with a conversation between himself and a notorious old warrior chief, Gumi, who 'became one of [his] earliest friends' ('The Solomon Islands', p. 562). As befits the then–and–now structure, they talked about a headhunting raid ('Some of them . . . jumped into the water . . . But we took 200 heads back to Roviana!').

One of the perpetrators is thus now a reflective old man, a domesticated heathen, but the story is completed by Goldie's drawing us into the present: 'It is nearly ten years since the old chief told me this story. As I pen these words his son is sitting at my elbow typing the translation of Mark's Gospel. Leaning over his shoulder, I read in his own language, "All things are possible to him that believeth"' (ibid., p. 563).

53 *AMMR,* 4 April 1912.

54 Goldie, 'Industrial training in our Pacific missions', *AMMR,* 4 July 1916, p. 2, quoting Kipling, 'The white man's burden' (see *Rudyard Kipling's Verse – Definitive Edition* (London: Hodder & Stoughton, 1940 and reprints), pp. 323–4).

55 Dudley Kidd, *The Essential Kafir* (London: Adam & Charles Black, 1904), p. 406.

56 Crowder, *Senegal,* p. 2.

57 It is clear for instance that much of Livingstone's writing needs to be interpreted within the framework of exploratory rather than missionary literature: *Missionary Travels and Researches in South Africa* was in fact dedicated to Murchison, then President of the Royal Geographical Society. Although observations characteristic of missionary writing are certainly not absent, these are less conspicuous than objectivist descriptions of places visited, notes on natural phenomena and disquisition on topics such as the divisions of southern African tribes (David Livingstone, *Missionary Travels and Researches in Southern Africa* (London: John Murray, 1857), pp. 201–2). The fact that the book was published by Murray, rather than one of the usual presses associated with the London Missionary Society, such as John Snow, or the Religious Tract Society, is telling in itself, while the book's main orientation is also reflected in the frontispiece depicting Livingstone's 'discovery' of Victoria Falls; frontispieces of other mission works were often portraits of prominent converts (see, for example, T. Williams, *Fiji and the Fijians* (London: Heylin, 1858), J. Williams, *A Narrative of Missionary Enterprises in the South Sea Islands* and William Ellis, *A History of Madagascar* (London: Fisher, *c.*1838).

58 Kidd, *The Essential Kafir,* p. 407.

59 M. V. Portman, *A History of Our Relations with the Andamanese* (Calcutta: Government Printer, 1899), i, p. 33.

60 Henry M. Stanley, *In Darkest Africa, or the Quest Rescue and Retreat of Emin, Governor of Equatoria* (London: Sampson Low, 1890).

61 Livingstone, *Missionary Travels and Researches,* p. 28: 'The laws which still prevent free commercial intercourse among the civilized nations seem to be nothing else but the remains of our own heathenism. My observations on this subject make me extremely desirous to

promote the preparation of the raw materials of European manu-
factures in Africa, for by that means we may not only put a stop to
the slave-trade, but introduce the negro family into the body corporate of nations, no one member of which can suffer without the
others suffering with it ... neither civilization nor Christianity can
be promoted alone. In fact, they are inseparable.' For further discussion see John Comaroff, 'Images of empire, contests of con-
science'.

62 Goldie, 'Industrial training in our Pacific missions', pp. 2–3.
63 For parallels with the Presbyterian mission in southern Vanuatu
    (then the New Hebrides) see Margaret Jolly, 'To save the girls for
    brighter and better lives', *Journal of Pacific History* 26 (1991), 36–7.
    As is shown in *The Transformed Isle*, there were also classes given in
    mat-weaving by the wives of teachers, in this case a Tongan woman.
    The importance of dress was such that in Fiji the idiom in oral
    traditions for adopting Christianity is 'taking the sulu' (a sarong-
    style piece of fabric worn around the waist by men and to cover the
    breasts by women). In a number of these cases it was the local
    people rather than the missionaries who made the abandonment of
    local for introduced clothing a necessary element and marker of
    'conversion'.
64 *The Transformed Isle.*
65 Goldie, 'The Solomon Islands', p. 584, transposed.
66 Judith A. Bennett, *Wealth of the Solomons*, chs 2–4, *passim.*
67 A second sequence relates a parallel story. In this case the whites
    land and attempt to entice young women with similar trinkets.
    'Intuition caused their victims to remain aloof,' but a trader seizes
    his chance, grabs one of the women by the arm, and drags her into
    one of two waiting boats. They row rapidly out into the bay, shooting
    numerous warriors who pursue them into the surf. This elaboration
    of the kidnapping theme thus emphasizes the base sexuality and
    immorality of these other white men. The mission's construction
    stipulates that sexual relationships between foreign men and is-
    lander women took the general form of kidnapping and rape. It can
    be argued instead that women may have actively wished to engage
    either in casual sexual contact with whites or to form longer-term
    relations with them. Comparatively stable relations with native wives
    do not figure in the mission depiction, but were by no means
    uncommon (Bennett, *Wealth of the Solomons*, pp. 69–72, 179–81). In
    so far as women entered into such liaisons and *de facto* marriages
    voluntarily, their diverse motives must usually have included an
    interest in acquiring foreign manufactured articles. While the ab-
    sence of evidence for women's perspectives obviously constrains any

understanding of these early twentieth-century relations, there is thus evidence that their involvement had a basis other than mere coercion.

68 This issue has been debated extensively in Pacific history. See, for a general discussion, Clive Moore, *Kanaka: a History of Melanesian Mackay* (Port Moresby: Institute for Papua New Guinea Studies/ University of Papua New Guinea Press, 1985), and Margaret Jolly, 'The forgotten women: a history of male migrant labour and gender relations in Vanuatu', *Oceania* 58 (1987), pp. 119–39.

69 There are parallels in nineteenth-century photography in the contrast between the bourgeois subject of a carte-de-visite portrait who reflectively looks away from the camera, but not towards an object which can be seen, and whose vision is hence not contained by the image or act of photography, and on the other hand the official photos of those such as criminals who appear either in profile or looking directly at the camera (or both). In the latter case the subordination of the individual to the state, in the person of the police photographer, is manifest (cf. Tagg, *The Burden of Representation*, pp. 35–6 and ch. 3).

70 The practical workings of the project to 'rescue children' or 'gain control of the means of social reproduction' are discussed by Michael Young, 'Suffer the children: Wesleyans in the D'Entrecasteaux', in Jolly and Macintyre (eds.) *Family and Gender in the Pacific*, pp. 108–34.

71 Cf. Margaret Jolly, 'To save the girls for brighter and better lives'.

72 See for instance George G. Carter, *Tie Varane: Stories about People of Courage from Solomon Islands* (Rabaul and Auckland: Unichurch Publishing, 1981), which includes interesting if constrained life histories of a number of local teachers.

73 John Comaroff, 'Images of empire', p. 678, quoting George W. Stow, *The Native Races of South Africa* (London: Swan Sonnenschein, 1905), p. 268. On the Moravians and Boers, see, for instance, *Travels in the Interior of Africa by Mungo Park, and in Southern Africa by John Barrow* (Glasgow: A. Napier, 1815), pp. 452–5.

74 Hugh Honour, *The Image of the Black in Western Art*, vol. 4, part 1: *Slaves and Liberators* (Houston, Texas: Menil Foundation/Cambridge, Mass.: Harvard University Press, 1989), pp. 59–60.

CHAPTER 5

1 [Robert Fletcher], *Isles of Illusion: Letters from the South Seas* (London: Constable, 1925), p. 51.

2   John Buchan, *Prester John* (London, 1910; reprinted Pan Books, 1950), p. 9.

3   Ibid., p. 14.

4   Ibid., pp. 24–5.

5   Ibid., pp. 23, 96, 165. Note the exhausting xenophobia here; presumably the half-caste's colour might equally have been that of English or American mustard, but why pass over an opportunity to arouse further displeasure through reference to the national enemy?

6   Ibid., p. 79.

7   Janet Adam Smith, *John Buchan: a Biography* (Boston: Little, Brown & Co., 1965), p. 142.

8   *Prester John*, p. 82.

9   Ibid., pp. 82–3.

10 Ibid., p. 206. This directly reflects Buchan's own response to the place described; see Adam-Smith, *John Buchan*, pp. 128–131, and Buchan, *Memory Hold-the-Door* (London: Hodder & Stoughton, 1940), pp. 124–5, quoted below.

11 *European Vision and the South Pacific*, 2nd edn (New Haven: Yale University Press, 1985), p. ix. On pioneer constructions of the Australian bush, see also Deborah Bird Rose, 'Nature and gender in outback Australia,' in *Colonialism and Culture*, ed. Nicholas Thomas (special issue, *History and Anthropology*, 5 (1992), 403–25).

12 Ibid., p. 220.

13 Ibid., p. 221.

14 Buchan, *The African Colony*, 2nd edn (Edinburgh: Blackwood, 1913), p. 184. I am grateful to Donald Denoon for drawing this to my attention.

15 This is echoed in Buchan, *A Lodge in the Wilderness* (London: Nelson, n.d., [reprint of work originally published in 1906]), p. 77.

16 Leo Amery, quoted in Walter Nimocks, *Milner's Young Men: the 'Kindergarten' in Edwardian Imperial Affairs* (Durham: Duke University Press, 1968), p. 16.

17 Lord Milner, 'Introduction', in *The Nation and the Empire* (London: Constable, 1913), p. xxxii.

18 Donald Denoon, *A Grand Illusion: the Failure of Imperial Policy in the Transvaal Colony during the Period of Reconstruction, 1900–1905* (London: Longman, 1973), p. xii.

19 Quoted in Thomas Pakenham, *The Boer War* (London: Weidenfeld & Nicolson, 1979), pp. 119–20.

20 Ibid., p. 96. See also J. A. Hobson's perspicacious critique: 'Both white races are strongly opposed to the liberation and elevation of the native, and the British are no more likely to lend their aid to carry out an Exeter Hall policy than the Dutch' (*The War in South*

Africa: its Causes and Effects (London: James Nisbet, 1900), p. 289; pp. 279–295 *passim* are instructive). 'Exeter Hall' referred to philanthropic and missionary opinion.

21 Shula Marks and Stanley Trapido, 'Lord Milner and the South African state', *History Workshop* 8 (1979), 54. See also the same authors' essay, 'The politics of race, class and nationalism' in *The Politics of Race, Class and Nationalism in South Africa*, ed. Marks and Trapido (London: Longman, 1987), especially, pp. 8–10.

22 Smith, *John Buchan*, pp. 122–3; Buchan, *Memory Hold-the-Door*, p. 119.

23 Compare Edward Said on Rudyard Kipling's *Kim* (Introduction to the Penguin edition, 1987, p. 12).

24 Though, acting as a mouthpiece for Milner's views, he had discussed this more directly in *The African Colony*.

25 *Memory Hold-the-Door*, pp. 129–30; on Milner's influence see Denoon, *A Grand Illusion*, p. xiii, and Nimocks, *Milner's Young Men*.

26 *The Milner Papers: South Africa 1899–1905*, ed. Cecil Headlam (London: Cassell, 1933), ii, 467–8.

27 *The Milner Papers*, ii, 314. On the extremely limited and meaningless exemption of some 'civilized' Africans from pass laws, see Denoon, *A Grand Illusion*, pp. 104–5. For an echo of the general political principle, see Buchan, *A Lodge in the Wilderness*: 'Remember, our democracy is a white man's democracy, and we are not moved by any foolish Rousseauism about the rights of man' (pp. 83–4; cf. p. 138).

28 'Such a race will not of itself develop great men or new ideas, or take a leading part in the progress of mankind. But under proper guidance it is capable of enjoying much simple content' (Milner, *England in Egypt* (London: Edward Arnold, new edn., 1894), pp. 386–7).

29 *A Lodge in the Wilderness*, p. 139.

30 Ibid., p. 140. Compare *The Milner Papers*, ii, 307, and Rhodes's own remarks on the 'peculiar class of human being, the Kaffir parson' (quoted in Hobson, *The War in South Africa*, pp. 290–1).

31 Ibid.

32 *Imperialism: a Study* (London: George Allen and Unwin, 1902, revised edn, 1938), p. 243.

33 F. D. Lugard, *The Dual Mandate in British Tropical Africa* (Edinburgh: William Blackwood, 1923), p. 197.

34 John Kelly, 'Fear of culture', *Ethnohistory* 36 (1989), 372–91.

35 Ibid., p. 311.

36 *The Nation and the Empire*, p. xxxi.

37 Ibid., p. xxxiv. Cf. Bernard Semmel, *Imperialism and Social Reform* (London: George Allen & Unwin, 1960), pp. 183–4, though this is on the whole disappointingly shallow.

38 *A Lodge in the Wilderness*, p. 158.
39 *The Age of Empire: 1875–1914* (London: Weidenfeld & Nicolson, 1987), p. 69.
40 *Memory Hold-the-Door*, pp. 124–5.
41 See particularly Charles and Elsa Chauvel's films, *Heritage* and *Sons of Matthew* (these are discussed by Stuart Cunningham in *Featuring Australia* (Sydney: Allen & Unwin, 1990)).
42 Lugard, *The Dual Mandate*, pp. 67–8, 196–200.
43 Cf. Marks and Trapido, 'Lord Milner and the South African state', p. 72.
44 E.g. Gayatri Chakravorty Spivak, 'Who claims alterity?', in *Remaking History*, ed. Barbara Kruger (Seattle: Bay Press, 1989), pp. 269–92.
45 See especially Sara Suleri, *The Rhetoric of English India* (Chicago: University of Chicago Press, 1992).
46 Vernon Lee Walker manuscripts, Rhodes House Library, Oxford. I am in the process of preparing an edition of these letters.
47 Anon., 'A trip to Fiji', *Age* (Melbourne), 19 January 1876.
48 Ibid.
49 J. M. Walsh, *Overdue: a Romance of Unknown New Guinea* (Sydney: States Publishing, 1925), p. 59.
50 See for example Simon During on F. E. Maning's remarkable *Old New Zealand, by a Pakeha* [i.e. white] *Maori* (Auckland: Whitcombe & Tombs, 1930, 1st edn 1863) in 'What was the West? Some relations between modernity, colonisation, and writing', *Meanjin* 48 (1989), 759–76.
51 Howard Walker, in Walker manuscripts, Rhodes House Library, Oxford.

CHAPTER 6

1 For the critical literature on 'development', see Hamza Alavi and Teodor Shanin, eds, *Introduction to the Sociology of 'Developing Societies'* (London: Macmillan, 1982). Though it seems hardly necessary to cite commentaries on the Gulf war, some comments that relate to the theoretical perspectives I have discussed in this book appear in *Public Culture* (section entitled 'War talk', 3 (2), (1991), 119–64); see also W. J. T. Mitchell's 'Culture wars', *London Review of Books*, 23 April 1992, 7–10.
2 It might be noted in passing that Marianna Torgovnick's useful and readable discussion of twentieth-century primitivism (*Gone Primitive: Savage Intellects, Modern Lives* (Chicago: University of Chicago Press,

1990)) neglects representations of contemporary native peoples, focusing instead on literary and ethnographic discourses such as the writings of Michel Leiris, Bronislaw Malinowski, D. H. Lawrence and Roger Fry. The issue that I am concerned with, of the significance of representations of native peoples in (former) colonies of settlement, thus does not enter into her discussion.

3 In the new series of *Transition*, for example, the first five numbers (51–5) range widely over postcolonial literature and film, AIDS, southern Africa, the Caribbean, Britain, Israel, Lebanon, Japan and so on, but included no articles whatsoever on native Americans. Gates's collection, *'Race', writing, and difference* (Chicago: University of Chicago Press, 1985) did slightly better in including one essay, Jane Tompkins's '"Indians": textualism, morality, and the problem of history'.

4 Stephen Greenblatt, *Marvelous Possessions: the Wonder of the New World* (Chicago: University of Chicago Press, 1991), pp. ix, 3–5.

5 An honourable exception is Clifford's chapter on 'Identity in Mashpee' in *The Predicament of Culture* (Cambridge, Mass.: Harvard University Press, 1988). There is of course an enormous range of other literature in the ethnohistory and anthropology of native Americans; what I am drawing attention to is their marginalization in cultural studies and critical theory, not of course a total absence from current discourse.

6 Robert Bage, *Hermsprong, or Man as He is Not* (London: William Lane, 1796), ii, p. 21.

7 Robert Lawlor, *Voices of the First Day: Awakening in the Aboriginal Dreaming* (Rochester, Vermont: Inner Traditions International, 1991), pp. 19, 51–9, 20, 10.

8 Ibid., p. 30.

9 Ibid., p. 30–1.

10 Ibid., pp. 211, 213. It is important to note that Australian patterns of gender relations varied considerably: see Diane Bell, *Daughters of the Dreaming* (Melbourne: McPhee Gribble and Allen and Unwin, 1983) and Fay Gale, ed., *Woman's Role in Aboriginal Society* (Canberra: Australian Institute of Aboriginal Studies, 1970).

11 Lawlor, *Voices of the First Day*, p. x.

12 Ibid., p. 137.

13 A caption to an article in *Le Monde* entitled 'Hollywood focus on the real Indians' read 'The film showed the American Indians in their true light for the first time' (*Guardian Weekly*, 5 July 1992, p. 15).

14 For one of the few more critical comments in the mainstream press, see Michael Dorris, 'Indians in Aspic', *New York Times*, 24 February 1991, section 4, p. 17.

15 See for example, Jean Fisher, 'Dancing with words and speaking with forked tongues', *Third Text* 14 (1991), pp. 29–30. Although Fisher offers a somewhat different argument to that presented here, I have drawn on this useful article at several points. It should be pointed out that while the revisionist view of frontier history seems an unsophisticated inversion from some points of view, it nevertheless remains contentious, as was attested by the controversy over the 1991 exhibition, 'The West as America – Reinterpreting Images of the Frontier', at the Smithsonian Institution (see Martin Walker, 'Westward Oh!', *Guardian Weekly*, 30 June 1991, pp. 25–6).

16 Torgovnick, *Gone Primitive*, pp. 88–9.

17 See Florence Curtis Graybill and Victor Boesen, *Edward Sherriff Curtis: Visions of a Vanishing Race* (New York: Thomas Crowell, 1976).

18 *Taonga Maori: Treasures of the New Zealand Maori People* (Sydney: Australian Museum, 1989), pp. 20–1.

19 Ibid., p. 25.

20 George French Angas, *New Zealanders Illustrated* (London: Thomas M'Lean, 1847), caption to pl. xxxiv.

21 *Taonga Maori*, p. 27.

22 Cf. Ruth Brown, 'Maori spirituality as Pakeha construct', *Meanjin* 48 (2) (1989), 252–8.

23 *Taonga Maori*, pp. 62–3.

24 For a useful overview see Ranginui Walker, *Ka Whaiwhai Tonu Matou: Struggle without End* (Auckland: Penguin, 1990).

25 Alan Duff, *Once were Warriors* (St. Lucia, Queensland: University of Queensland Press, 1991).

26 Clifford, *Predicament of Culture*, pp. 271, 275.

27 Edward W. Said, 'Yeats and decolonization', in *Remaking History*, ed. Barbara Kruger (Seattle: Bay Press, 1989), pp. 15–16.

28 Paul Gilroy, 'It ain't where you're from, it's where you're at: the dialectics of diasporic identification', *Third Text* 13 (1990), 5.

29 Gilroy, 'It ain't where you're from', 3–6. See also Paul Gilroy, *There ain't no Black in the Union Jack* (London: Hutchinson, 1987; Chicago: University of Chicago Press, 1991).

30 Maori woman quoted in Toon van Meijl, 'Political paradoxes and timeless traditions: ideology and development among the Tainui Maori, New Zealand', PhD thesis, Australian National University, 1990, p. 140.

31 Published as *Bran nue dae: a musical journey*, by Jimmy Chi and Kuckles (Sydney: Currency Press/Broome: Magabala Books, 1991). Tom Zubrycki made a film about the musical, also entitled *Bran nue dae*, released through Ronin Films, Canberra, 1991.

32 Gyan Prakash, 'Writing post-Orientalist histories of the third world:

perspectives from Indian historiography', *Comparative Studies in Society and History* 32 (1990), 398–402. See also Rosalind O'Hanlon and David Washbrook's critique, 'After Orientalism: culture, criticism, and politics in the third world', *Comparative Studies in Society and History* 34 (1992), 141–67, and Prakash's reply, 'Can the Subaltern ride?', ibid., 168–84.

Notes to Plates

Frontispiece   On Lindt's work, see Shar Jones, *J. W. Lindt: Master Photographer* (Melbourne: Currey O'Neill Ross/Library Council of Victoria, 1985).

Plate 4   The frequent feminization of 'Hindoos' is effected here by the way in which the central man's pose echoes that of the woman, and by the appearance of the fabric. Compare William Hodges's responses on arriving at Madras in 1780: 'Some time before the ship arrives at her anchoring ground, she is hailed by the boats of the country filled with people of business . . . This is the moment in which the European feels the great distinction between Asia and his own country. The rustling of fine linen, and the general hum of unusual conversation, presents to his mind for a moment the idea of an assembly of females' (quoted in Harriet Guest, 'The great distinction: figures of the exotic in the work of William Hodges', *Oxford Art Journal* 12 (2), 36–58). On the Daniells, see Mildred Archer, *Early Views of India* (London: Thames & Hudson, 1980).

Plate 6   Javanese physique was not graphically represented in Raffles's plates, which included images of 'Javans' in war and court dress, and 'a Javan woman of the lower class'. He did, however, understand them as a distinct race: 'of the three chief nations in these islands, occupying respectively Java, Sumatra, and Celebes, the first has, especially by its moral habits, by its superior civilization and improvements, obtained a broader and more marked characteristic than the others. Both the Malayan and *Búgis* nations are maritime and commercial, devoted to speculations of gain, animated by a spirit of adventure, and accustomed to distant and hazardous enterprizes; while the Javans, on the contrary, are an agricultural race, attached to the soil, of quiet habits and contented dispositions, almost entirely unacquainted with navigation and foreign trade, and little inclined to engage in either. This difference of character may perhaps be accounted for, by the great superiority of the soil of Java to that of the other two islands.' Thomas Stamford Raffles, *The History of Java* (London: Black, Parbury, and Allen, Booksellers to the Hon. East-India Company, 1817), i, p. 57.

Plate 7   '[I]t may not be uninteresting to introduce to the reader a native of *Papua* . . . stolen from his country in the course of this [slave] traffic. The lad represented in the annexed plate came into my service at *Báli* under very peculiar circumstances, and has accompanied me to England. Since his arrival he has excited some curiosity, as being the first individual of the woolly haired race of Eastern Asia who has been brought to this country. It is known, that on the Malayan Peninsula, in Luconia, Borneo, and most of the larger islands of the Eastern Seas, there are occasionally found in the mountainous tracts a scattered race of blacks entirely distinct from the rest of the population. Some have conceived them to be the aborigines of these countries; others considering them as of the African race, adduce them in proof of an early and extensive intercourse between Africa and these islands. I shall content myself with observing, that they appear at the present day to form the bulk of the population of Papua or New Guinea. The following remarks upon the individual now in England, whom we sometimes call Papua, and sometimes (more to his satisfaction) Dick, were obligingly communicated to me by Sir Everard Home, Bart.

"The Papuan differs from the African negro in the following particulars. His skin is of a lighter colour, the woolly hair grows in small tufts and each hair has a spiral twist. The forehead rises higher, and the hind head is not so much cut off. The nose projects more from the face. The upper lip is longer and more prominent. The lower lip projects forward from the lower jaw to such an extent that the chin forms no part of the face, the lower part of which is formed by the mouth. The buttocks are so much lower than in the negro as to form a striking mark of distinction, but the calf of the leg is as high as in the negro"' (Raffles, *History of Java*, ii, p. ccxxxv).

There are several aspects of this depiction that are characteristic of the time: first, although Raffles notes that the boy came into his service under 'very peculiar circumstances' he does not explain these, but instead takes the individual as a specimen and a curiosity. Secondly, the interest in this exemplar of a 'lower race' is immediately related to physical distinctness, whereas the civilized Javanese are discussed more in terms of character and customs. Thirdly, there is a discrepancy between the textual and visual representations: while the former is coldly generalizing and scientific, the aquatint romantically depicts the melancholy victim of slavery, gazing out to sea, presumably in the direction of his homeland.

Plates 8 and 9   A wider range of these propaganda photographs is reproduced in Thomas, 'Colonial conversions: difference, hierarchy, and history in early twentieth-century evangelical propaganda', in *Comparative Studies in Society and History* 34 (2) (1992), which this section draws upon.

Plate 11   'The concept behind this series of studio portaits of black male dancers came about in reaction to images of black Australian people I was continually seeing presented around me by photographers in books, magazines, and galleries. These images tended always to fit into the realist documentary mode usually reserved for the "ethnographic subject".

'Such examples of this style of representation of indigenous groups exist in all European-colonised countries, e.g. North America, Brazil, etc. Thus this "record them now before they die out" mentality has never been exclusive to Australia.

'*Some Lads* takes the utmost example of such a preoccupation – being the mid-nineteenth century scientific studio studies of Aborigines by early pioneer photographers – but changes the intentions.

'Here I use a studio situation, the lighting flat, and a similar blank backdrop. The voyeuristic quality remains . . . Here I encourage my subjects to enjoy the staring camera (in contrast to the uncomfortable glaring in the earlier century photographs), to intentionally pose and show off. In an attempt to dispense with the seriousness and preciousness, it captures a lyricism and rarely assigned bold sensuality' (Tracey Moffatt, 1987). Tracey Moffatt's comments are quoted in Helen Ennis, *Australian Photography: the 1980s* (Canberra: Australian National Gallery, 1988), p. 28.

Index

Aborigines 28–31, 173, 174–8, 191–4
Achebe, Chinua 110
Acosta, Jose de 75–6
Adanson, M. 215 n.42
Africa, representations of 52, 54, 80–1, 86–7, 115
agency 59–61
Aguirre 58, 210–11 n.53
Algeria 124
America, conquest of 52, 72–5, 173
Andamanese 134
Andrew, Thomas Pl. 2, 33–5, 54, 55, 63, 78, 133
Angas, George French 185
anthropology 6–7, 96, 192
and colonialism 201 n.14
Artikeln furniture 29
assimilation 49, 116, 134, 152, 167
Auden, W. H. 12
Australia 28

Bage, Robert 31, 174
Bali 92–3
barbarian, figure of 72
Barrow, John 157
Bhabha, Homi 8, 39–59

Bloch, Maurice 216 n.56
Boas, Franz 89
Bolla, Peter de 50–1
Bourdieu, Pierre 8, 21, 58–61
Bran Nue Dae 191–2
Buchan, John 143–53, 155, 156, 157, 159, 160, 167
Buffon, Comte de 81–3, 91, 92
Bula, Daniel 132

census, colonial 38
Certeau, Michel de 21
Chi, Jimmy 191–2
Christianity 61–4, 72–7, 119–20, 124, 146, 191–2
Clifford, James 24, 187–8
Cohn, Bernard 38–9, 40
colonial discourse theory 3, 8, 39–60, 158, 172–3
colonialism, limited effect of 15–16
administrative 109–25
in anthropology 13–14, 18–19
failure of 159–69
in literary studies 18
stereotypic view of 12–13, 170–1
Columbus, Christopher 72, 85

Conrad, Joseph   160
Costner, Kevin   178–83
Crowder, Michael   134
Crusoe, Robinson   5
Curtin, Philip   68, 69

Dances with Wolves   16, 31,
    178–83, 192
Daniell, Thomas and William
    54, Pl. 4, 208–9 n.47
Das, Veena   47
Derrida, Jacques   44–5
difference vs. similarity, in
    colonial discourse   51–2
discourse, concept of   50–1, 143
Duff, Alan   187
Dumont, Louis   92, 93

essentialism *see* typifications
evolutionism   109–10, 151–2,
    156–7
exoticism   53, 94
    different from primitivism
    173, 182

Fabian, Johannes   7, 70–1, 76
familial metaphors, in colonial
    discourse   98
'Fanonism'   47
'fatal impact' of colonialism   15
feminization of colonized   56,
    73, 231
Fiji   33–5, 48, 107–25, 154, 160,
    164–5
Fiji Indians   117–18, 124–5, 154
Firth, Raymond   185
Fisher, Michael   91
Fletcher, Robert ('Asterisk')   143
Forster, Johann Reinhold   77,
    84–6, 89, 91, 155
Foucault, Michel   4, 12, 20, 21,
    24, 39, 40–3, 58, 70, 98
Fraser, James   54

Freud, Sigmund   12
Fry, Roger   94

Gates, Henry Louis, Jr.   33,
    197 n.4
Geertz, Clifford   90–4,
    215–16 n.56
gender, in colonial discourse
    98–102, 132–3, 137
Gilchrist, John   39
Gilroy, Paul   189–90
Goldie, John F.   112–13,
    127–32, 135, 156
Gordon, Sir Arthur   109–25,
    154, 156, 157
government   4–5, 38–40,
    109–25
governmentality, concept of   4,
    40–3, 50, 116–17
Grand Tour   5
Greenblatt, Stephen   68, 69
Guha, Ranajit   57
Gulf war   95–6, 170

Herodotus   72
Herzog, Werner   210–11 n.53
Hobsbawm, E. J.   107, 155
Hobson, J. A.   153–4
Hodges, William   54, 231
hooks, bell   20
Hulme, Keri   186
Hulme, Peter   37
Hurley, Frank   26

imperialism, doctrine of   150–5
India   38–9, 53, 54–5, 108–9
indirect rule   107–25
infantilization, in missionary
    representation   129–33,
    134–5, Pls 8, 9, 140

JanMohamed, Abdul   8, 37, 43,
    44, 51–3

journalism, colonial 164–5

Kidd, Dudley 133, 134
Kipling, Rudyard 135
Kolben, Peter 84

Lagusu, Hudson 55, Pl. 5
Lawlor, Robert 174–7
Lestrade, G. P. 49
Lindt, J. W. 7
Linnekin, Jocelyn 103–4
Livingstone, David 136,
 222 n.57, n.61
Long, Edward 49, 78
Lugard, F. D. 157
Lyautey, L. H. G. 124

McGrane, Bernard 67–8, 70
Maori 28, 127, 183–90
Marcus, George 91
masculinity, colonial 81, 160,
 167
Marx, Karl 23
Mead, Margaret 104
Memmi, Albert 13
Middle East 25–6, 95–6
millenarian movements 122
Miller, Peter 45–6
Milner, Alfred 145, 150–5, 157
mimicry 40, 46–7, 48, 56–7, 59
missionaries 62, 125–44, 153,
 155–6, 168
modern/premodern distinction
 3, 49, 67–71, 77–8, 125, 141
modern/premodern, as analytical
 fiction 69
Moffatt, Robert 136
Moffatt, Tracey 193–4, 233–4
Moravians 136, 141–2
Morocco 124

New Hebrides (Vanuatu) 160–9
New Zealand (Aotearoa)
 183–90
Nicholson, R. C. 132
'noble savage' 22, 99–104, 179

Orientalism (discourse) 6, 23,
 25, 32, 46, 53, 54,
 208–9 n.47
Orientalism (book) 8, 21–7, 31,
 37, 46
otherness, Renaissance concept
 of 72–4

Pacific Islands 31, 35, 85–6,
 98–104, 109–10, 157, 163–5
Pagden, Anthony 68, 69
Park, Mungo 5, 86–7
Parry, Benita 55
population, in colonial discourse
 112–23
Portman, M. V. 134
postcolonialism 7, 30–1, 194–5
Poulantzas, Nicos 42
Prakash, Gyan 19
Prescott, W. H. 75
Prester John 143–53, 163, 181
primitivism 28–32, 53, 171–85,
 188–9
project, notion of 105–6, 158
Pryce-Jones, David 25, 95–6
psychoanalysis 47
Pufendorf, Samuel 84, 91, 104

racism 14, 33, 37, 53–4, 77–80,
 89, 150–1, 196–7 n.4
Raffles, Thomas Stamford 87–9,
 Pls 6 and 7, 231–2
Ralegh, Walter 73
Rhodes, Cecil 145, 150, 151
Rose, Nikolas 45–6

Said, Edward 5–6, 7, 20, 21–7,
 38, 46, 98, 187–8, 192
Salt, Henry 54, Pl. 3
sanitation 118–25

Sartre, Jean-Paul   13
savagery, representation of
    33–5, 72–3, 99–104, 127–8
segregationism, colonial   48–9
Smith, Bernard   68, 69, 98–103,
    148
Snowden, Frank   78
Solomon Islands   61–4, 109,
    126–41
southern Africa   143–53
Spivak, Gayatri Chakravorty   8,
    51, 55–6, 209–10 n.49
Stanley, Henry   78, 80–1, 134–5,
    Pl. 10, 160
Stepan, Nancy   78
stereotype, concept of   37,
    99–104
Stoler, Ann   13–14
Subaltern Studies group   47, 57

Tanganyika   115, 120
Tanner, Tony   45

Thurston, J. B.   108
Tierra del Fuego   85–6
Todorov, Tzvetan   52, 68–9, 72,
    77, 141, 196 n.4
Torgovnick, Marianna   94, 179
Trinh Minh-ha   144
trout-fishing in colonial culture
    149
typifications, racial and cultural
    24, 36–7, 71–2, 79–80,
    84–96, 129, 132–4, 157–8,
    190–1, 194–5

Wagner, Roy   182
Walker, Vernon Lee   160–9
Watt, Ian   5
White, Geoffrey   61–4
Williams, Raymond   20
writing, failure of   160–9

Zionism   17